From Vietnam to El Salvador

From Vietnam to El Salvador

*The Saga of the FMLN Sappers
and Other Guerrilla Special Forces
in Latin America*

David E. Spencer

PRAEGER

Westport, Connecticut
London

Library of Congress Cataloging-in-Publication Data

Spencer, David E.
    From Vietnam to El Salvador : the saga of the FMLN Sappers and
other guerrilla special forces in Latin America / David E. Spencer.
      p. cm.
    Includes bibliographical references and index.
    ISBN 0–275–95514–1 (alk. paper)
    1. Fuerzas Populares de Liberación Farabundo Martí. Fuerzas
Especiales Selectas—History. 2. Special forces (Military science)—
Latin America—History. I. Title.
UA607.S2S64 1996
356'.167'097284—dc20   96–13555

British Library Cataloguing in Publication Data is available.

Copyright © 1996 by David E. Spencer

Library of Congress Catalog Card Number: 96–13555
ISBN: 0–275–95514–1

First published in 1996

Praeger Publishers, 88 Post Road West, Westport, CT 06881
An imprint of Greenwood Publishing Group, Inc.

Printed in the United States of America

The paper used in this book complies with the
Permanent Paper Standard issued by the National
Information Standards Organization (Z39.48–1984).

10 9 8 7 6 5 4 3 2 1

Contents

Acronyms

ATS	See BATS.
BATS	Anfres Torres Sanchez Battalion of the FPL (also called SS-20).
BRAC	Rafael Aguiñada Carranza Battalion of the FAL.
BRAT	Rafael A. Torres Battalion of the FAL.
BRAZ	Rafael Arce Zablah Brigade of the ERP.
CEMFA	Military Training Center, located in La Union.
COBRAC	Commandos of the BRAC.
DLAD	Luis Alberto Diaz Detachment (PRTC).
DRU	Unified Revolutionary Directorate, military command of the FMLN (later changed to CG).
EEBI	Escuela de Entrenamiento Básico de Infanteria, Somoza's Basic Infantry Training School that housed his most elite units.
EMCFA	Armed Forces High Command.
ERP	Popular Revolutionary Army, one of the five FMLN factions.
ETA	Separatist Guerrillas from Spain.
EZLN	Mexican Zapatistas.
FAL	Armed Forces of Liberation, one of the five FMLN factions.
FES	Special Select Forces, the generic term for special forces of the FMLN.
FMLN	Farabundo Marti National Liberation Front.
FPL	Popular Liberation Front, one of the five FMLN factions.

GEC   Special Combat Group (Argentine Montonero guerrilla special forces).

GOE   4th Brigade Special Operations Company.

JCR   Junta Coordinadora Revolucionaria, an alliance of Chilean, Argentine, and Uruguayan guerrillas.

JTP   Juvented Trabajadora Peconista, a Montenero mass front.

K-93   Alejandro Solano Battalion (BAS) of the FPL.

M-19   Colombian Guerrilla Movement.

PRAL   Long Range Reconnaissance Patrol, EASF special forces.

PRTC   Central American Workers Party, one of the five FMLN factions.

PSR-ML   Peruvian Partido Socialista Revolucionario (Marxista-Leninista).

RN   National Resistance, one of the five FMLN factions.

S-7   Ernesto Morales Sandoval Battalion (BEMS) of the FPL.

SS-20   Anfres Torres Sanchez Battalion of the FPL (BATS).

TECMA   Comandante Manglio Armijo Special Troops, FES battalion of the ERP.

TOC   Tactical Operations Center.

X-21   Juan Mendez Battalion (BJM) of the FPL.

Introduction

During the armed conflict carried out in El Salvador against International Communism during the decade of the 1980s, both the armed forces and the FMLN continually developed the use of special forces as the mechanism to defeat strategic objectives. However, the FMLN FES also played an important role at other levels, such as the operational and tactical levels.

The concept of the use of the FES by the FMLN came onto the Salvadoran scene as one of the contributions of Cuba during 1981 and 1982. Insurgent elements from the ERP and the FPL were given training in the school at Matanzas, Cuba. Later, this program was extended to the other organizations of the FMLN such as the FAL, RN, and the PRTC. However, these latter groups did not produce as spectacular results. The politico-military leadership of the ERP and FPL did apply the special forces concept in the strategic context. They used the FES against big objectives in the rear areas of the armed forces, especially against economic objectives that affected things on a national scale. Examples of this are the downing of the Oro and Cuzcatlan bridges. In real terms, the destruction of these bridges was an attempt to isolate the eastern region of the country and establish liberated territory.

In simplified form, the FMLN FES applied their efforts on the different war fronts in the following manner.

On the strategic level, they made efforts against strategic targets such as the vital installations of the Air Force, the Third Brigade, the Fourth Brigade, and the CEMFA (Armed Forces Training Center). They attacked the headquarters of these units, causing terrible damage to equipment and personnel.

At the operational level, the FES acted with less intensity against the operating units of the armed forces. In other words, they attacked the immediate reaction battalions, fixed positions such as radio repeater stations, and units temporarily stationed at different places. These attacks were usually carried out in conjunction with the guerrillas' strategic mobile forces.

At the tactical level, the FES acted as urban commandos. In this role they acted against political and military personalities, which at times produced losses of a strategic nature in the political and military leadership of the country. However, in practical terms the planning and execution of these actions was designed at a tactical level and did not obey strategic requirements of the FMLN high command.

Also at the tactical level, the FES coordinated their efforts with other types of forces, such as the local guerrillas and clandestine militias.

The former indicates that the dynamics of the application of the FES obeyed three basic principles: (1) use little force against superior forces; (2) coordinate attacks with other types of forces; and (3) initiate attacks from the inside out.

One of the characteristics of the FES that is most important to emphasize is the base ideology, a determining aspect in the final production of the trained combatant. This concept made it possible to train and use small children as first-line combatants, equipping them with small arms and explosives to accomplish their missions. One example of this was the second attack against the Third Brigade base, located in San Miguel. Here a unit known as the Samuelitos, made up entirely of children, threw explosives into the barracks where the soldiers were sleeping. This caused very serious damage.

After five years of very positive results, the High Command of the FMLN, in June 1985, established in its military guidelines the priority to dedicate more effort to the development and creation of FES units and make it the highest combat echelon of irregular warfare in the Salvadoran war.

José Angel Moroni Bracamonte

From Vietnam to El Salvador

CHAPTER I

Guerrilla Special Forces of El Salvador: The FPL, Vietnam, and Cuba

In 1982 the Salvadoran army captured a large cache of documents from a safe house in San Salvador belonging to the high command of the Popular Liberation Forces (FPL), one of the five guerrilla factions. Among the numerous documents were several with dates from early 1980 through mid-1981. They were letters and notes from meetings in which the creation of special forces units were discussed. Due to the triumph of the Sandinistas in Nicaragua and the greatly increased interest of Cuba and the international socialist community in Central America, the guerrillas of El Salvador were anticipating a qualitative and quantitative leap in force levels and combat in their tiny Central American nation. Open maneuver warfare was expected by the beginning of 1981, and the documents anticipated the need for guerrilla special forces, and discussed the concept, composition, and missions of the anticipated special units. Forseeing the guerrillas' lack of heavy weapons, the documents explicitly outlined the role of the special forces as tactical balancers for the guerrillas. In the documents' own words, the guerrillas called them "tubeless artillery" and "planeless bombs."[1] The special forces would be the initial answer to the armed forces artillery, armor, and aviation.[2] Other documents captured in this haul outlined how the special forces would counter the army's advantage in heavy weapons. Essentially, the proposed units would combine the abilities of two military skills: infiltration and explosives. In other words, the proposal was to create sapper units that could infiltrate enemy positions and blow up their support weapons and hardened positions.

This was by no means a new concept. The Germans had developed storm trooper battalions in World War I. Their mission was to infiltrate enemy trench lines and knock out key positions with explosives, grenades, flame throwers, and small cannon to allow following infantry forces to assault through to the objective. The Soviets developed elite demolition units during their own civil war, the subsequent wars with Poland, and during the Spanish Civil War to infiltrate across enemy lines and conduct sabotage operations of all types. However, it was the Viet Minh and later the North Vietnamese that developed the concept to its full expression and gave it its unique characteristics. The previously described units were very skilled with demolitions, and not as skilled at infiltration. The Vietnamese turned this around. They concentrated heavily on infiltration and were less skilled with the demolitions. Essentially, they integrated principles from the German storm troopers and the Soviet demolition units with advanced infiltration techniques. Most infiltration techniques taught in conventional special forces schools emphasize finding where the enemy is not and crossing his lines at these points. However, few special forces schools teach techniques of infiltrating into an enemy position by moving directly under their guns without being detected. This was the unique characteristic developed by the North Vietnamese. Reportedly, the North Vietnamese made a deal with some highly skilled professional thieves and robbers. They granted them amnesty or rewarded them in some way for becoming part of the special sapper units and teaching their techniques of breaking into houses and crossing security barriers undetected to the men of those units.

The result was that the North Vietnamese special forces could regularly cross triple-strand concertina fences, minefields, and other obstacles without being detected. They would often conduct or spearhead devastating attacks against American and South Vietnamese army and air bases. While few of these attacks successfully overran American bases, they would often inflict devastating damage, knocking out command posts, artillery positions, parked aircraft, supply dumps, and other targets. Often the first indication of attack was the first explosion of a sapper satchel charge within the perimeter, after the attack was well under way.

Some American studies of the overall effects of these attacks dismissed them as largely ineffectual.[3] In the long run, they caused less damage than North Vietnamese artillery and rocket attacks. However, the Vietnamese did not feel that their efforts had been wasted, as they continued to train and teach these tactics after 1975, when they toppled the Saigon regime after 21 years of war. The Communist and Warsaw Pact countries did not agree with the American assessment either. The Vietnamese special forces had a reputation for being the best in the world.[4] The American disdain for these tactics and techniques would cost their Salvadoran allies dearly in the 1981–1991 civil war.

Essentially, the special forces being proposed by the FPL in their documents was a proposal for the transposition of the special forces techniques used by the North Vietnamese to El Salvador. Success against the Americans and their allies in Vietnam made it likely that the techniques could be used successfully against the Salvadoran army, which was for the most part

American trained. Time would show that this proposal would prove to be one of the most successful ideas to emerge from the Salvadoran experience. The majority of the spectacular blows suffered by the Salvadoran government forces would be at the hands of the guerrilla special forces using Vietnamese techniques.

It was no accident that Vietnamese concepts like those of the sapper special forces should show up first in the ranks of the FPL. The FPL had been formed in 1970 by Cayetano Carpio, alias Marcial. The press often called him the Ho Chi Minh of El Salvador because of his affectation of a scraggly goatee, and his admiration for all things Vietnamese when it came to revolution. Carpio established direct ties with the Vietnamese, and the ties between the Vietnamese and the FPL would remain strong through the end of the Salvadoran conflict. Carpio was obsessed with Vietnamese methods and modelled his own forces and war plan on the lessons learned from Vietnam. He rejected the Cuban concept of a *foco* or small group of guerrillas causing revolution from the distant hinterland, and the idea of quick insurrection as advocated by urban guerrillas. His strategy was modelled on Ho Chi Minh's adaptation of Mao Tse-tung's concept of prolonged popular war. He was convinced that the Americans would never allow a revolution in El Salvador to succeed without a struggle. The Marines would land first. However, the lesson from Vietnam was that while the Americans were militarily powerful, they could not withstand a prolonged war. The guerrillas could lose every battle, but as long as they continued fighting and inflicting American casualties, the American political environment could not endure a protracted war. The Vietnamese special forces techniques were a spectacular way of inflicting the type of casualties that sapped American political will.

Exactly when the FPL was first exposed to the Vietnamese special forces concepts and techniques is unknown. However, it was probably sometime between 1975 and 1979. A handwritten conceptual manual, captured at the same time as the documents mentioned above, showed an intimate familiarity with the Vietnamese techniques. Whoever wrote that document had either gone through training and/or had access to a Vietnamese technical manual.

This might have come indirectly through the Cubans. The Cubans had maintained ties with the Vietnamese since the early 1960s. The 1966 Tricontinental conference served to strengthen and consolidate these ties. It was at this time that Che Guevara developed the revolutionary strategy for Latin America of creating "one, two, three, many Vietnams." The Cubans sent personnel to Vietnam to carry out a variety of functions. In addition, Vietnamese personnel came to Cuba to teach their revolutionary techniques to the Cuban armed forces. After the 1975 fall of the Saigon government, Cuban enthusiasm for Vietnamese tactics and strategy increased manifold. The Vietnamese showed the world how a Third World country could defeat the United States. It is no coincidence that after 1975 the Latin American revolutionary groups favored by the Cubans were those which had an affinity for the Vietnamese. In Nicaragua the Cubans were closest to the faction of the Sandinistas led by Tomas Borge. This faction was known as the Prolonged Popular War faction, the strategy advocated by the Vietnamese. In El Salvador, the guerrilla faction that enjoyed the closest relationship with the Cubans between 1975 and 1980 was the FPL, led by Cayetano Carpio.

Sometime before 1979, Cuban military personnel were trained in Vietnamese special forces techniques, and further, how to set up a school to teach these techniques to others. According to Miguel Castellanos, the Vietnamese special forces were considered, in the socialist world, to be the best special forces in the world. The Cubans sent their men to be trained by the best, and then turned around and taught these techniques to the Salvadorans.[5]

The captured documents indicate that the FPL held several meetings and developed several different concepts about special forces simultaneously. These can be divided by categories of speciality: sappers, combat swimmers, urban commandos, and snipers. These categories would essentially remain constant for the entire FMLN throughout the war, with little modification.

SAPPERS

The sapper concept was the most important of the four categories and would reach the highest levels of development within the FPL and the FMLN. Because of this, the special forces sapper can be considered to be representative of overall FMLN special forces efforts. The concept of the special forces sapper was a direct import from the Vietnamese conflict. The carefully developed techniques that proved successful against the French, South Vietnamese, and the Americans in Vietnam would prove to be successful again against the American-assisted Salvadoran armed forces.

Most of the initial FPL sappers were trained in Cuba, causing some to question the Vietnamese origin of the FMLN special forces techniques. There are a number of indicators that leave no doubt that these techniques were indeed developed in Vietnam. First, according to several sappers captured later in the war and the FPL commander, Miguel Castellanos, a number of sappers were trained in Vietnam.[6] The course in Cuba and the course in Vietnam were considered by the FMLN to be equal in terms of value and techniques taught. That the techniques taught in Cuba were Vietnamese is evidenced by the fact that many of the techniques described in sapper manuals use the prefix "Vietnamese"—the "Vietnamese crawl," for example. Parallels between the techniques used by the Vietnamese sappers and the FMLN sappers are too close to be merely coincidental.[7] Prior to

El Salvador, these techniques had been used exclusively by the Communist Vietnamese or their allies in Southeast Asia. So whether vicariously or directly, there is no doubt that the origin of the special forces sapper tactics and techniques lies in Vietnam. These techniques will be described more thoroughly in Chapter 2.

The FPL came up with the name Fuerzas Especiales Selectas, in English, Special Select Forces. This name was shortened to the acronym FES.[8] Eventually, this FPL acronym for its sappers would be adopted by all of the guerrilla factions and become the generic term for special forces of all types throughout the FMLN. The Salvadoran armed forces learned to respect the FES, and always spoke of them with a mixture of fear, loathing, and admiration.

An interesting conceptual twist that was characteristic of the Marxist approach to warfare is that special operations were conceived of more as political operations than purely military endeavors. Where Western nations put a division between warfare and politics, the Marxists have always blurred the distinction, more fully complying with the Clauswitzian axiom that warfare is merely politics by other means. To the Salvadoran guerrillas, the potential political impact of an operation was regarded to be equally if not more important than the purely military effect. Great emphasis was placed on the role that special forces could play by enhancing the psychological, and thus political impact of a guerrilla attack or operation.

Interviews with captured FPL special forces personnel indicate that sapper recruits were being sent to Cuba for training as early as May 1980. As mentioned before, some FPL cadres had either received the sapper course or had been thoroughly briefed on sapper techniques prior to this date; the early documents mentioned above show a high degree of conceptual maturity on the subject, prior to the formation of the actual units. However, there is, as yet, no record of this. An alternative possibility is that the FPL documents were straight copies of Cuban or Vietnamese manuals. At any rate, what is clear is that by mid-1980, FPL sapper units were already well in the process of formation.

All of the original sapper cadres were trained in Cuba and Vietnam. Later schools would be set up in the strategic rearguard of the guerrilla zones of influence. Since it is difficult to synthesize this experience, it is useful to allow one of the Cuban-trained sappers to recall his own experience here.

I was recruited in 1980. In November of 1980, I was sent to the San Pedro Hills where I participated in the January 1981 "final offensive." After this failed, I went through a training course in political indoctrination and military tactics. Because I excelled, I was made a squad leader. Because of my actions in this position, I went through a month-long training course in January 1982, after which I was made platoon leader. Because of my distinction in this position, I was chosen by Commander Camilo to get ready for a course in Cuba. On October 19, I finally left the San Pedro Hills for a safehouse in Ciudad Delgado, a suburb of San Salvador. However, I received a message to return to the front, as there was an urgent need for trained combat leaders. On November 12, I again left for San Salvador. At San Rafael Cedros I made contact with Manolo, who drove me to the suburb of Soyapango, where he turned me over to Oscar, who took me to the suburb of Mejicanos to a safehouse there. A family lived there, but I never learned their names. After several days Oscar came to get me and introduced me to Ernesto, who gave me instructions on how to get the right papers. He also gave me 200 Guatemalan quetzales and 100 Salvadoran colones to grease the bureaucratic red tape. Later Anselmo and Belisario came and picked me up and dropped me off at the western bus terminal, where I caught a bus to the Comalapa International Airport. Here I caught a flight to Managua. This was on the evening of November 26. At the Managua airport I was met by Gerardo, who took me to a safehouse at a place called Crucero. Inside were several Salvadoran guerrillas. We waited until December 24 with nothing to do, except greet new arrivals. All of us were from the same organization, going to Cuba to go through the Special Forces course. While we were in Nicaragua, Gerardo was in charge of doing all the necessary paperwork so we could continue the journey. On December 24, Gerardo finally came and told us that all the paperwork had been done and that we could now continue our journey to Cuba. He took us to the airport and handed our papers to a Cuban, who took them and gave them to immigration. There were ten of us. When we reached Havana, we were met by Rene, who drove us in a Cuban military vehicle to the Che Guevara School. We were assigned to Area 93. There were six more guerrillas from the FPL there. Our routine ran from Monday through Friday. From 6:00 to 8:00 A.M. we had physical training followed by breakfast until 9:00 A.M. We had theoretical and practical instruction from 9:00 A.M. to 1:00 P.M., after which we ate from 1:00 P.M. to 3:00 P.M. and then had siesta from 3:00 to 5:00 P.M. From 5:00 to 6:00 P.M. there was mandatory study hall followed by dinner until 7:00 P.M. Between 7:00 and 9:00 P.M. there was mandatory study hall again. Lights out was from 9:00 P.M. until 5:00 A.M. This schedule lasted four months. The basic topics covered by our training were tactics, infiltration and explosives techniques, topography, first aid, physical training, and marksmanship. There were guerrillas from three organizations at this course: the FAL, the FPL and the ERP, about 30 total. The course ended on May 5, 1983. The other organizations made travel arrangements for their people earlier, but I did not leave Cuba until August 1983. We travelled back to Nicaragua and were sent to the same safehouse in Crucero that we had stayed at before. There were about 15 other guerrillas at the safehouse in Nicaragua, all returning from courses in Cuba and the USSR. From Nicaragua I flew to Guatemala and stayed in the Posada Real hotel in zone 1 for three days. Finally, on October 3, 1983, we took a bus to El Salvador and arrived at the western bus terminal the same day. I was taken to a safehouse in Soyapango for a week. Finally, I was picked up in a small white truck and taken to San Vicente where I was received by my commanders.[9]

FROGMEN

El Salvador has numerous lakes and rivers along its major routes of communication. In addition, many of the most important geographical divisions are made by these bodies of water. El Salvador also has a relatively long coastline. Aquatic capability is a minimum necessity for any military force serious about fighting on this terrain. As such, it is not surprising that the FPL, which was most influential in El Salvador's region of greatest lakes and rivers, Chalatenango, would think about acquiring cadres with special forces training in waterborne operations. An FPL document from early 1980 gives a list of "frogman equipment," diving masks, air tanks, fins, and outboard motors in inventory.[10] The initial attempts to form combat swimmer units probably tried to incorporate guerrillas that already had aquatic skills and experience. This is very reminiscent of similar attempts by the Argentine Montoneros that will be discussed in a later chapter. However, not discounting the Vietnamese influence, it should be mentioned that the Vietnamese special forces also had combat swimmer sections that conducted a number of operations in the rivers of Vietnam, Cambodia, and Laos. A number of river craft were mined and damaged by these units. However, the concept and mission of combat swimmers was fairly straightforward, and there were a number of good sources that could have provided the inspiration to the FPL, aside from the Vietnamese.

The FPL envisioned the combat swimmers carrying out amphibious raids on different targets. These could be conducted from the lakes and rivers in central El Salvador, and from off the Pacific Coast. The initial attempts to form a unit without special training may have been a failure. The FPL persisted with the idea of a combat swimmer unit and apparently discussed the possibility of training some men in Cuba. The Cubans agreed, and several men were subsequently sent to Cuba to undergo a naval commando course. The naval commandos would carry out the first spectacular special forces operation for the FMLN. The experience of one of the early recruits for the Cuban course is illuminating.

In May 1980, the FPL selected eight of us for special courses in Cuba. Those of us selected were not told that we were going to Cuba, but only that we were going to Nicaragua, and from there we would be given further instructions. I was chosen to be leader of the group and was given a packet of cigarettes. On the inside of one of the cigarette wrappers were telephone numbers that I was told to call once inside Nicaragua. In case of capture, or danger, I was to smoke the special cigarette to destroy the evidence. All of us were given money. The eight of us were to meet at the bus terminal with another three comrades and travel to the port of La Union.

At La Union, the eleven of us tried to act as if we were travelling individually and told the authorities we were going as tourists to either Costa Rica or Nicaragua to visit relatives. Once we had gone through immigration, we took the ferry to Nicaragua where we stayed in a predesignated hotel. At the hotel, the group of three comrades revealed to the rest of us that they were going to Cuba to participate in a sapper course. Our group of eight did not yet know what our mission was. The next day I went to the phone and called my contact. Speaking in code we agreed to meet alone at a church in Chinandega, Nicaragua. Once we met and established identity, the contact told me to go get the rest of the group and get into a small bus being driven by the contact.

From Chinandega we were driven to a safehouse in Managua. On the road we were asked who could swim. When four of us answered, we were taken aside. The four nonswimmers were told they would be given a platoon leader's course, while the four swimmers were told we would be trained as combat swimmers.

On May 19, our group was flown to Cuba on the Cuban commercial airlines. Here we met another contact who was an intelligence officer of the Cuban army. This man drove us to a safehouse where he picked up some other Salvadorans that had arrived earlier and then drove all of us to a training base known as Area 100 in Mariano Province. There were other nationalities at Area 100, including Chileans, Nicaraguans, Haitians, Ethiopians, and so on.

The frogman course, officially called combat swimmer's course, was tough, consisting of arduous sessions of physical training, swimming, and training with weapons, explosives, and boats. Mornings were spent in exercise and swimming, and afternoons in the study of Marxism, and other subjects such as explosives, weapons, navigation, topography, and so on. We were trained in the use of limpet mines and the destruction of docks, ships (wood and steel hulled), and bridges. We were trained in the use and maintenance of Soviet-manufactured open and closed circuit breathing gear. Weapons familiarization training included a variety of weapons: AKM rifles, M-16s, FN FALs, G-3s, Garands, UZI submachine guns, M-3 grease guns, Browning 9mm pistols and Colt .45 pistols. We were also trained to carry out amphibious landings from small launches and rubber boats.

Dive training and landings were carried out from a boat called the "Vietnam," manned by the course instructors. Protection was provided by Cuban coastal craft.

In August or September of 1980, a huge parade was held at Area 100. Nine hundred members of the FMLN trained in different specialties (special forces, infantry, women, artillery, frogmen, etc.) paraded for the FMLN leadership, which included Shafik Handal and Raul Castro.

After the parade we went back to training. Of the ten of us who started the course, several finished the course work but couldn't pass the qualifying exams. Only four men, including myself, made it.

In December 1980, we finished our training and flew back to Managua, Nicaragua on the Soviet commercial airline, Aeroflot. From here we were sent back to El Salvador by different routes. Some went by normal commercial routes, bus, and airplane. However, some returned to El Salvador by rowing dugout canoes called "cayucos" across the Gulf of Fonseca.[11]

THE URBAN COMMANDOS

The urban commandos were units which were to conduct terrorist warfare in the heart of the enemy stronghold. The most common method of operation was to be the use of bombs and selective assassination. Among the urban commandos was to be a special unit attached directly to the FPL high command, which was then operating clandestinely within the captial city, San Salvador. Their mission was to provide security for the leadership. However, they would also carry out assassinations, bank robberies, and other special urban operations. They were to be provided with bulletproof vests, pistols, submachine guns, silencers, disguises, and individual communications gear.[12] It is not known if this unit was ever formed. The FPL leadership was forced to leave San Salvador and the other urban areas by the government intelligence units and independent vigilantes. The higher echelons went to Nicaragua, while the lower field commanders established command posts in the rural areas of the country. The FMLN high command personnel did use special forces troops for their bodyguards when they were in country, but it is not known if these bodyguards were part of a special unit, or if they were just special forces troops, detached from their units for bodyguard duties.

Other urban commando units were formed following the same guidelines, except that of serving as bodyguards. It is not clear that these units received any specialized training abroad for their mission. Most training seems to have been acquired on their own, and picked up through experience. There were specific FPL manuals on such subjects as security, disguise, sabotage, and intelligence, techniques practiced by the urban commandos. It is known that members of the urban commandos were chosen from among the most experienced and dedicated combatants. They were organized as cells of only a few people, four or five at most. These cells were strictly isolated and only the leader had contact with the outside organization. Each member of the cell was supposed to make daily contact with an assigned member of the cell. If for any reason that person failed to show up, or gave a warning signal, the cell was supposed to disperse, and the now isolated individual members were supposed to make contact with the organization on their own. Some provisions were made for contact, such as special rendezvous points, and so on. In the early days, the urban commandos carried out many missions of sabotage, kidnapping, and assassination in all of the major urban centers, but especially in the capital of San Salvador.

The tactics and the organization of the urban commandos were evocative of the tactics used by the Junta Coordinadora Revolucionaria (JCR)[13] guerrilla groups in South America. The Salvadoran guerrillas had been great vocal supporters of the Argentine Montoneros, the Uruguayan Tupamaros, and the Chilean MIR during the 1970s; however, it is not known how much contact the groups had with each other at this time. It is known that the JCR made contact with the FMLN in early 1980 and offered to provide material and instructional support to the FMLN.[14] While there is no proof that the JCR trained the FPL urban commandos, it is highly likely because of the similarity of the operations, and the fact that in 1982, an urban warfare manual of the Chilean Resistance was captured in an urban commando safehouse in Santa Tecla, a town contiguous to San Salvador.

The intelligence services of the armed forces and security forces launched a concerted and ruthless campaign in late 1980 against the urban commandos. By mid-1981 the security forces had destroyed most of the urban commando cells and the clandestine guerrilla organizations in the major cities. However, they did not totally disappear and would make a comeback with a vengeance in 1988.

THE SPECIAL OPERATIONS DETACHMENT

An FPL document dated August 1980 proposed the creation of a Special Operations Detachment of "battalion" strength, divided into two "detachments" of six "sections" each.[15] If later FPL battalions created in 1981 and 1982 can be used for reference, this meant that it would contain somewhere between 200 to 250 men organized into two detachments of company size, divided into three sections, each equivalent to a platoon. In addition, the battalion would have an artillery platoon of light mortars, recoilless rifles and machine guns, a communications platoon, a first aid platoon, and a training school platoon. The special forces unit was to be under the direct control of "Marcial," an alias for Cayetano Carpio, the maximum leader of the FPL. A member of the high command under Marcial would have central control over all special operations forces. He was to work intimately with the intelligence and counterintelligence structures within the FPL. The unit was to be formed by October 15, 1980.[16] The detachment was originally thought to consist largely of specialists in urban operations. Specialists were called for in explosives, sniping, interrogation, the use of light artillery, driving, lock picking, and so on. Equipment called for in the table of organization and equipment included: 27 rifles, submachine guns and sawed off shotguns, 100 pistols, hand grenades, smoke bombs, a bazooka, a .30 or .50 caliber machine gun, a motorcycle, a car, binoculars, wigs, beards and mustaches, hand-held radios, tape recorders, and body armor.

At least one section of this unit was formed by August 1980, but it is not known if the entire detachment was ever completed. By late 1980, the military intelligence services and private "death squads" had waged a fierce campaign against the FMLN in the cities. For the most part, the guerrillas were forced out into the countryside. This may have had an effect on the concepts of organization of the special forces as the emphasis was less on urban commando skills and more on a wider range of specialist skills.[17]

Urban commandos were designed to infiltrate and survive in the enemy rear areas, causing as much confusion and pandemonium as possible among the enemy ranks. They were to hamper enemy movement and lower morale by disrupting the tranquility of his rear areas. This would force the enemy to move slowly and devote resources he would normally assign to combat, to provide security in these places.[18]

SNIPERS

The concept of sniping was implemented. However, at this stage of the war it appears that a special sniping unit was not formed, special sniper rifles were not obtained, and no one received specialized training. Sniping was instead implemented as a specialized form of attack on army installations. The favorite mode was to send out a pair of combatants who were good shots, with ordinary rifles (preferably in 7.62mm NATO or larger because of the increased range), who would quietly set up within rifle range of a military installation and take potshots at the sentries, and any other military personnel that were unlucky enough to be walking around. After a few shots, the two snipers would quietly and quickly slip away. This method was undoubtedly demoralizing to the army troops, and conversely was a great morale booster for the guerrilla forces. Some passages from a guerrilla commander's diary captured in Chalatenango in late 1981 show clearly how sniping was implemented.

April 7th, 1981. We sent comrades Geremias, Geronimo and Demecio to snipe at the enemy sentry at San Isidro. They fired but missed.

April 8th. At 3:00 A.M. we sent Geremias and comrade Pedro to snipe from the same place as before. The target was on the edge of the hilltop that is behind the mayor's building. Comrade Pedro realized that the target was a very long distance from where they were set up. They decided to shoot anyway. Pedro did the shooting, and hit the feet of the enemy sentry. All of the enemy positions blindly opened fire in retaliation.

April 9th. We sent comrades Pedro and Geronimo on a mission to snipe at the sentry post in San Isidro. They made an uneventful approach, but set up too far away so that when they fired they didn't hit their target.

April 11th. Rene took his squad of Demecio, Geremias, Pancho and Javier out to set up an ambush at 4:00 A.M. When the enemy didn't come after two hours, Rene sent Geremias and Javier to snipe at the sentries at San Isidro. The pair got close to the sentry. Javier raised his rifle and fired, killing the sentry. They then returned quickly to the ambush position hoping to draw the soldiers out. When no one had come by 8:00 A.M., Pancho and Javier returned to snipe. They could see no one. The two guerrillas yelled, "Out here are the guerrillas. You soldiers only kill old ladies!" After yelling they set their weapons on automatic and fired up the army trenches. The soldiers did not move and the two guerrillas left.

April 12th. I sent Mauricio, Mundo and Arcadio out to snipe at the Amates post of San Isidro. They set up too far away, fired six 7.62 NATO rounds and didn't cause any casualties.[19]

While these FPL guerrillas were not very skilled at sniping, this short passage shows the demoralizing and paralyzing effect that daily harassment can have on a superior number of soldiers, even when the snipers are mostly missing their targets. Sniping would remain a special tactic, and not something worthy of specially trained personnel or a special purpose force, until approximately 1988. At this time, the FMLN began to import specialized sniper weapons, specifically the Soviet-made Dragunov, and train special forces personnel in sniper techniques. While the Dragunov rifle is not favored by expert snipers in the West, it is acknowledged as an adequate weapon for the mission for which it was designed. A unique target assigned to the guerrilla snipers was to fire at aircraft in the hopes of hitting a pilot or vital part of the aircraft. This met with some success as several aircraft were holed and some pilots were wounded by Dragunovs. However, the most effective use of snipers occurred during the November 1989 urban offensive. This will be discussed in a later chapter.

By 1982 there were two FPL FES units known as F-30 and J-28. The F-30 were the FES unit subordinate to the high command of the FPL. The F-30 had a platoon whose mission was to provide security for the high command of the FPL in the department of Chalatenango. There were two platoons that were located near the border with Honduras in subzones 1, 2, and 3 of the Apolinario Serrano Northern Front that covered the department of Chalatenango. The F-30's strength was approximately 100 guerrillas.

The J-28 FES units were those FES troops subordinated to the brigade of the FPL. There were two groups corresponding to each FPL brigade group. Group No. 1 operated on the Western, Northern, Central, and Metropolitan fronts. Their home base was in the Northern Front in Chalatenango in subzone 1. The strength of Group 1 was approximately 30 guerrillas. Group No. 2 consisted of approximately 40 guerrillas and operated in the Para-Central and Eastern Fronts in San Vicente and Usulutan, and their permanent base was in subzone Marcial Gavidia and subzone Jaragua. The combat swimmers were located in Chalatenango and were part of the Northern Front forces.[20]

The documents and experiences of the FPL, mentioned above, are a good window on the total picture of special forces development in El Salvador. The irony is that despite the FPL's pioneer work, it was the ERP faction of the FMLN that really first explored the full possibilities of FES tactics. A spectacularly successful raid on the Ilopango air base, described in a later chapter, opened the door for future development and operations. The ERP were so pleased with the results of the air base attack that they formed an entire FES battalion known as the "Special Troops Comandante Manglio Armijo," known by the Spanish acronym TECMA. The TECMA battalion was distributed on three fronts. The first and second sections were located on the Northeastern front. The third section was located on the Southeastern front. The fourth section was based on the Western front. The TECMA had a total of two commanders and 240 combatants. Each section consisted of 60 combatants. A unique aspect of the TECMA was that they were assigned organic support weapons, 81mm mortars, 90mm recoilless rifles, and heavy machine guns. This gave them an independence and capacity for operations not enjoyed by any of the other organizations' FES units. Perhaps as a consequence, the ERP FES were the most active of the war, carried out the most spectacular operations, and were the most feared.[21]

Later, organizations such as FAL, RN, and the PRTC also sent personnel to Cuba or the ERP and FPL schools to be trained in FES techniques, but these units did not receive the same support and priority as those of the

FPL and ERP. As a result, the high command of the FMLN lost faith in them except for use in small, localized actions. This was because many of their operations in larger and more sophisticated actions had been less than successful.

The start-up work of the FPL, the training in Cuba, and the initial success and enthusiasm of several groups, but particularly of the ERP, set the stage for the most thorough development and employment of guerrilla special forces in Latin America. The following chapters will describe the tactical methods of the various special forces units and give a partial operational history of the special units of the FPL, ERP, and FAL. These were the guerrilla factions that most successfully developed the special forces concept and conducted the most successful special forces operations.

While not all of the FMLN factions initially embraced the concept of FES and special forces guerrillas early in the war, their enthusiasm grew as the special forces carried out spectacularly successful operations. Ironically, while the FPL did the initial development work on the ideas and concepts of special forces, it was the ERP that would actually develop the largest FES units and conduct the most special forces operations. The FPL would develop the next largest units, following in descending numerical order and operational success by the FAL, RN, and PRTC. The FPL developed conceptual work for four types of special forces: sappers, combat swimmers, urban commandos, and snipers. Operational and political situations in El Salvador would dictate that only the sapper concept would be fully developed during the war. The concept of the urban commandos would be watered down and delegated to the clandestine militias, the FMLN's irregular, part-time urban members. Highly sensitive urban operations were delegated to the sapper units, which, because of their higher level of training, could be trusted to operate successfully in an urban environment.

The FAL organized their special forces along similar lines to the FPL. Consequently, the U-24 organization and equipment mirrored those of the J-28. The U-24 was based on Guazapa Mountain and participated in the first attack on the 4th Brigade. They were decimated during the army Fenix operations from 1985 to 1987, but were reorganized and fought in Soyapango during the 1989 urban offensive. Another special forces unit of the FAL was known as the COBRAC (Commandos of the BRAC, the FAL battalion). This unit operated on the Para-Central Front and was approximately a platoon-sized element. It was also devasted by the Fenix operations. After Operation Fenix, the FAL dissolved the COBRAC and transferred all of the personnel to the U-24. In addition, the FAL had a unit known as the Pedro Pablo Castillo Urban Commandos that operated on the north semiurban periphery of San Salvador and were trained in FES techniques, although their missions were more oriented toward the urban setting.[22]

The RN had the J-27 and Unit September 15 (U-S-15), consisting of two platoons, and was based on Guazapa Mountain. The J-27 was initially trained by the FPL J-28. This is the origin of the designation J-27. The J-27 and J-28 operated jointly for a time.[23] The PRTC didn't organize an FES platoon until 1987. This platoon operated in eastern El Salvador and was largely used to provide security for the PRTC high command. By 1988 the PRTC FES unit had approximately 30 members. Meanwhile, the FES of the FPL and the ERP enjoyed some fairly spectacular success. Attacks on the 4th Brigade base at El Paraiso, the Puente de Cuscatlan Bridge, Cerron Grande, and several other minor actions convinced the FMLN of the importance of special forces.[24]

In May–June of 1985, a meeting of the high command of the FMLN was held, in which military guidelines were established, including the priority of developing and creating more FES units, and to designate these units as being the highest category of combat unit of irregular warfare in El Salvador.[25] This was the first formal recognition by the FMLN high command of the permanent institutional elite status of the FES.[26] Ironically, just as they became an institutional elite, the number of spectacular actions they carried out declined. This was mostly due to the fact that the army had developed tactics that forced the FMLN to split up into small units. The FMLN, in the same meeting mentioned above, adopted new tactics. It abandoned the semiconventional tactics it had adopted in 1982 and reverted to purely guerrilla tactics. Attrition was the word of the day. Instead of battalion against battalion, the ambush, harassing attack, mine warfare, and sabotage were used. It was rarely after this that the FMLN was able to concentrate for a full-scale attack, and the results of these attacks were mixed at best. Another aspect to this was that although the FES had been highly successful, they had suffered fairly heavy attrition. Since there were not too many of them, even a small number of killed and wounded in an operation was a heavy loss. Little by little, the Cuban-trained personnel were lost, and although the FMLN set up its own schools and trained replacements, these were never of the same calibre as those originally trained in Cuba. The men chosen for training in Cuba had been guerrillas with proven combat skills and ideological commitment. The new recruits were often very young, inexperienced, and not as reliable. This is a common phenomenon in armies around the world. As wars progress and the best soldiers are killed, wounded, or returned, armies are forced to employ men that fall below desired standards.

However, the FES did continue to operate. Mostly, they were assigned special reconnaissance missions and other missions, such as sabotage, assassination, ambushes, and so on, that required more skill, daring, and training than was the norm among regular guerrilla forces. However, it was often very difficult to distinguish these actions from those of regular guerrilla units. This is reflected in this work. It will be noted that very few operations after 1986 are discussed.

NOTES

1. Artilleria sin cañon y Bombas sin Avion.

2. FPL, *Notes from the Meeting with David on the Special Select Forces*, April 15, 1981.

3. Alan Vick, *Snakes in the Eagle's Nest: A History of Ground Attacks on Air Bases* (Santa Monica, CA: Rand Corporation, 1995), pp. 67–103, 127–165.

4. Courtney E. Prisk, ed., *The Comandante Speaks: Memoirs of an El Salvadoran Guerrilla Leader* (Boulder, CO: Westview Press, 1991), p. 67.

5. Prisk, *The Comandante Speaks*, pp. 66–67.

6. Ibid.

7. Similar conclusions are found in Major Victor M. Rosello, "Vietnam's Support to El Salvador's FMLN: Successful Tactics in Central America," *Military Review* (January 1990), pp. 71–78.

8. FPL, *Notes from the Meeting with David*, April 15, 1981.

9. Interrogation Transcript of RAA, May 11, 1987.

10. FPL, untitled document listing diving equipment in the guerrillas' inventory, August 1980.

11. Interrogation Transcript of SSG, April 5, 1982.

12. FPL, *Project of the Special Operation Detachment*, August 1980.

13. An alliance of four South American guerrilla groups: the Argentine Montoneros and ERP, Bolivian ELN, Chilean MIR, and the Uruguayan MLN Tupamaros.

14. Servicio de Inteligencia del Estado (Argentine Intelligence), file entitled *JCR*, given to the author by a former SIE operative in 1991.

15. FPL, *Project for the Special Operations Detachment*, August 1980.

16. Ibid.

17. Ibid.

18. Ibid.

19. FPL, *Centeno Clandestine Archive*, captured from the FMLN in 1982.

20. Special Operations Group, *Know the Enemy* (Armed Forces of El Salvador, 1986).

21. Ibid.

22. Armed Forces of El Salvador, *Activities in Which the Terrorist Guerrillas Have Participated*, March 1990.

23. Interrogation Transcipt of TA, September 17, 1987.

24. Armed Forces of El Salvador, *Activities in Which the Terrorist Special Forces Have Participated*, March 1990.

25. FMLN, *Military Line of the FMLN: High Command Meeting, May-June, Morazan 1985* (Sistema Venceremos, Morazan, 1986).

26. Ibid.

CHAPTER 2

FMLN Special Forces Techniques

SAPPERS

The sappers were the most important and common specialty within the FMLN special forces. Sappers were considered strategic forces that used special irregular tactics independently or in conjunction with the regular units. Their mission was to attack and destroy objectives, deep in the enemy rear, where they would attempt to eliminate the army's strategic and tactical advantages by penetrating at the weakest points. In other words, their role was to act as equalizers. They were the guerrillas' substitute for heavy artillery and aviation.[1] Sapper personnel were selected from among the best of the regular guerrilla units.

The sappers were assigned the task of breaking the enemy's defenses of the cities or economic centers by the destruction of fixed, fortified positions and the enemy's support weapons, planes, armor, and artillery. This included attacking the very center of the armed forces and the government zones of control. Highly destructive attacks in the "safe areas" of the enemy would cause both physical and psychological damage. If the enemy had nowhere to rest, he would begin to lose confidence in himself and his leaders. Loss of morale would lead to loss of the war.

All the objectives of the sappers were assigned by the high command of the FMLN. The FMLN high command based its orders on those objectives which would produce the greatest political and psychological repercussions and economic damage, and that would inflict the greatest military defeat on the enemy. The political impact of the operation was usually the first consideration. The FMLN was struggling for political power, and as such the political effects of its military operations were usually the most important objective. The FMLN took Clausewitz's maxim about the relationship between politics and warfare very seriously.

Basic sapper objectives included destroying enemy combat forces, command posts, small enemy bases, or small units in the guerrilla zones of persistence; destroying equipment such as helicopters, armored vehicles, and artillery; anti-aircraft ambushes; intelligence through the taking of prisoners, documents, and reconnaissance; planning and facilitation of operations by regular forces; eliminating and disrupting enemy reconnaissance units and intelligence networks.

The advantage of the sappers was their simplicity. Essentially, they were an effective, low-tech commando force. They concentrated on a few skills which they learned to perfection and carried out with a high degree of discipline. There were two main areas of specialization: infiltration and the manufacture and use of explosive charges.

Infiltration was for two purposes. First, it was the means by which the sappers' main weapon, explosives, was delivered to the target; and second, it was the means by which a sapper unit reconnoitered a target to plan and prepare for an attack. An outgrowth of sapper infiltration skills was that they were employed by the chain of command to conduct tactical and strategic reconnaissance for the regular guerrilla units.

A key aspect of infiltration was patience. To give an example, the penetration of 100 meters of perimeter might take an hour or more. To do this effectively, sapper commandos were taught a series of drills in which they carried out very precise physical movements to overcome a variety of obstacles. They drilled in these movements repeatedly so a sapper commando would automatically know which technique to use when faced with a particular obstacle, without having to think about it. In other words, these techniques became second nature to the sapper special forces man. Among the types of obstacles that could be crossed with these techniques were all types of fences, wire obstacles, minefields, areas covered by bright lights, walls, ditches, and so on.

Sapper penetration operations were always carried out at night, when it was darkest, usually between the hours of 12:00 midnight and 2:00 A.M. This was also found to be the time when the sentries and soldiers were the least alert. The guerrilla sappers conducted penetration operations nearly naked. This was so they could better feel the obstacles they were crossing. For these missions, the guerrillas were taught to rely heavily on their tactile senses. Their uniforms consisted of a pair of tight, dark (usually black) shorts or briefs, and thorough camouflage body paint. The body paint depended on the terrain and could be charcoal, mud, or multicolored paint. A well-trained sapper soldier could, with little difficulty, routinely penetrate an army base or position without being detected.

If the army discovered sapper/commandos penetrating its perimeter, the FMLN did not cease to plan the attack on that objective. Blowing the cover of a sapper operation merely delayed the attack. The sappers might cease penetration operations for several weeks, and then resume them, as soon as the initial excitement had died down. Examples of this were the attacks on the CEMFA and the second attack on the 3rd Brigade. Reconaissance was discovered for both objectives in 1982–1983. In 1985 the sappers attacked the CEMFA, and in 1986 the sappers attacked the 3rd Brigade. Few sapper attacks were cancelled, they were merely delayed. The sappers did not attack until they calculated they had at least a 90 percent chance of success. Therefore, thorough reconnaissance was usually considered more important than speed. As stated before, patience was key to sapper operations. The overall guerrilla strategy was "prolonged popular war," so the FMLN could wait to strike at the right moment. This combined with self-discipline made the low-tech sapper commandos a formidable enemy.

Modes of Attack

There were three modes of attack using penetration. The first was clandestine penetration, clandestine extraction. The second was clandestine penetration, violent extraction. The third was violent penetration, violent extraction. The first mode was for clandestine attacks. The sappers employed clandestine attacks in operations where the objective was to destroy enemy equipment housed in fortified bases, such as parked aircraft or vehicles, ammunition dumps, and fuel depots. A common attack using this mode of penetration was known as the "Fan" method. This was used in attacks against airfields. Penetration was made at the center of the strip. The attacking unit divided into two groups. One group would then move to one end of the airfield, and the other to the opposite end. Once in position, they initiated the attack inward to the point of penetration, whereupon they would exit the airfield. The objective was to maintain the secrecy of the operation until the explosives went off, destroying the equipment sometime after the guerrilla force had already made its exit. The principle weapon in this type of attack was explosives with Soviet PUT-02 time delay fuses.

Usually, the second mode of penetration, penetrate secretly, withdraw violently, was the favored mode of action for a sapper unit. This was used for attacks on fixed army positions with perimeter obstacles and defenses. The objective of these attacks was to annihilate enemy personnel. Sapper teams would infiltrate the base along predetermined routes and then attack outward toward the perimeter. The months of stealthy penetration and exfiltration spent on reconnoitering and objective were finally put to use, and what might have taken six months of patient reconnaissance would be over in a few violent minutes. Attacking from the center out had several advantages. Normally, bases are set up so that the most vulnerable and important equipment or personnel to protect are placed in the center with defenses on the perimeter to stand between them and the enemy. This would include command personnel, communications, and heavy weapons. By eliminating these elements first, the sappers would effectively cut off command, control, and support for the remaining elements within an army camp. The second purpose for attacking from the center out to the periphery was to disorient and frustrate the defensive plan of the objective. Most defensive works face outward, not inward, and have little or no protection to the rear. Attacking from behind took advantage of this vulnerability and allowed the sapper commandos to make their escape by blasting a path through the rear of the defensive perimeter back out to safe territory. This technique against fortified positions was known to the sappers as the "Flower" method. This mode of attack was usually carried out in conjunction with a regular guerrilla unit employing artillery. If, when the operation was discovered, the sapper commandos were still located inside the objective or perimeter of the objective, support artillery would go into action to distract and confuse the garrison, allowing the sappers to exit the objective.

The final mode of penetration, violent in and violent out, was used only when conditions didn't allow for secret penetration. Usually, this would be against lightly defended objectives located in towns. However, it could also be used for attacks on larger objectives. Attacks of this nature were only carried out when there was 100 percent knowledge of the enemy forces at the objective. This mode of attack was always carried out with popular artillery support, ramps, mortars, and rifle grenades. In this case, sapper units almost always operated in combination with regular units. The regular units would lay down a heavy barrage on the objective to pin down the enemy defenders. While they were hunkered down in their bunkers and trenches, the sappers would rapidly penetrate and blast a path through the defenders to the center of the objective. Here they would attack command, control, and support elements and then withdraw, blasting their way back out.

MOVEMENT TECHNIQUES

As mentioned above, one of the primary techniques that enabled the sappers to penetrate military bases and installations for reconnaissance and attack were their special movement techniques. There were numerous drills, many still unknown, but the following descriptions taken directly from a sapper's notebook shed much light on the methods.

The basic movement was the "crouched advance." This position was used to advance great distances such as from the departure points to the forward edge of battle (FEBA). It was also useful in the approach to attack objectives. This was the starting position for all other movement techniques. The technique was done by bending the knees and bending the trunk forward. Arms were tucked in and the rifle was held tight to the chest with the muzzle pointing forward. The weight of the body was supported by the leg to the rear. High steps were taken to avoid bushes, branches, or other things on the ground that could cause noise. The forward foot searched for a quiet place to rest the foot and then planted it slowly to make sure it would not make noise. The weight was then shifted to the recently planted foot and the process was continued.

The next movement was the "advance on one side." This movement was used to advance short and medium distances in those areas where there was short vegetation, that were under enemy observation. From the crouched advance the commando laid down on the left side. The left leg was moved forward and bent at the knee. The left arm was bent and the weight of the body rested on the forearm. Movement was made by pushing the heel of the right foot against the ground as close to the body as possible. The right leg was straightened, which causes the body to advance forward. The position of the left leg was not changed. The weapon was held with the right hand holding the forward hand guard with the stock resting on the left thigh. This kept it from striking objects and making noise, and also kept the muzzle out of the dirt.

A third movement technique was "the crawl." This was used during penetration, for deactivating minefields, and for approaching the line of departure for assault. From the crouched advance the sapper laid prone on his stomach with legs slightly apart. The rifle was taken in the right hand by the sling, and held as close to the muzzle as possible. The arm was laid flat to the ground and bent forward at the elbow. The weapon was laid across the crook of the forearm and the bicep to keep it out of the dirt. The right leg was bent forward and the left leg extended with the foot resting on its side, flat on the ground. At the same time, the left arm was extended forward, palm down, flat on the ground. Movement was made by pushing off the right foot and pulling with the left hand. The head was kept down, face toward the weapon.

A variation of this was the "high crawl." The prone position on the stomach was assumed, with the legs apart and knees bent. The body rested on the forearms with arms bent and elbows out. In the crook of the arms the weapon was carried, muzzle off the ground. Movement was made by pushing off the elbow and the foot opposite from each other. The head was held up and the buttocks kept down.

A further variation was known as the "Vietnamese crawl." This movement was done by lying face down on the ground with legs and heels together. The arms were bent with elbows out, resting on the forearms. The hands were in, fingers open. The fingers met forming a heart shape. Movement was made by moving the hands forward, pulling with these, and pushing the body up off the ground with the feet, toward the hands.

The head was kept low, but still looking forward. The rifle could be laid on the ground to one side and pulled up every two or three pushes.

The "movement on three points" was used to recon objectives. This was a variation of the advance on the side. The same position was taken up. Generally, the arm was straightened, but for a lower profile, the body could rest on the forearm. The movement was made by using both feet to push the body off the ground to where only the feet and one hand (or forearm) were touching the ground. The body was moved forward and then rested back on the ground. The arm was moved forward to find another position, and the feet pushed off again. The rifle could be carried either across the thigh of the left leg, with the hand on the muzzle, elbow tucked in, or tucked under the armpit.

Special movements were developed to overcome base lights. The basic principle was that where there was light, there was also shadow. All of the movements were made starting from the crouched advance.

The "lights in front" movement was done by going down on the knee of the foot that was behind at the time the light appeared, and lowering the buttocks until they touched the foot. Simultaneously, the sapper stretched out the free arm and with the finger, covered the rifle muzzle. The face was covered by bending the head and torso downward. When the light appeared the commandos would say "light in front," to warn the others and when the light passed, the commando would say "the light has passed," for the same reason. When a light appeared from the side the commandos would say "light from the side." The movement was made by going down on the knee of the leg behind and touching the buttocks to the foot. The free arm reached forward and covered the muzzle of the rifle with the finger. The foot in front was then stretched backward, and the torso bent down to the ground. The face was turned away from the light.

When an overhead flare appeared the commandos would say "overhead flare." The movement was made by going down on the knee of the back leg, but not touching the buttocks to the foot. The free arm covered the rifle muzzle with the hand, and the torso was bent forward until it was resting on the forearms. The front leg was stretched backward, and then the leg on the knee was stretched back as well until the commando was in a prone position.[2]

The above is probably not a comprehensive list of the different types of movement techniques, but does cover some of the most important types. These movements were practiced over and over again until they were second nature. When employing these movements during an operation, every movement was made very deliberately and patiently. It could take hours for a sapper team to penetrate to the interior of an installation. Body and mind control were fundamental qualities that each sapper had to possess.

The special movements and techniques were largely taught to allow the commando to infiltrate enemy positions and cross his perimeter undetected. One of the principal obstacles encountered by the FES troops were different types of wire fences. The following excerpt from an FPL FES man's captured notebook reveals some of the techniques for breaching this obstacle.

Breaching a Wire Obstacle

There are generally three types of fencing used by the enemy: cyclone, barbed wire, and concertina. There are two types of methods for breaching these obstacles: destructive, and nondestructive. Nondestructive methods should always be used for reconnaissance, while destructive methods can be used for assault.

Almost all wire fences can be breached nondestructively. This depends upon their flexibility and the gaps between the strands. The commando should always attempt to slip his body in between the gaps. This can be done by taking time and making very deliberate movements.

Cyclone fencing can generally be unhooked from its stakes and stretched to open a hole big enough for a man to squeeze through. Care must be taken to not cause noise. This can be done by using stakes, or having a comrade hold the fencing while the other comrade goes through. During a recon, the commandos must be careful to return the same way and return the fence back to its original position. Another possibility is to dig a hole underneath the wire. However, this takes time, and can often be detected by the pile of dirt produced. Often in our country, holes can be found underneath fences because of water drainage. These should be searched for before digging a hole.

Barbed wire can generally be penetrated by stretching the strands apart. However, often it is electrified. Electrified wire can be stretched apart and held with wooden stakes. Care must be taken not to touch the wire when passing in between. Nonconductive material may also be placed over the bottom strand to allow the commando to crawl through.

Concertina wire is probably one of the easiest to penetrate. Gaps are often large enough to crawl through. However, one should take care, as the concertina is often combined with mines and booby traps. If the gaps aren't big enough to crawl through, little wire clips can be carried to clip strands together and create a larger gap. This method is often undetectable, and can be left in place after a recon for a future attack. It is preferable to go under or through wire obstacles, as going over them leaves one vulnerable to observation and fire. For all types of wire during a recon, extreme care must be taken to return the fence to its original state. This helps avoid detection.

The destructive method is divided into two categories: wire cutters and explosives. Wire cutters cause the least noise and are preferable where speed and silence are required. Wire cutters should have wooden or rubber handles to avoid electrocution. Care must be taken that the wire not snap and make further noise. This can be assured by having another comrade hold the strands being cut. Holes should be large enough to permit the rapid deployment of the troops.

The same type of explosive used for breaching minefields is used for breaching wire obstacles. One advantage of this method is that often a wire obstacle and minefield can be breached with one explosion. This type of explosive should only be used during an attack where obstacles are relatively shallow, and speed is of the essence.[3]

CAMOUFLAGE

To aid their movements, the sappers were also heavily drilled in camouflage techniques. They were taught that camouflage consisted of a combination of coordinated measures applied to insure the concealment of the action of their forces to disorient the enemy as to the composition of the guerrilla forces and their military intentions. Camouflage allowed the sappers to gain the element of surprise, confuse the enemy, and exact maximum efficiency of their own forces. When the sappers conducted operations, they always used camouflage. For night penetration missions there were four types. The sappers knew these as (1) grassy—vegetation; (2) multicolor— paint; (3) earth—mud; and (4) carbon or ash.

Grassy camouflage was used in places where there was heavy vegetation, or in areas where the only vegetation was grass. The sapper would wear olive green or camouflage pattern clothing, overalls, or shirt and trousers, and a cap. Strips of burlap cloth 10 cm long by 1 cm wide were sewn onto the back of the pants and shirt in a diamond pattern. Strips were also sewn onto the cap and equipment bag and added to the rifle. This was the only type of camouflage clothing worn by sappers. The other types of camouflage were painted directly on the sapper's naked body.

What the sappers called multicolor camouflage was used where there was no foliage and very little vegetation. The camouflage was painted on the body and the equipment and consisted of a mix of different colored inks such as black, green, brown, and blue; and different plant juices such as those from cassava and sweet potato leaves. The only clothing worn was briefs. The whole body, equipment, and weapons were painted in flower patterns, called "tiger spots" by the sappers.

Mud or slime covering was used where the terrain was tilled or cleared of vegetation. Mud made from the soil taken from the objective of operation was used. Only shorts or briefs were worn. The mix was applied to the body, shorts, bag, and on the explosive charges.

Carbon or ash was used where the terrain was burned or paved. Only briefs were worn. The substance was smashed into powder and applied to the combatant's entire body, bag, briefs, and the explosive charges.[4]

EXPLOSIVES

The main weapon of the sapper was the explosive charge. It was also the principal weapon in the enemy arsenal that could hamper and endanger sapper penetration missions. Sappers were thoroughly trained in the theory of explosives, their uses, manufacture, and deactivation. The sappers were taught that explosives were mixes of chemical substances which, upon being initiated by an external agent in the form of gas and heat, released great amounts of energy at high speeds, the volume of the gasses being much greater than the space occupied before the reaction. The destructive power of the explosive was not due to the large amount of energy it produced, but rather to the velocity at which the energy was released. This rapid expansion produced a mechanical, destructive effect.

The sappers primarily used explosives that they called initiators and penetrators. Initiators were those explosives that were sensitive to heat, chemical buffeting, and electrical sparks. These explosives were used to make detonating caps and to detonate other explosives. Penetrators were explosives that were extremely powerful, but not very sensitive to the action of external agents. They could only usually be set off through the explosion of an initiator explosive.

The most common type of explosive carried by the sappers was Soviet TNT. This was considered a medium explosive. It was yellow in color, came in small rectangular cakes, and remained stable in temperatures under 81.2°C and lower. It could be burned at temperatures above 81.2°C, but would not explode until it reached an initiation temperature of 290°C. Once it exploded, the gasses expanded at a velocity of 7,000 meters per minute. This was adequate for most of the sappers' needs. The one drawback was that it was not flexible (plastic) like American C-4, so it was difficult to modify or shape at the moment of placement. However, it could be cut or melted at low heat and poured into a mold. The sappers did have other types of explosives such as C-4, exogene, nitroglycerine, and so on, but they were in shorter supply because of the difficulty to obtain them.

The sappers were trained to make their own explosive charges according to their needs. The sappers were trained to determine the amount of explosive, size, and shape of their charges according to the particular construction of the objectives the explosives were designed to destroy or damage. Explosive charges were to always be placed on the vulnerable points of the objective. This is where they caused the greatest destruction.

For greater effect and to insure initiation, the sappers often used a reinforcer. This was an additional amount of high explosive that was placed on a charge. For each kilogram of charge, the sappers were taught to add 25 grams of reinforcer up to a total of 200 grams of reinforcer explosive. Exogene, PENT, picric acid, and plastic explosive were among the explosives used as reinforcers.

The sappers were taught to make four types of charges: (1) concentrated, (2) adjusted to construction, (3) elongated, and (4) accumulative. Concentrated charges were those charges whose length was no more than five times their width. Most of the charges used by the sappers were of this type. They were used to kill or destroy anything in the interior of buildings and bunkers. Among the favorite concentrated charges used by the FMLN sappers were what they called "hand charges," and "square charges." The hand charges could be of 100, 200, 400, 800, and 1000 grams. Each sapper unit made its own and came up with different sizes that it preferred for different tasks. The square charges varied from two to four kilos of explosive, and were the ones that the FES initially tossed into barracks and bunkers to annihilate the occupants and equipment and produce the greatest initial shock.

Adjusted charges were those explosives used to destroy complex constructions of metal such as hangars, bridges, and warehouses; any construction with a metal frame.

Elongated charges' length exceeded five times their width. These were used to breach obstacles, similar in concept to the bangalore torpedo. Usually, they were from three to nine kilos. The explosive was encased in a plastic or metal tube, or a piece of hollow bamboo. In the center of the charge a waxed paper tube or plastic tube, often a straw, was placed. Inside of this tube was the reinforcer and at least three blasting caps apart from the one used to initiate the explosion.

Accumulative charges were those used to open breaches or holes in metal or reinforced concrete. They were equivalent to what was called "hollow" charges in Western armies. The basic principle was that of a concentrated stream of explosive energy. Because of their shape, the energy developed concentrated at one point, which allowed it to penetrate armor. The FMLN sappers used these charges for the destruction of fuel storage tanks, armored vehicles, cisterns, and fortifications. When used against armored vehicles, they were to be placed on the fuel tank, motor, or side-skirts, where the vehicle was most vulnerable.

The sappers used three methods of initation: mechanical, electrical, and chemical. Mechanical was the most common, and was used in conjunction with a striker. Most mechanical blasting caps were factory-made types, brought in from Nicaragua, but the guerrilla sappers were taught to make their own. They also made their own strikers, which was a device that through friction produced the necessary heat and light to ignite time fuse crimped to the mechanical blasting caps attached to the explosive charges. For more delicate timed explosions, the sappers usually employed the PUT 01, a Soviet-made multiuse striker.

For electrical detonation, the sappers set up a complete electrical circuit and then ran energy through it to produce the explosion. The common way that electrical detonation is initiated in Western armies is by means of a hand-cranked dynamo. The other alternative was to set up a device where the continuous energy supply (a battery) was connected to an incomplete circuit. To initiate the explosion, means were provided to complete the circuit. This usually involved a device where a nonconductive wedge was placed between two pieces of conductive material attached to the battery. When the explosion was initiated, the wedge was removed and the circuit was completed.

The advantage of electrical initiation was that a number of explosives could be set off simultaneously on the same circuit. This means of detonation was highly desirable to blow down bridges, railroads, towers, and buildings, although mechanical means could be used as well. The biggest problem for these types of objectives was to find a sufficiently large source of energy. The sappers were taught to calculate 1.5 volts per electrical detonator and 20 meters of cable. All electrical detonators used by the FMLN sappers were factory made, connected by conductors of size 20, 22, or 24 cable of between 2 to 10 meters to number 10, 12, or 14 size main cable. The main cable was connected to the energy source.

The sappers also had access to the American M1 chemical initiator. It was used to detonate independent explosive charges that were placed on the weak points of enemy equipment: armor, artillery pieces, ammunition dumps, and so on. It could be activated by squeezing the upper part with the teeth or engineering crimps, which broke a vial containing acid, and then shaking it. The acid in the vial would then flow out and eat away a striker retaining wire. Once it was corroded, the striker would hit a fulminating cap and produce the necessary spark to initiate the blasting cap, burning the time fuse or det cord, which would then initiate the explosion.[5]

MINES AND BOOBY TRAPS

As mentioned earlier, one of the principal weapons used to deter the sappers were mines and booby traps. The sappers were trained that minefields used by the enemy were employed to protect sensitive objectives, as a defensive measure or as barriers to harass the guerrillas, and even fake minefields were used to confuse and disorient. The sappers had to be familiar with all types of mines, emplacement patterns, and booby trap devices. Thorough training was conducted on a number of U.S.-manufactured mines, since these were the types that were predominantly used by the Salvadoran military. They included M-14, M-16, M-18A1 anti-personnel mines, M-7 anti-tank mines, and a wooden anti-personnel mine of unknown designation. In addition, they were trained in all types of fuses and detonation devices such as mouse traps,[6] pressure release and pressure application devices, and so on.[7] To illustrate some of the FES techniques, the following extract from an FPL FES man's captured notebook is illuminating.

Breaching a Minefield

Minefields can be breached either silently or with noise. During a recon, we prefer the silent method. During an attack, either method can be used, largely depending on the nature of the attack and the distance covered by obstacles and mines between the attacking force and the objective.

For the silent method, there are two variations: deactivation and marking. Deactivation is normally used only during an assault. Marking can be used during either an assault or a recon. Deactivation requires knowledge of all the different types of fuses. During the advance, we should always be looking for trip wires. We should always move very slowly and deliberately. Furthermore, we should conduct recons barefoot and wearing only briefs, as the bare skin is one of the best detectors of trip wires. When a mine is located, we should always feel for trip wires by feeling delicately around the fuse with our fingers. If we are going through deactivation procedures, we need to be familiar with the various types of fuses, and carry the correct equipment to deactivate them.

If we are pressed for time, we can mark the mines. This is done by carrying several markers. On one side they are painted olive green or black. On the other, they are painted white. The white side is placed facing the rest of the comrades. The dark side is placed facing the enemy. Once a mine is located, the commando should pass over or underneath the mine if there is space. If not, he should find a way to go around it.

During a recon, the commandos should withdraw the same way they entered and pick up the markers to avoid enemy detection of the recon. However, during an assault, this is not a requirement.

To breach a minefield with noise, a special explosive is placed over the minefield and detonated. This charge consists of explosive inside a metal, plastic, or bamboo tube. The commandos must be careful once the explosive has detonated. Often it will not destroy the mines, but rather fling them out of path without deactivating them. The crater caused by the explosion is generally a good path to follow. This method can be used for shallow minefields or obstacles.

During an attack, command-detonated mines (claymores) should be deactivated (command lines cut). Another option is to turn them back toward their operators.[8]

RECONNAISSANCE PRINCIPLES

Thorough reconnaissance was regarded by the sappers as the principal insurance that allowed them to carry out their assigned missions. Because this was so important to the sappers, they became highly proficient at it. As a result, besides reconnaissance for their own missions, the sappers were assigned the mission of carrying out reconnaissance for the regular units.

Types of Patrols

The sappers carried out a number of basic types of reconnaissance missions. The standard reconnaissance was called an exploration patrol. During this type of reconnaissance, small patrols penetrated fixed enemy positions to collect information about the enemy and determine vital information about the surrounding terrain.

A second type of reconnaissance was the combat patrol. This was a raid or ambush of enemy forces after an exploration patrol. In other words, after a patrol had carried out reconnaissance, it organized a strike, to confirm information about the enemy. The raids always sought the element of surprise through expert camouflage and by taking maximum advantage of the terrain, the massive use of explosives, and maintaining the initiative until the raid was over.

The third type of reconnaissance patrol was the shadowing patrol. This patrol was used during army offensive operations against guerrilla areas of persistence. The objective was to study current enemy movement and behavior, to try to anticipate future enemy plans and actions, and to transmit this information to the guerrilla high command for the planning of defensive missions and counterattacks. Particular attention was to be paid to locating and anticipating the movement of command posts, artillery, mortars, heavy machine guns, and so on. At any time the high command might order the sappers to attack one of these objectives to cause havoc in the enemy rear and force the enemy to halt operations.

The sappers were taught that a lot of information could be learned by the signs that a unit left in its wake. Different units and types of units left behind different types of garbage: for example, leftover food. Elite and cazador units ate food out of bags. Tracks left by units on the terrain could indicate numbers, equipment, uniforms, and discipline. A wealth of information could be learned without ever seeing the enemy.

Sappers were trained to always keep in mind which regular and militia guerrilla units they could coordinate with to carry out different types of attacks. When the order came down, this gave them maximum flexibility to rapidly plan attacks on their own or in conjunction with other forces. Some of the principles used in this type of reconnaissance were to maintain constant observation of the enemy, always move parallel to the enemy force, and employ stealth to remain undiscovered.

Reconnaissance patrols were usually organized into two groups, a reconnaissance group and a support group. The reconnaissance group physically approached the enemy (objective) to observe, while the support group took up a position to reinforce the reconnaissance group in case it was detected. The support group provided support and cover for the reconnaissance group's withdrawal.

Reconnaissance of an Objective for Assault

The reconnaissance of an objective for assault was a long and tedious process that had various stages that were rigorously followed. First, a peripheral reconnaissance was carried out. Access roads, reinforcement routes, and withdrawl routes were located and noted. The sappers would then conduct a visual assessment of the exterior defenses of the objective. They would then tentatively select rally and dispersion points for both the sapper and support forces to take part in the attack. The sappers then began probing the perimeter around the objective to find the main and secondary locations best suited for breaching the outer defenses. The positions of bunkers, fences, and minefields were noted. The sappers then began to search out dead space not covered by the defenses, such as behind houses, trees, and where darkness and shadows obscured vision. The sappers would spend as much time as they determined necessary to conduct a thorough outside observation of an objective. When they felt they had enough information, and they had drawn an initial map, they would begin deep penetration reconnaissance missions.

This was considered most important, because the commandos would determine the likelihood of success during these missions. The precise location of the main objectives would be determined, and the position of secondary objectives would also be noted. A precise internal map would be drawn. The sapper commandos would note how long it would take them to penetrate the objective at different locations, and timetables would be made. Contingencies were planned for; peripheral and perimeter recons were made by lower echelons. However, in the deep recon operations, the overall commander of the operation personally led the missions into the interior of the objective.

Information that had to be compiled for an attack included: the quantity of troops, NCOs, officers, and commanders; the location of heavy equipment and assets (vehicles, planes, armored cars, etc.); the location of ammo dumps; the location of the communications shed; the location of the barracks and officers' quarters; the location of the support arms; and where internal defenses of the objective were located. Conditions of the objective were noted. Was the objective inside or outside the urban perimeter? What were the natural terrain features such as rivers, ravines, and so on? What were the artificial terrain features such as farm crops, mounds of earth, and so on? Was the first line of defense a wire fence, concertina wire, or a wall? Were there elevated guard platforms, nearby dense vegetation, trees or grass? What was the lighting situation of the objective? Did they have yellow lights or white lights? Were the lights fixed or mobile? Did personnel move during the late hours of the night? What were the natural noises made in each sector? What were the atmospheric conditions like? Was there rain, fog and cold, moonless nights, thunder and lightning? All of these things were noted and written down in a reconnaissance report, and those features that could be were drawn on an accurate map. The sappers found that the best time for recon and attack was always between 2330 and 0230 hours, the period of night when there is the greatest cold and when humans are usually the least alert.

Those items that presented the greatest obstacles to sapper troops included brightly lit objectives; multiple lines of defense with randomly scattered minefields; flat open terrain; dispersed location of support weapons and equipment; mobile sentries; places with no natural noise; first lines of defense consisting of tall walls, guard towers, or bunkers flush with the ground; no visible points of reference; the presence of dogs; and hidden positions.

The sappers would spend months penetrating a position to find out details that could not be determined by outside observation. It was not uncommon for a large objective to be reconnoitered over a period of several years before an attack was carried out, and just prior to attack, intensively for six months.[9]

PRINCIPLES OF ATTACK

The FMLN sappers adhered to a number of very well-thought-out operational principles that were designed to take advantage of their strengths and minimize their weaknesses. For any attack, the first principle was to have a thorough study of the operational situation. This included a complete knowledge of the enemy and knowledge of nuances and capabilities of their own forces. Once a thorough knowledge of the enemy was had, rigorous planning of each detail was required where the commander made sure that each combatant had a clear concept about his mission before the mission began. Part of this rigorous planning process included the thorough organization of forces and equipment to accomplish the mission. Planners were urged to be flexible enough to take timely advantage of opportunities presented; for example, attack when most of a base's troops were out on operations or on leave. The motto of the sappers was "Fight much with little." This was a primary attack principle and was meant to remind the sapper leaders to attack with the minimum force necessary. A smaller force on an objective such as an army base was easier to control in the type of night operations always carried out by the sappers. A smaller force was easier to infiltrate, and was more expendable. If a small force failed and was destroyed, it might be a tactical loss, but not a strategic loss to the guerrilla movement. The sappers calculated that 50 men could completely destroy a military base of more than a thousand men. This was a ratio of 1:20.[10]

To have success with these ratios, the sappers were taught to conduct "close in raids." This was the idea of "hugging" the enemy perimeter. Attacking close allowed the sappers to make maximum use of their main weapon, explosives. At the same time, hugging the enemy perimeter negated the enemy's main weapon of advantage, heavy support weapons such as artillery, armored vehicles, and aircraft. Most army forces under attack would try to break contact and put enough distance between themselves and the guerrilla attackers. This would allow them to identify the attacking force and use their heavy weapons without endangering their own force.

By hugging the enemy perimeter, the sappers would neutralize these attempts.

To get in that close, the sappers had to strictly keep the principles of secrecy and compartmentalization during planning. As will be seen, some operations did not go according to plan because there were leaks or detections. Only those that had a need to know were to be involved in planning an operation. Only the overall commander would know the plan for the entire operation, while his subordinates would know only their specific missions and sectors.

During the reconnaissance and attack, every man had to be thoroughly and adequately camouflaged and had to take maximum advantage of terrain, using every fold and nuance of the terrain that might allow him to get in close without being seen. This required extremely brave and resourceful men, and a maximum use of human resources and equipment. All of these precautions, in planning, reconnaissance, and attack allowed the sappers to get in close, and more importantly, gain the element of surprise. Without at least partial surprise, the likelihood of success was severely diminished.

If surprise were lost, or the plan went awry, the sappers were taught to always have an offensive mind. If they hesitated or hung back in a difficult moment, they would be killed. However, if they took the initiative, they might be killed but had a much better chance of living and saving the mission than if they did nothing. If possible, coordination and cooperation with other types of forces, regular guerrillas or militias, was desirable. While these forces did not accompany the sappers onto the objective, at least initially, they were useful for providing fire support to distract the enemy on the objective, or to supress points of resistance that the sappers had either failed to subdue or that had appeared unexpectedly.[11] (For a good example of FES planning see Combat Order #5 in Chapter 4 on the ERP FES.)

THE GROUP DURING THE ATTACK OF ENEMY COMBAT FORCES

Sapper attacks were clandestine surprise actions carried out through special techniques against objectives located in the rearguard of the enemy. Sapper attacks required careful preparation, rapid execution, and rapid withdrawal.

The objective of the attack was to inflict devastating strikes against enemy combat forces, equipment, and installations through small, but well-trained forces. Unit tactical principles to accomplish this objective were to destroy enemy combat forces within the attack objective, secretly penetrate deep into the objective to gain surprise and annihilate the enemy in the first moments of attack, attack from deep inside the enemy position toward the outside, maintain firm control of the overall operation as well as in the individual actions of the teams, and never lose the initiative.

SAPPER PLATOONS DURING ATTACKS

The most common sapper unit was the platoon. Although there were sapper companies and even a battalion, the basic unit was the platoon. This usually consisted of between 15 and 30 men, divided into between three and seven teams. The attacking platoon would receive its verbal combat order from the commander at its base. The verbal combat order indicated: the main objective and its distance; topographical information; a brief enemy situation report that indicated composition of the enemy forces and their equipment; how the sentries were arranged; enemy movement; the number of wire entanglements and fences in the defense system; lighting system; support weapons; bunkers; and so on. The order contained a brief description of the overall unit mission and the subunit and individual missions. It included a mission timetable. This indicated when the unit should be ready for departure to attack; how much time they had on the objective; projected withdrawal time; and so on. Finally, the verbal order indicated a chain of command, in case the leader should be killed or incapacitated. The unit commander's assignment was to make sure that every man completely understood his part of the plan before the unit was allowed to break up to prepare.

Once this was done, each team and man prepared the equipment and assembled to march to a predesignated point of departure. The equipment had to be simple and light, easily transportable, but of sufficient power to fulfill the mission. At the base each team commander and the platoon commander carried out a thorough inspection of each man and his equipment.

At the departure point, the operation became serious. Security was set up and unit and subunit meetings were held to drill the men on their individual and group missions. Once the leaders were satisfied, orders were given for the march to the start point just outside the perimeter. Camouflage was touched up, and the leader sent a team out to conduct a last reconnaissance of the objective perimeter.

At the starting point, the unit waited until the last reconnaissance team returned and reported any last-minute changes in enemy dispositions. From the start point, the unit would approach the outer fence under the cover of the designated team rocket launcher operators. Once this was reached, the operators would move up to cover the team during penetration of the perimeter. Once the outer wire fence was reached and the breach was opened, the leader stepped aside and ordered the subunits to penetrate through the perimeter to their jumping-off points and wait for the attack signal. Once the teams reached these points, each individual sapper located his objective and kept it under observation. They also looked to see where they would throw their explosive charges. Finally, the explosive charges were primed and given a final check.

There were a number of types of subunits or teams that normally had between two and five men. In a few cases six to seven men were used, depending on the requirements of each case. A perimeter group would be assigned to attack and occupy the perimeter, bunkers, and trenches that could impede penetration or extraction. The main group attacked the primary unit objective within the objective, a company command post, battalion command post, or the command post of part of a regiment, where they might have the mission to annihilate 15 to 20 officers and leaders in one or two installations. An anti-armor group would be assigned to attack armored and motor vehicle parks. In El Salvador these could consist of between three and ten vehicles. A reserve group would be kept to deal with any unexpected contingency that might come up during the action. They could be used to reinforce other groups so they could fulfill their missions, help transport dead and wounded, and carry out diversions. Flanking groups would attack objectives on the flanks of the main group, annihilate the forces on these objectives, and then occupy them until the end of the attack to drive off and defend the main effort.

Once their missions were over, the subgroup leaders would inform the unit leader on the status of their assignment. Communications between the unit leader and his groups were done through runners. The teams did not normally carry radios onto the objective. Communications outside the objective, between the unit leader and the overall leader or supporting regular forces, were done by radio. The distances involved outside the objective made sending runners for personal contact communication prohibitive and impractical. After the team leaders reported to the unit leader, this information was transmitted to the higher echelons. If the higher echelons were satisfied, they would issue a withdrawal order. When the order for withdrawal was received, the unit would withdraw to a predesignated rally point. This withdrawal was carried out by subunit according to an assigned sequence. Once all the groups arrived at the rally point, the group withdrew to its base and conducted an after action report and analysis on the results of the attack. This report was immediately sent to the high command. Once this was done, the unit was free to reorganize and begin preparing for future missions.

To further illustrate the subunit and individual tactics during the attack, the following was extracted from the notebook of an FPL sapper, captured by the Salvadoran army.[12]

Attacking a Bunker

To attack a bunker, the commandos first explore and reconnoiter the terrain thoroughly, then the missions are assigned to each man. These are distributed as follows: One man kills the sentry, one man is designated as the explosivist, and one man is designated as the support man. The last man's job is to support the explosivist. An option is to take a fourth man who will carry a rocket launcher. He will fire at the target when he hears the shots fired to take out the sentry. The explosives carried are to be made ready at as close a distance to the bunker as possible.

As soon as the rocket is fired, or the sentry is killed, the explosivist and his support man run as quickly as possible up near the firing ports. The explosivist feels in front of the ports to see if they are covered with wire mesh that might stop the introduction of the explosives. If not, he throws the first charge in and then grabs a second charge and throws it in. He then makes his way around and throws a charge in through the bunker door, and then returns around throwing in charges through the firing ports, one by one.

Once the charges have gone off, the support man moves up and fires a burst of rifle fire into each of the openings through which the explosivist has just thrown explosives. If it is necessary, he can also hurl in backup explosives. Meanwhile, the explosivist returns to the leader and reports on the status of the mission. Once the report is given, the leader orders the explosivist to go get the support man who is still firing bursts, or is finishing throwing charges.

This is the basic format for almost all assault missions. Other attack missions will be minor variations on this pattern. One note of caution needs to be emphasized. Never put your body up against the walls of the bunker, as the shock wave from the explosives will cause you injury, and possibly death.[13]

LEADERSHIP

An interesting aspect of sapper training was that each man was trained to be a leader. Leadership was a major section of nearly every sapper manual captured by the armed forces from the FMLN guerrillas. While interviews with former sappers make it clear that there was a formal hierarchy within the sapper units, it is apparent that each man was trained to take command if it was required. Furthermore, the size of a sapper operation could involve anything from an entire battalion, of a couple of hundred men, down to a team of between three and seven men. Since operations were compartmentalized, anyone from a battalion commander to a team leader could be completely in charge of an operation. Furthermore, as mentioned earlier, one of the main principles to guarantee success was the sappers' ability to maintain initiative during an operation, even if things went wrong. With each man trained as a leader, any man could potentially take charge of an operation to keep it going, despite setbacks to include the death of key personnel. Since sapper leaders were taught to lead from up front, this was not an unlikely scenario.

There were essentially three principles of leadership that were ingrained into each sapper: continuity, flexibility, and persistence. Continuity meant that a leader should be constantly reviewing unit plans and movement. The leader should be in control of any changes and make sure the orders that were given are carried out by his subordinates. Continuity involved the leader being responsible for the accomplishment of the mission. Flexibility meant that the leader should be able to change his plan. If he saw that the plan was likely to fail, he should have enough character to cancel the plan, and make another decision or alternative plan which would still accomplish the mission. He should also be flexible in making individual assignments, and make sure they were fair. If an assignment was unfair, he should redistribute the work load. Flexibility involved being sensitive to the needs of the unit and the men while still carrying out orders. Persistence was the principle that the leader should persist and never rest until the assigned job was done.[14]

AMPHIBIOUS TECHNIQUES

Much less is known about the guerrilla combat swimmers. As far as is known, only the FPL had combat swimmers, and as can be seen from the subsequent chapter, their employment was more limited and less successful than the sappers. However, as has been stated, this book is not the final word on guerrilla special forces during the war in El Salvador, and information may be revealed in the future that will complete the picture.

The only manual captured from the guerrillas that detailed combat swimmers was a handwritten manual in a spiral notebook captured in northern Chalatenango in 1983. Curiously, the notebook did not describe river operations, as one might expect given the nature of the terrain in El Salvador, but rather beach landings. This section is an edited excerpt from this notebook, and gives an idea of the type of training that was received by FPL combat swimmers.

The following is a description of the theoretical organization of an amphibious landing. The boats, presumably rubber rafts, would be disembarked from the mother ship out at sea with the entire commando crew. The boats would then make their way to a point several hundred meters offshore. The first men in were the scout swimmer team or teams consisting of two or more specialists who were assigned to swim ahead and scout out the situation. In theory, all members of the unit would have been capable of this mission. The manual indicated that if men were not specifically designated, just before the landing members of the ground patrol should be designated to carry out this mission.

The task of the scout swimmer team was to conduct an immediate reconnaissance of the landing beach, set up security for landing, mark the landing point and any dangerous places where the boats could be damaged, hide the boats during the land action, prepare the boats for the withdrawal, and provide security for the withdrawal.

During the reconnaissance of the landing zone, the boats would remain 300 to 500 meters out in the water. Here the boats would wait for the scout swimmers. The scouts would swim until they reached the surf without passing through it. The scouts would rendezvous here and then carry out the reconnaissance of the beach by deploying 50 meters apart and swimming in together, moving parallel in a line. Together they would reach the beach and move 200 meters inland. From this point the team would spread out 50 meters apart to each side, and then come back together to communicate to each other what they had seen. If all was clear, they then gave the landing signal. One of the team members would also facilitate the landing of the assault boats by signalling possible rocks and dangerous points. Meanwhile, at the landing point, once the men had disembarked, the scout swimmers would hide the boats of the ground patrol. The ground patrol would immediately form a rally point perimeter. This place might or might not be used later during the withdrawal. From here, the ground patrol would go and carry out its mission. Meanwhile, the scout swimmers would set up security and anticipate the moment of withdrawal. The boats had to be ready to go into the water at the exact moment that the ground patrol returned so as to not delay the evacuation of the mission. While the boats were making their way out to sea, the scout swimmer team remained on the beach as security until the boats passed the surf. Once the boats crossed the surf, the swimmers would leave and swim until they reached the boats that would wait for them beyond the surf.

This passage describes techniques, but mainly concentrates on the role of the scout swimmers and not the other elements of an assault. Fortunately, on another set of pages, either a real or a practice mission against a railway bridge was outlined that is reproduced below.

Unit Organization

Spec. team: Carrasco

Scout team: Muñoz, Mora

Demo team 1: Hooker, Vargas F/leader

Demo team 2: Cifuentes, Gomez/leader

Demo team 3: Soto, Suarto (Sudao)/leader

Sec. team 1: Parra, Quintanilla

Sec. team 2: Vidal, Ordonez

Sec. team 3: Reyes, Chandia

Sec. team 4: Valdez, Ortiz

Asst. team 1: Jaramillo, Lagos, Vaso Alto

Asst. team 2: Mendoza, Cabrera, Gallardo, Chomania

General Organization

Command: 1

Security Element

Team 1: 2

Team 2: 2

Team 3: 2

Team 4: 2

Total: 8 commandos

Combat Element

Suppt. 1: 3

Suppt. 2: 3

Demo 1: 2

Demo 2: 2

Demo 3: 2

Total: 14 commandos

Team missions. Suppt. team 1: Participates in fire concentration, assaults bridge and sets up immediate defensive position. Suppt. team 2: Participates in fire concentration, assaults rail line and sets up immediate defensive position. Demo. 1: Participates in fire concentration, assaults with Assault Team 1, and places charges on right side of bridge. Demo 2: Participates in the fire concentration and assaults with Assault Team 1, and places charges on left side of bridge. Demo 3: Assaults with Assault Team 2, and participates in fire concentration against rail line. Scout: Will recon the beach, mark the boats every 30 degrees, short distances, one long. Will secure beach, will hide the boats and await the return of the patrol. Password: Lizard/Red. Boat formation will be in a single line (string). Meeting Points: Will be determined en route. Fire concentration signal: Whistle blast (by leader). Assault signal: End of concentrated fire. Signal to board boat: ———. Will not carry rank or identification documents.

Things to do before the mission. Coordination meeting between the mother boat captain and the patrol leader. Landing point: Quintero. Landing time: 2200 hours. Evacuation time: 0230 hours. Signal by means of radio—Quantity of men, boats. Ask for distance from coast where boat stops (going, return). Support of embarkation (launch). Help to prepare for embarkation. Help in case of accident (flare night or day). Hot coffee for the return trip. Radio function check. Ask for radio frequency.[15]

While these passages provide a glimpse into the methods and training of the FMLN combat swimmers, the information is far from complete. Hopefully, these passages will provoke further revelation of the operations and training of the these little-known special forces.

THE SNIPER

Several FMLN documents mention snipers as a special force, but as yet there is little evidence to suggest that there were units of guerrilla special forces snipers. Rather, men from both regular guerrilla units and from among the sappers were given special training and returned to their normal units. In many cases no special training was received. Sniper operations were carried out by the best shots within the guerrilla units. In many ways, "sharp shooters" would be a more accurate description than "snipers" for much of what the FMLN designated as "snipers."

A guerrilla manual on snipers defines the sniper as an expert rifleman who was capable in any situation to deliver well-aimed precision fire; accurately estimate distances and conduct reconnaissance; locate and identify sounds; rapidly recognize enemy personnel and their equipment; move without being discovered by using cover and camouflage; use protected and covered firing positions; be able to use maps, sketches, compass, and binoculars to locate and identify the objective; have much patience to wait for the enemy; and be deeply loyal to the revolution with full conviction of the mission he carried out. Many of these characteristics were similar to those required for sappers, so sappers that were good shots made good candidates for sniper training.

Tactical Use of the Sniper

Sniper assets were specialized units whose use was to be only for special and specific missions. Snipers could operate alone or in combination with other forces. The presence of snipers, for an operations commander, was an opportunity to strike the most vulnerable and sensitive points of the enemy. However, the FMLN warned unit commanders that they had to use their snipers properly and not assign them to carry out other missions and waste their skills. Snipers could be employed in offensive actions and defensive actions. In offensive actions they could be used in attacks, ambushes of harassment and containment, coups de main, harassments, and so on.

During the attack, snipers could be used against objectives such as sentries, advantageous positions held by the enemy, entrenched objectives, support weapons crews such as machine gunners, and so on. Snipers could be used against objectives that were hard to approach and needed to be eliminated or neutralized from a distance. Another profitable use of snipers was to support an attack by covering the flanks to contain enemy reinforcements.

In an ambush a sniper would be used to shoot the driver of a vehicle, the vehicle windshield, and tires when the enemy used vehicles. When the enemy advanced on foot the objective was to shoot the officers, the radioman, crews of support weapons, and so on. In other words, take out the enemy's command, communications, and support elements. The objective was to completely disorganize the the enemy's ability to act and react.

In a coup de main, the use of snipers was considered limited because of the nature of the mission (rapid). In this type of attack, snipers were considered useful only to eliminate different kinds of obstacles that impeded the penetration of the objective without setbacks: reflectors, lights, and sometimes sentries that blocked the point of penetration.

Snipers were useful for harassment, against enemy concentrations, sentries in barracks or guard houses, support weapons crews, and so on. The objective was to terrorize the military installation with random but deadly sniper attacks.

During offensive maneuvers, the use of snipers was determined by the leader of the operation or the leaders of the different sectors or directions of attack, according to needs that were anticipated during planning, or from contingencies arising during the development of the action. During maneuvers, leaders kept the snipers nearby to be available on call.

Snipers could also be used for defensive actions, especially against enemy actions against the guerrilla zones of persistence. Sniper operations in general had the objective of containing the enemy advance through causing demoralizing casualties. They were to search and take out enemy sentries, scouts, special forces and enemy snipers. Snipers were also used to fire at low-flying enemy planes and helicopters.

Snipers were to be assigned based on the information provided by the reconnaissance units on the behavior of the different units of the enemy. The idea was to take full advantage of the enemy's weaknesses and strike where it would do the most damage.

Snipers could be particularly effective during enemy offensive patrols. The combination of snipers and minefields was recommended because it was thought to produce highly favorable outcomes. The sniper would take advantage of an enemy unit blundering into minefields and create more casualties by firing at the soldiers attempting to rescue the mine victim. Although this was a cruel tactic, it was particularly effective because it had a devastating effect on enemy morale. This would effectively contain the enemy advance. Another sniper tactic in the face of an enemy advance was to conduct a methodical withdrawal, letting the enemy advance as close as possible to the guerrilla sniper nest and then shooting a couple of his men. The sniper would then withdraw to the next position. The snipers would make successive withdrawals from nest to nest, taking advantage of the vegetation, so the enemy would not detect the source of his casualties.

Although guerrilla manuals indicated that sniper equipment depended on the mission, the enemy, terrain, and resources, basic items included a weapon, binoculars, maps, drawings, compass, and a watch. Weapons favored by the sniper were those with heavier caliber bullets such as the Garand, the Mauser, FAL, and G-3. M-16s were used on occasion. In 1988 the FMLN obtained quantities of Soviet-made Dragunov rifles. Around this time it also obtained a number of silencers to use on the AK family of weapons. Sniper weapons could be equipped with either an optical sight or infrared sight, according to an FMLN manual. However, in practice the FMLN did not use many optical sights until the last few years of the war, when it received the Dragunovs, and very rarely used night vision devices. Most of the latter seemed to have been captured from the military. Radios were carried on special missions.

Very important to sniper operations was the use of the sniper's nest. The sniper's nest could be a constructed or a natural postion. It was a position that was chosen with considerable care that had a clear field of fire, cover, a covered approach route, and that was inconspicuous. The position would be within the normal range of the anticipated objectives. When the sniper was operating in advance of the main guerrilla force a place was to be selected that was covered from the flanks, and could not be picked out on the horizon. Under these circumstances the sniper was not to occupy a permanent position. This would attract greater enemy fire and allow the enemy to encircle and cut off the sniper.

In the nest, the sniper was taught to obey all of the principles of camouflage and cover. Camouflage was designed to avoid observation from both the air and the ground. This was done by attempting to take advantage of all of the natural cover possible as well as altering shapes, shadows, and the texture of the men and the equipment to blend in with the surrounding environment. If the sniper wore clothing, it was either olive green or dark in color. Ten-centimeter by one-centimeter-long strips of burlap cloth could be sewn to the back of the shirt and the pants. Snipers could also use the camouflage of the sappers and paint their bodies with paint made of ash, mud, or colored ink mixed with plant juices. When using this camouflage they wore nothing but dark shorts that were painted in the same manner. Movements had to be slow, cautious, and deliberate. Fast and jerky movements would give the position away. The sniper was not to expose his body or equipment. Care was to be taken with shiny objects, noise, and smoke. Often, more than one sniper occupied the same nest. When this was the case, the snipers would take turns looking for enemy troops. As this was a tiring occupation, one sniper would rest while the other was on duty. When the snipers switched turns, they were not to exchange positions. The nest was to be chosen or built so that both men had clear fields of fire and observation.[16]

URBAN COMMANDOS

Urban commandos operated in the heart of enemy territory. Because of this they had to take more precautions than normal guerrilla units that operated in mostly rural areas of El Salvador. The first security measure was that every commando be known by a code name or pseudonym. This also applied to every clandestine base and unit. These were never to be referred to by their real names or designations.

Every unit and mission operated on the basis of compartmentalization. Information was to be distributed and disseminated on a strict need-to-know basis. The leaders were to make sure that the different teams, support units, bases, allied political groups, and so on, did not know of each other. In case any guerrilla was captured, he was thoroughly prepared with a consistent cover story, a continually rehearsed statement about his identity, work, and so on. These were calculated to last at least 48 hours, more than enough time for the guerrillas to break up the organization and move all of the cadres and equipment.

The urban commandos used camouflage and disguise. The objective was to alter their normal appearance. One of the easiest methods was to alter hair. If the guerrilla had a beard, he was to shave it, or grow one if he shaved. They would also alter the length and cut of the hair. Hats, different clothing, and glasses both clear and dark were also used. During all operations it was mandatory to wear hats and handkerchiefs to cover the face. Ski masks were also recommended, but in the heat of El Salvador's tropical climate, were impractical. The fundamental principle of disguise in the urban area was to blend in and not be recognized. During operations the guerrillas were visible, but they dressed and took measures so that when the action was finished they would merely slip back into the faceless crowds from where they had come.

Urban commandos carried out continuous check and countercheck operations. These were drills to make sure that intelligence operations were not being conducted against them. The urban commandos made mental censuses of the neighborhoods in which they lived, operated, and had their secret bases and caches. This was done by making frequent strolls through the neighborhood and seeing who worked and lived where. If any changes occurred, they were to be noted. The newcomers were to be watched to make sure they were not enemy operatives. These drills had to be conducted in the most natural manner possible so as not to arouse suspicion, since neurotic behavior would give them away.

Compartmentalized cells communicated with the central organization through daily contact. At very precise times one person from the cell and the contact would meet to pass information and status reports. To avoid enemy intelligence the place and time of the meeting was changed, but the contacts had to be punctual. If they could not meet for some reason, the urban commandos established alternative meeting points and other means of signalling such as dead drops where the contact could check for a sign that would indicate danger, or other reasons why the contact was not made. This guaranteed that units did not lose communication with each other over problems like a traffic jam, mechanical breakdown, or other normal complications. If contact or a sign were not made in a 24-hour period, this meant that something serious was wrong and the cells would assume that they were compromised and split up.

Signs were used for unknown guerrillas to identify themselves. This could be the use of a specific type of clothing, or clothing worn in a certain way, a magazine or newspaper carried in a certain way. These were usually combined with some type of verbal code such as a certain answer to a specific question, and so on. Combining both physical and verbal codes guaranteed that mistakes were not made.

Every guerrilla cell had a cache ideally located somewhere between the area where the guerrillas lived and their zone of operations. Caching was an art, the trick being to build it without giving it away, and keeping it hidden from the enemy and curious passersby. Although El Salvador's cities were full of concrete structures, there were a lot of empty and overgrown lots, stream beds, and other areas that made perfect areas for caches. Because El Salvador is a tropical country, special methods had to be used to protect the cached material. Most equipment, books, documents, and so on had to be stored in sealed plastic containers or bags. Grease or pitch was used as an additional protectant.

One of the principal tasks of the urban commandos was to gather information. What made the urban commandos unique was that they operated in the enemy cities where most of the political, economic, and military activity of the enemy took place. Information was gathered on all of the government branches, the presidency, the courts, the city officers, the national legislature, and the directors of the major government bureaus and enterprises. Information was gathered on the telephone and electricity grid, including everything to do with the national communication and power system. Information was gathered on military officers, where their families lived, their cars, property, vehicles, what they did during their off time, and more. Special attention was to be paid to the pilots. Information was to be collected on U.S. diplomats, particularly the military advisers. All of these people were considered high profile targets. The most difficult information that the urban guerrillas were tasked to gather was information on the military intelligence nets, spies, and collaborators. The objective was to discover the nets and watch them without their realizing it. This way they could avoid "being fingered" by the enemy nets.

Urban guerrillas were trained to know their cities intimately, how to calculate direction, distance, and size by just a glance, so as not to raise suspicion. This could be done by knowing one's pace count, how long it took to walk a certain distance, the size of objects in the vicinity, and the size of standard things like the height of telephone poles, or the standard length of a block. In a single pass, the commando was trained to gather a lot of information without raising suspicion and to be able to describe what he saw verbally to his cell leader after the pass. A lot of emphasis was placed on the need for the information gathered to be both accurate and timely.

The commandos were trained to order the information in their minds so that it would be operationally useful. Different types of reports were to be made for different categories of objectives, and the commandos were trained to look for different types of information, depending on whether the objectives were fixed objectives, units, vehicles, people, and so on. If information was missing, the category was to be placed on the report and left blank to let higher command know what further reconnaissance needed to be done. Every report was to carry the date and time, so it would not be confused with earlier or later missions.

Operations

All of the information gathered was to be submitted through contacts to the higher-ups in the chain of command. They would select targets and pass the orders back to the units responsible to carry out the missions. Missions carried out by urban commandos included the assassination of military officers or pilots; destruction of military officers' property or businesses; kidnapping or assassination of important military, political, or business figures, or civilian collaborators and spies of the government; ambushes; sabotage of economic targets, infrastructure, or military targets. The first task was to obtain any missing information and corroborate information obtained in earlier patrols. In addition, the state of the objective was observed: how alert the defenders were, what the security was like, what vehicles were parked outside, were there any nearby bus stops, and what was the lighting around the area. Most observation was carried out when there was the most traffic and congestion near the target. This allowed the patrols to gather the most information, and loiter the longest around the target without being detected. However, attempts were also made to observe the target during the time frame that the attack was going to take place, so that the members of the mission would know what the conditions would be like at the time they carried out their operation. In addition to information on the objective, at this point the commandos would begin to note information on external factors that could affect the operation such as traffic patterns; the hours of stores, businesses, and schools that might be nearby; police and military posts; and so on. Also, places that could serve as concentration points, routes, and alternate routes would be chosen at this time.

During the planning period, pseudonyms and code words were used to describe the objective and the major characteristics of the same. This would prevent the enemy from discovering the plan even if he captured some of the paperwork. As with the sappers, urban commandos never stopped planning operations; they merely delayed them if they were discovered.

Once the information was gathered, it was thoroughly studied and the plan was made. Because of the nature of urban guerrilla warfare, the plan had to be good the first time, as often there was no time to change or modify the plan, both because of changing circumstances and because of government counterintelligence operations. Once the plan was finalized, the missions were assigned to each member of the cell or unit. If possible, simulations were carried out. This was highly desirable, but again, because of circumstances was not always possible. Equipment was gathered and checked and rechecked. Weapons had to be thoroughly cleaned, disguises repaired and tested, camouflage prepared, and, if explosives were used, they needed to be checked and rechecked along with their blasting caps, detonation cord, time fuse, strikers, and so on. Twenty-four hours before the operation the commandos would stop carrying out activities that might wear them down physically, such as doing exercise or playing sports. They would also refrain from tobacco, coffee, and alcohol or any other substance that might alter their senses or state of being.

Once the operation got under way, the commandos would first send out at least one man to make a last-minute patrol around the objective to make sure that everything was as anticipated. This was done as the cell or unit was concentrating. The different teams or individuals would then take up their positions. The leader would take up a position from which he could control the entire operation and personally reinforce any of the teams if the development of the action required. All positions were taken up as secretly as possible to catch the enemy by surprise. All missions were composed of action and security teams. The signal to go into action was always the firing or action of the action group. No one was allowed to begin the mission until the action team did. All advances were to be made in an organized fashion with one man or team advancing under the cover fire of the other man or team. Withdrawals were carried out the same way. The interaction between the security teams and the action teams was based on the same principle, with the security teams covering the flanks and rear of the action teams during the attack and withdrawal.

Once the action was ended, each team would withdraw by routes previously and carefully chosen. Withdrawals had to be quick, but also appear normal enough that they would not arouse suspicion or pursuit. The same day or the next day, the leader would make contact with all of the cells to make sure that the missions had been carried out, to find out what their needs were, and to get the impressions and evaluations of the different teams and individuals. This contact could be personal, direct, or indirect.

The leader would then take all of this information and carry out an evaluation. A meeting of the entire unit would be held to check the leader's information and point of view against those of his team leaders and men. This was also an opportunity to share impressions, talk about improvements, and plan for future operations.[17]

NOTES

1. FPL, *Notes from the Meeting with David on the Special Select Forces*, April 15, 1981.

2. The movement section is a composite from three documents: FPL, *J-28 Commando Course*; ERP, *Training of Special Forces*, captured in Morazan in 1988; Unknown FPL FES student, *Commando Course of July 7, 1989*, notebook captured by armed forces in 1989 in Cinquera.

3. Unknown FPL FES student, *Commando Course of July 7, 1989*, notebook.

4. FPL, *J-28 Commando Course*.

5. Ibid.; and FMLN, *Manual de Instruccion Para los Comandos Urbanos: El Explosivo Como Arma Popular* (El Salvador: Publicaciones FMLN, 1987).

6. The mousetrap is an anti-handling device placed on the bottom of a mine that is designed to activate when the mine is lifted out of its hole. It is called a mousetrap because it acts on the same principle and even resembles a conventional mousetrap.

7. FPL, *J-28 Commando Course*.

8. Unknown FPL FES student, *Commando Course of July 7, 1989*, notebook.

9. FPL, *J-28 Commando Course*; and Special Operations Group, *Know The Enemy*, Armed Forces of El Salvador, 1986.

10. Interrogation Transcript of AIA, June 5, 1985.

11. FPL, *J-28 Commando Course*.

12. Ibid.

13. Unknown FPL FES student, *Commando Course of July 7, 1989*, notebook.

14. FPL, *J-28 Commando Course*.

15. FPL, *Spiral notebook*, handwritten document containing a variety of subjects, captured by the armed forces in 1983.

16. FMLN, *Sniper Shooting*, printed document captured at an unknown date by the Salvadoran army.

17. FMLN, *Instruction Manual for Urban Commandos #3* (El Salvador: Publicaciones FMLN, 1987).

CHAPTER 3

FPL Special Forces Operations

THE FINAL OFFENSIVE (SAN SALVADOR, JANUARY 1981)

FPL special forces, perhaps the special forces detachment described in Chapter 1, were slated for action during the January 10, 1981 offensive in San Salvador. This is the first documented combat action of these forces. There were two groups, probably each of about platoon strength. One group was concentrated in the San Marcos neighborhood, and another near Ciudad Delgado. Initial plans were frustrated because the army had been informed about guerrilla plans to attack the air force base at Ilopango, and the National Guard headquarters. The military launched spoiling incursions against suspected guerrilla points of concentration on January 10. One of the places attacked was the special forces point of concentration in the San Marcos neighborhood. They were forced to spend the day evading army forces. Men and weapons became completely scattered and disorganized, so the men were not able to carry out their assigned task. The group leaders lost control. On January 11 the army returned to its barracks, thinking that because of the lack of guerrilla action, it had successfully prevented the offensive. However, this lull allowed the guerrillas to reorganize and attack. Action was especially strong and successful in Soyapango and Ciudad Delgado. On Monday January 12 the army began to send out patrols. They began to surround the city by taking the San Jacinto and Soyapango hills and the San Salvador volcano. The army made another incursion against San Marcos where the special forces were concentrated, apparently to prevent guerrilla forces from massing. This again prevented the special forces in that neighborhood from acting. In addition, the leader of the San Marcos group, Joaquin, proved to be incompetent, and was never able to regain control of his troops and weapons. The FPL leadership finally stripped him of his rank and appointed comrade Rafael as the new leader. Meanwhile, of the second group, under comrade Calin, 15 men were sent into Ciudad Delgado to support the militias and masses that were acting there. The men were equipped with two RPG-2 launchers and assigned to knock out the armored vehicles the army was using to patrol the area. These vehicles had caused the most trouble for the guerrillas. Special forces men were also assigned the missions of blocking roads, firing homemade artillery at army installations, and sabotaging the electrical power grid. It is not known what the outcomes of these missions were. Special forces were also assigned to support militia forces in the San Sebastian neighborhood. An army force ambushed some FPL militias in this area, killing some and pinning down the remainder. The special forces were sent to counterattack. Four special forces men were killed, but they managed to extricate the militias and set up a roadblock by crossing public transportation buses.[1]

The special forces were essentially used as regular guerrilla forces during this offensive. One of the major problems for all the forces of this offensive was bad planning, coordination, and leadership. The Salvadoran army was tipped off, which eliminated the element of surprise, one of the crucial elements for guerrilla success. In addition, the guerrillas were plagued by problems with their weaponry. For example, the homemade cannon, basically consisting of a mechanical catapult that launched explosive charges, failed to work because the detonators failed to set off the charges once they reached the target. The 1981 offensive did not provide a very glamorous beginning for FPL special forces.

FPL FROGMEN AND THE PUENTE DE ORO BRIDGE (OCTOBER 15, 1981)

The FPL combat swimmers would have a little more success than the special forces detachment. They had been slated to participate in the Final Offensive as well. Originally, the frogmen were assigned the mission of swimming into the docks of the Salvadoran navy and sabotaging the boats used for patrolling the Gulf of Fonseca. The objective was that the elimination of the boats would allow a massive influx of weapons into El Salvador from Nicaragua by boat across the Gulf. The possibilities were subsequently expanded. The combat swimmers developed a list of possible targets. These included: the Cerron Grande hydroelectric dam, the 5 de Noviembre hydroelectric dam, the navy boats at Acajutla and La Union, major bridges, navy installations, and docks. However, when the frogmen submitted their list of materials required, the FPL high command cancelled the mission because it was having enough logistical problems just arming the regular guerrilla forces that would carry out the Final Offensive. It was already having space problems for bringing in conventional weapons and equipment. The operations were further impeded when one of the frogmen deserted and revealed the plans to the military. The great January 1981 offensive went ahead without the participation of the FPL combat swimmers in their designated role. The failure of the Final Offensive and the lack of resources caused the FPL high command to hold up the development of the combat swimmers. All of the equipment that was coming into the country from Cuba and Nicaragua was being used to arm the regular units of the FMLN. These units were barely holding their own against the military, who were aggressively conducting search and destroy missions against the Guazapa volcano and Morazan. There is evidence that the few swimmers in the FPL organization were dispersed to the various fronts. One frogman, whose pseudonym was Mauricio, was assigned as a squad leader of a regular unit in the Gallinero area of Chalatenango near the Honduran border. Here he fought to resist several army incursions to clean the guerrillas out of the area. His special skills were put to use retrieving lost equipment from the rivers and lakes. The fate of the other frogmen was probably similar to Mauricio's.

Finally, the Salvadoran army began running out of ammunition and supplies without having eliminated the guerrillas, and was forced to considerably slow down operations. The FMLN took advantage of this lull and began to plan an offensive for the latter part of that year. The goal was to liberate eastern El Salvador and gain international recognition of that territory. To do this, they would have to cut off and isolate the eastern part of the country. The plan was to isolate the east by destroying the key link on the highway that connected the eastern part of the nation to the west. This was the Puente de Oro bridge over the Rio Lempa. The FMLN joint command, or DRU, assigned the task of blowing up that bridge to the FPL frogmen.

The FPL would have liked to have used only national assets, but when they assembled the frogmen that were left, there was not enough men to carry out the operation. Low graduation numbers in Cuba, desertions, casualties, lack of practice, and the lack of equipment forced the FPL to ask the Cubans if they would help. The Cubans agreed, and at least three Cuban instructors were sent over with their equipment to help the Salvadorans. There are rumors that a member of the Basque ETA with the pseudonym "Lucas" participated as well.[2]

The guerrilla planners were aided by an army sergeant from the nearby Nancuchiname hacienda post that deserted 11 days before the attack. This deserter gave the FPL all of the details they needed on the defense of the bridge and the habits of the military forces in the area.

A large and well-armed FPL force escorted the Cubans at all times. On October 14, guerrilla forces from a number of different camps massed and began approaching the bridge and its surroundings. Approximately 500 guerrillas massed for this attack. They began to attack the soldiers and paramilitaries guarding the bridge, and posts in the immediate vicinity of the bridge that might be able to rapidly render assistance. At the bridge there was a National Guard position with 18 agents, and 8 army soldiers from Nancuchiname that had been assigned to guard the bridge. Nearby at the Nancuchiname hacienda were the remaining 22 men of a 30-man platoon of soldiers from Military District 4 in Usulutan and 24 men from the Treasury Police were at the Tierra Blanca hacienda post. All of these forces came under attack simultaneously. The 8 soldiers were on one end of the bridge, while the National Guardsmen defended the other. After beating off the initial onslaught, some of the Guardsmen crossed the bridge to assist the soldiers. One man had already been killed. The defenders were nearly pinned down by the massed guerrilla forces armed with rifles, machine guns, rocket launchers, and explosives. The defenders only had rifles, and no grenades. This became apparent because the guerrillas got very aggressive and continually shouted to their comrades to not worry because the defenders lacked explosives. The battle lasted all day and into the night. The guerrillas reached the ANTEL telephone exchange and blew it down, as well as the train platform.

Meanwhile, a large force escorted the Cubans and the FPL combat swimmers to a point on the river close to the bridge. Then, the combined Cuban and Salvadoran swimmers loaded 8 large explosive charges of 500 sticks of TNT each on a boat and floated downstream toward the bridge. The swimmers reached the bridge as the bright streaks of tracers, the bang of grenades, and the staccato of machine gun fire sounded overhead. A soldier looked over and noticed the boat gliding toward the bridge. He fired at the occupants with no effect. The boat then went under the bridge and landed on the shore. The soldier fired several times at this boat, but his fire was inaccurate and elicited no response. The soldier then turned his attention elsewhere. While the bridge defenders were occupied by the diversionary attack from the ground, the frogmen attached the explosives to all of the pylons and supports. They ignored the fire from the soldier on the bridge. The frogmen methodically began placing the explosives. The rest of the bridge guards were not even aware of the commandos' presence, and the man who had fired on the raft had no idea of the significance of what he'd seen. He didn't report it until afterward. Concentration was on the guerrillas firing from the road and the land approaches. After about two hours, the frogman commander gave the signal and the time fuses on the charges were set. The men slipped back into the boat and took it downstream. The guerrilla attackers continued to fire, but did not press home their attack. At this stage their mission was to keep the defenders on the bridge away from the explosives. At 3:00 A.M. a huge explosion knocked down one of the main support pylons and the anchoring cables and a 500-meter stretch of the bridge plummeted into the river. One of the soldiers either fell or was thrown into the river. Hours later he dragged himself back to his position, completely wet, missing his boots, and with a wound in the right foot, but otherwise unscathed. At 5:30 A.M. the guerrillas attacking from the land finally withdrew, leaving the shocked defenders to sort through the debris. Despite the huge explosion and the fierce battle, only one soldier was killed and two were wounded. Two civilians from the area were also wounded by all of the fighting. The guerrilla objective was accomplished; the only way now into eastern El Salvador was by air, or boat across the Lempa.[3]

The dramatic success of this operation opened the way for further development of special forces troops. In particular, the other factions of the FMLN became more favorable toward the concept. They had seen that under the right conditions, spectacular results could be accomplished. Ironically, it was the ERP that would more fully develop special forces operations, even though the FPL had been the initial organization to adopt these methods.

SAN ISIDRO LABOR (APRIL 3, 1982)

Perhaps because of their negative experience during the 1981 offensive, and the fact that Cuban combat swimmers had assisted the FPL frogmen with the Puente de Oro bridge operation, the FPL did not seem to fully realize the potential of special forces units. At this stage they largely used their units for limited tactical operations in combination with other forces. This may have been due to their overall strategic bias toward prolonged warfare, which called for victory through a war of attrition that would cause the gradual collapse of the government. An example of the kind of typical operation carried out by the FPL FES was the taking of San Isidro Labor. This town was 18 kilometers north of Chalatenango city along the road to San Jose Las Flores. San Isidro Labor was a jumping-off point for many of the army's offensives into Chalatenango, and a key point of access to San Antonio de la Cruz, Nueva Trinidad, Nombre de Jesus, and Arcatao, near which the guerrillas had many camps. The garrison in San Isidro had been a major thorn in the guerrillas' side, and impeded the free movement in this area that the guerrillas desired. Taking San Isidro Labor would mean cutting off access to this region by ground transport. Once the garrison fell, the region would only be accessible to the army by helicopter.

The guerrillas had been reconnoitering this base since 1980. Guerrilla patrols, guerrilla sympathizers in the town, and FES patrols had compiled a complete dossier of the garrison, its numbers, habits, and defenses. The current defenders of the town consisted of 50 soldiers and paramilitaries armed with new M-16s, G-3s, and M-1 carbines. They also had new M-79 grenade launchers, a 90mm recoilless cannon, a .30 calibre machine gun, an M-60 machine gun and an 81mm mortar. Three times a week, a helicopter came to the town to deliver supplies.

The mission to take the garrison was led by comrade German, the military commander of all FPL forces in what the guerrillas called the "northern sector." An FES group was to attack in combination with two platoons of regular guerrillas and an undetermined number of popular militias. The regular troops would be responsible for physically taking the garrison and town, while the militias were assigned to set up roadblocks and ambushes outside the town and sabotage the electrical lines. In essence, the militias were to cover the attacking forces' flanks and rear, serving as a buffer and early warning if the government proved capable of reacting quickly.

On the night of April 2, the guerrillas took up strategic positions around the town. At midnight the FES moved in to annihilate the sentries and outposts of the first lines of defense. Simultaneously, the lights were cut by the militia. Cutting the electrical lines blacked out the town and alerted the garrison that the guerrillas were up to something. However, since the guerrillas frequently knocked out the power lines, this did not cause as much concern as one might expect. The advantage was that it greatly facilitated the stealthy advance of the FES teams. As a consequence, the FES were able to move undetected right up to their objectives. With small explosives and rifles they easily annihilated the outer sentries and blockhouses with hardly a struggle. The regular units, consisting of two platoons, took advantage of the FES action and surrounded the barracks without being opposed. It happened so quickly that no soldiers were able to escape. Once in position, the guerrillas opened fire. A furious exchange of fire took place between the attackers and the defenders. Even though their situation was nearly hopeless, the soldiers would not give in without a fight. Initially, the soldiers responded with fire from the machine guns and recoilless cannon. They managed to pin down the guerrillas with fire from their M-60 machine guns. The soldiers also used their 90mm recoilless cannon, which initially caused the guerrillas a lot of concern. However, luckily for the attackers, the soldiers' aim was off and the rounds fell short. However, the machine guns were causing more trouble. The FES were ordered to take out these points of resistance. Their RPG operator fired a rocket at the M-60 machine gun position, and scored a direct hit. The guerrillas thought they had silenced it, but a few seconds later it sputtered back to life and continued to fire. Another rocket was fired with the same results. This continued several times until finally, the last RPG-2 rocket the guerrillas had took the troublesome gun out permanently. Meanwhile, the .30 calibre machine gun was still making things difficult. Since all the rockets were used up, the FES had to find another way to take out the .30 calibre gun. Using their techniques of stealth, and the cover of darkness, they managed to get close enough to knock out the .30 calibre gun with hand-thrown blocks of TNT. This turned the balance of the battle in favor of the guerrillas, because it allowed them to now maneuver. However, the soldiers refused to give up and resisted to the very end with grenades and recoilless rifle fire through the night. The guerrillas responded with hand-thrown explosives. When the soldiers ran out of ammunition around 4:00 A.M., and most of the garrison were dead, resistance ceased. The army suffered 35 dead and 5 captured; the guerrillas suffered 5 dead. After the barracks were taken, the population was gathered and comrade German gave them a political speech about the strength and just cause of the revolution.[4]

In this attack, the FES were used in a secondary support role to support the regular guerrilla forces. They facilitated the guerrilla battle plan by opening the way for the regular forces to approach their objective and took out troublesome enemy strong points when these held up the regular forces' advance. FPL special forces operations were of this nature up to 1983. The limited and support nature of their activities was probably due in large measure to the FPL's concept of prolonged war as a more realistic strategy than insurrection and spectacular military action as advocated by the ERP. The strategic objective was to consolidate control over the zones of persistence. This would change in 1983.

DESTRUCTION OF THE 4TH BRIGADE BASE AT EL PARAISO (DECEMBER 30, 1983)

During 1983, the FMLN began to acquire new strength, both in numbers and equipment. The flow of weapons from the Socialist bloc through Cuba and Nicaragua was steady, and was supplemented by quantities of weapons captured from the government. Furthermore, the FMLN had finally begun to overcome its factional rivalries and conduct coordinated operations.

From late 1981 through 1982, the different factions of the FMLN organized large units. These consisted of battalions and brigades of between 300 and 800 men. The high command of the FMLN felt that it needed to prove its new large units, and its newfound cooperation in a spectacular operation. The decision was made to attempt to overrun an army base. However, it could not be just any base; it had to be a base of symbolic importance. It was more important that the operation strike a political blow than that it inflict a purely military defeat on the armed forces. The 4th Brigade headquarters at El Paraiso fit the requirement.

This base had been designed and built with U.S. aid. It used a defensive layout that had been developed in Vietnam. However, it had some major flaws. FES recon elements had been probing the base, which lay along the main highway from San Salvador to Chalatenango city in a valley surrounded by high peaks. There were no fortified positions on the hills and ridges above the base. These ridges and hills were too far away for effective small arms or homemade artillery fire. What the planners had not counted on was the possibility of the guerrillas using massed artillery.

The FMLN had some infiltrators inside the base that were providing accurate information. In addition, since the base straddled the main road as it did, it was a simple task for FES recon elements to dress as civilians and casually stroll or drive by to observe defenses without raising suspicion. The operation was so big that FES elements of three of the guerrilla factions, the FPL, FAL, and RN, cooperated and spent months mapping out the base, its defenses (wire entanglements and minefields) and choosing the best routes of penetration. Initial perimeter reconnaissance and penetration reconnaissance were made to draw a general outline of the base and make an initial feasibility study. This was then submitted to the high command for approval. From the moment this study returned to their hands approved for attack, the FES elements spent over six months carefully learning every detail of the installation. They could not afford failure. During these six months at least one FES team, and usually more, penetrated the installation every single night to find out, check, and recheck every piece of data they gathered. It is a credit to the FES commandos that, in all of that time, they were not detected. Some of the FES men were able to crawl around so close to military positions that they could have reached out and touched the men inside the trenches and bunkers. Often they found them sleeping.

The guerrilla infiltrators at the base provided the FES with some very useful information; information about the interior layout and defenses. However, information that would prove most useful included leave schedules, and information about current and upcoming operations. The FMLN high command stipulated that if it was possible, the attack on the 4th Brigade base should take place at a time when the most number of soldiers were either on operations outside the base or on leave. A number of diversionary actions were carried out in the north of Chalatenango to draw as many troops of the brigade as possible out of their base. The infiltrators within the brigade suggested that the period between Christmas and New Year's 1983 would be an ideal time for the attack. They proved to have suggested the perfect date as only one company of infantry would turn out to be providing base security during the attack.

The distraction operations were successful. The FMLN was able to transfer entire battalions completely undetected from the area around San Vicente to Chalatenango and the Guazapa volcano in preperation for the attack. The operation was so big that the guerrilla forces of the Chalatenango front would not suffice. The FPL had formed a brigade, the Felipe Peña Mendoza Brigade of four battalions. The K-93 battalion and the X-21 battalion operated in Chalatenango. The SS-20 and the SA-7 battalions operated in San Vicente. For the 4th Brigade attack, the FPL brought the entire brigade together. In addition, the FAL brought up their battalion, the BRAT from the San Vicente area. All the factions in the area, the FPL, the FAL, and the RN would participate in the attack. The FES units and the regular FPL battalions from Chalatenango, the X-21 and K-93, would attack the El Paraiso base. Simultaneously, the combined forces of the FAL and FPL, the BRAT, BRAC, SS-20, and SA-7 brought in from San Vicente would launch an attack on the city of Chalatenango. The SS-20 would attack objectives in Chalatenango city proper, and the SA-7 would hit objectives outside to cover the flanks and rear of the attack. These included El Limon and the Azambio bridge. Chalatenango city is located a few miles north of El Paraiso. The mission of the attack on the city was twofold. The first purpose was to attack the barracks of Military District 1 (DM 1) in Chalatenango city proper, to prevent these forces from aiding El Paraiso. The second purpose was to provide cover for a combat swimmer unit assigned to blow down the Colima bridge. This would block the army's key route into the FPL's main area of influence, northern Chalatenango. RN forces would conduct operations to the south of El Paraiso. They would make incursions from their strongholds on Guazapa volcano to block reinforcements from the 1st Brigade in San Salvador. Simultaneously with the combined FPL, RN, and FAL operation, the ERP FES and artillery units would conduct an attack further to the east and attempt to blow down the Cuscatlan bridge. This attack will be discussed later in Chapter 4. A Cuban advisor arrived in Chalatenango and helped the FES prepare for the attack. Eight separate rehearsals were made on mock-ups of the base on El Comun hill.

On the night of December 30, 50 FPL FES, dressed only in shorts and painted completely in mud from head to toe, assembled at El Plan del Horno. Each man carried an MP-5, Uzi, or CAR-15 and two U.S. M-26 grenades. From their assembly point they marched to within 500 meters of the base. At this point they divided into teams and began their penetration around 10:00 P.M. They silently cut holes in the wire and marked the minefields. The paths they made through the obstacles were then marked for the follow-up forces. Two hours later, when the FES teams reached their objectives inside the base, they began to attack. The combined FES commandos of the three organizations would use approximately 1,000 blocks of TNT before the operation was over. The first to go off were some three kilo charges. While the FES were penetrating the wire, heavy mortars had been set up silently on the hilltops surrounding the base. The explosions set off by the FES signalled the mortars and artillery to open up. The guns on the hills opened up a barrage of concentrated mortar fire on the outer perimeter defenses. Amid the noise of the explosions, the FES charged forward and began to throw charges into the barracks and command posts of the installation. In the pandemonium, the soldiers began screaming and running in confusion. Most didn't survive. The FES were ruthlessly efficient. Those that survived the first blasts of the explosives hurled into the barracks were subsequently cut down by additional explosives and bursts of automatic rifle fire. A few lucky men were able to flee. Some ran to their perimeter positions and attempted to resist. Only a few soldiers were able to fight; five FES men were killed.

While this was happening, the mortars on the hills continued their bar-

rage on the base perimemter defenses. With the accurate coordinates provided by the FES recon units, they laid down a murderous fire. The FES
attack lasted approximately 45 minutes. Meanwhile, under the cover of the
mortars and the FES commandos, the 330 regular guerrillas of the X-21
battalion assembled at openings in the wire cut by the FES teams. The
mortars stopped, the FES came out and the X-21 rapidly assaulted through.
They made quick work of army diehards. However, some of the government soldiers proved very difficult, as a number of the X-21 were killed
and wounded.

Meanwhile, outside the base, the K-93 attacked and took objectives immediately around the base to prevent relief forces from reaching El Paraiso
on land. Detachment 3 attacked El Refugio, Detachment 2 attacked El
Barrancon in La Reina, Detachment 1 attacked the Soyate bridge.

After the last resistance had ceased, the guerrillas rapidly ransacked the
base and policed up all useful material. Around 600 weapons were captured
including 500-plus M-16 rifles. All other equipment and buildings, not useful to the FMLN, or too heavy to carry away were destroyed. The FMLN
forces then withdrew. Meanwhile, the relief forces attempting to reach the
base had to fight their way through road ambushes and harassing attacks
along the roads. By the time relief forces were able to get through, all they
found were dazed survivors, and the smoking wreckage of what had once
been one of the most modern military bases of El Salvador.[5]

FAILURE AT THE COLIMA BRIDGE

Things did not go as well elsewhere. The combat swimmers failed to
blow down the Colima bridge. Because it was a failure, the army and the
public never knew it had been a target until one of the participants was
captured and interrogated. As mentioned before, one of the purposes of
the Chalatenango city attack, carried out in conjunction with the El Paraiso
attack, was to provide cover for the frogmen of the FPL while they blew
down the Colima bridge to physically prevent forces from Military District
1 from reinforcing the brigade headquarters. It would also serve to prevent
troop movement into Chalatenango department. This would allow the
forces participating in the El Paraiso and Chalatenango attacks to withdraw
with little fear of serious government pursuit. The target was considered to
be fairly soft and not well defended. Four men were assigned the original
mission, all of which had received combat swimmer courses in Cuba. One
had gone to Cuba in 1980 and come back in 1981. He probably had
participated in the destruction of the Puente de Oro bridge. Another had
gone in 1982 and come back in 1983. One of them completed two frogman
courses in Cuba.

The plan was to blow the bridge down with a 100-kilo charge of explosives. During the day of December 30, 1983, the charge was carried by the

frogmen in a hammock, slung from a pole, in the same way that the guerrillas carried their dead and wounded comrades from battle. When they reached the lake they formed a small raft consisting of two poles on either side with the explosive in the middle wrapped in plastic sheeting to provide buoyancy and keep the explosives dry. Each man was equipped with a mask, snorkel and fins but no diving tanks. Two men took hold of the raft on either side to tow it, with the third swimming ahead as a scout. This man carried a compass and a device to measure the depth of the river. The fourth man swam behind as security. Once they reached the bridge, the front and rear men set up security on either end of the bridge while the two men hauling the raft fixed the explosive charge to the main pylon. When the charge was ready, the two men gave the prearranged signal to the two security men that all had gone as planned, and they made their way to the rendezvous point. One of the men at the bridge activated a mechanical time fuse, and the frogmen swam to a predesignated spot to await the explosion. However, there was nothing but silence. The combat swimmers withdrew, leaving their explosive charge behind. After reporting on their failure, they were ordered to swim back, find out why the explosives had failed to detonate and retrieve the charge. It was determined later that the PUT 01 time fuse failed to detonate due to submersion. The swimmers had to retrieve the charge from the bridge the same way they had taken it in. After retrieval, and discovery of the problem, a new attempt was planned.

A renewed attack on Chalatenango city was planned for mid-January 1984. The attack was planned to provide a distraction to give the FPL frogmen another chance to attempt to blow down the Colima bridge. According to an FMLN defector, the main objective was the bridge, not the city, as some histories of the war claim.[6] This time a new American-made chemical fuse was used, provided with a special cover to keep it dry. This fuse used a small ampule of acid which broke when initiated. The acid cut through a metal plate. When the metal was eaten away it released a striker which initiated a blasting cap which lighted the time fuse and caused the explosive to go off. The frogmen again made their raft and swam to the Colima bridge in the same formation as before. There were no hitches and the approach was especially smooth as the men had swum that route at least twice now. However, this fuse also failed; this time when the blasting cap initiated, it opened up small holes to allow the fumes out. In this case these holes allowed water in, which soaked the time fuse and stopped the explosion. The frogmen again were sent in to retrieve the charge.

One of the frogmen was killed in a government operation, and a second man deserted. Some recruiting was done, and seven more men were brought in to train to blow down the bridge. This unit trained intensively under the leadership of "Augustin" on the Lempa river between the November 5 Dam and the September 15 Dam at a place called Los Amates. Another operation was planned, but it is not known if it was carried out. Meanwhile, one of the leaders was sent to Cuba to discuss their problems with the Cuban advisors. The Cubans said that the problem was that they were not using enough reinforcement explosive.

Most military explosives such as C-4 and TNT are favored because of their stability. They require very violent force and high heat to detonate. As a consequence, they can be carried under combat conditions without fear of accidental detonation. C-4 can even be lit with a match or cigarette lighter and it will burn and not explode. Because of this, many soldiers will shave off little pieces of this explosive and use it to heat their coffee or shaving water. The drawback is that to detonate these explosives requires a lot of force and heat. This can only be produced by a much more volatile and unstable explosive, for example, nitroglycerine. Blasting caps are filled with such an explosive, and this is the reason that they are handled with such care, kept separate from the explosives, and carried in a waterproof, shockproof carrying case. However, on occasion, depending on a number of conditions, blasting caps will explode but fail to detonate the more stable explosive. Reinforcers are often used to insure that the more stable compound does indeed explode. Reinforcers are small amounts of more unstable explosives that are wrapped up with the TNT or C-4 to insure their entire detonation. FPL combat swimmers had used 100 grams for a 100-kilo charge, and the Cubans advised 300 to 400 grams. Furthermore, the Cubans said that the Salvadorans needed to use at least 5 blasting caps on the explosive and use more than one fuse. The Cuban advice does seem to have been correct, but they gave it in an arrogant manner, making fun of the Salvadorans' failure. This caused a lot of resentment among the FPL, especially since the Cubans boasted so much of their superior ability, yet not one of these Cubans had actually participated in a combat operation. Not all was roses between the Salvadoran guerrillas and their international supporters.[7]

While problems continued with the combat swimmers, enthusiasm for large, combined operations with FES and regular guerrilla battalions soared. These were very heady times for the FMLN. It was stronger than ever and was now continually engaging the Salvadoran armed forces in open, conventional combat. Inspired by its success at the 4th Brigade, the FMLN began planning attacks on various high profile targets around the country. Planning began in earnest for an attack on the artillery regiment base within days of the success at the 4th Brigade. Simultaneously, plans began for an attack on the Cerron Grande dam. The priority was the artillery regiment. However, the FMLN high command needed a quick victory with high political impact. Cerron Grande was found to be an easier target, so the FPL attacked Cerron Grande instead, and postponed its plans for attacking the artillery regiment.[8]

ATTACK ON THE CERRON GRANDE DAM (JUNE 28, 1984)

More than a military operation, the attack on Cerron Grande was a political statement. Even though the guerrillas were now operating as conventional units, the armed forces had managed to limit guerrilla action to the remoter areas of Chalatenango, San Vicente, Morazan, San Miguel, and Usulutan. The army had successfully driven the guerrillas out of the major cities and the most important economic zones. Most people did not directly feel the effects of the war, and the elections of March 1982 and 1984 had done much to take away the fire and the appeal of the guerrilla political message. Cutting off much of El Salvador's electrical power for a significant period of time would seriously impede the economy and directly affect the lives of the common citizen. In effect, the war would be taken to the people. It was hoped that the success of this operation would provoke discontent with the government. In addition, it was intended as a demonstration of guerrilla strength and power.

As mentioned, the war was essentially a conventional war at this point. The FPL planned this operation as another large operation, and the Felipe Peña Mendoza Brigade was again brought together with forces marching in from the Para-Central Front (San Vicente) to assist in the operation. The objective of the attack was to knock out the electrical plant, which would cut off electricity to a large portion of the nation.

Large forces were needed to block off all of the access routes to the dam. In addition to the FPL, the FAL and the PRTC participated in the operation. Northern Front forces of the FPL attacked the dam, while forces of the FPL, FAL, and PRTC set up ambushes along the main routes to the dam. The 700 men of the FPL SA-7 and SS-20 battalions from San Vicente took up positions on the road from Sensuntepeque. Three hundred men of the FAL's BRAC battalion set up on the road from Cojutepeque at San Rafael Cedros. The 300-man PRTC battalion known as the DLAD set up on the road from San Vicente, at kilometer 51. The FPL's X-21 and K-93 battalions would attack the dam and its immediate vicinity. The X-21, which had so successfully overrun the 4th Brigade base was chosen to attack the dam itself. The K-93 battalion was assigned to attack the army's position at Monte Redondo, Ilobasco.

At 2:00 A.M. the FES attacked the defending army forces in their bunkers and barracks on the southern end of the dam with explosives and submachine guns. The defenders were a company element from DM 1, Chalatenango. The FES attack was accompanied by a simultaneous assault by the guerrillas from the X-21 battalion which fired mortars and followed the FES units in to attack the remaining government positions. The three-man FES teams were ruthless. One man killed the sentry while the other two men ran up to the positions and threw in satchel charges. Once these went off, the second man used his submachine gun to finish off anyone remaining. The FES showed no mercy, and made sure that no one survived at their objectives. As mentioned in the section on technique, this was not so much a means of cruelty, but a means of protecting one's rear. Since the FES were so small in number and operated on such a rapid and precise time schedule, they could not afford to leave survivors in their wake that might fire on them from the rear or set up resistance against the follow-on forces. In ten minutes the FES had eliminated or neutralized the security company.

The X-21 was not as efficient as the FES however, and let a large number of government troops escape their assigned objective, and these, instead of fleeing, continued to resist and impede operations. It took all day to root out and suppress these government resisters. Many took cover in the reinforced concrete buildings on the bridge. Because of this, the FES units were not able to move onto the bridge to sabotage the electrical facilities. However, the FPL regular battalion brought up its mortars and used these to lob shells into the equipment, accomplishing the mission of damaging the electrical station. However, the destruction was not nearly as thorough as if it had been carried out by the FES.

While this was going on, the government began to react. Local army forces began moving by road to save the bridge as soon as they could assemble their forces. At 5:00 A.M. an army unit ran blindly into the FPL battalion ambush on the road to Sensuntepeque and suffered heavy casualties. Over 75 rifles were captured as well as a 120mm mortar.

At 5:20 A.M. part of the Belloso Battalion ran into the FAL forces at San Rafael Cedros. The Belloso soldiers fought hard until noon, leaving four prisoners and seven rifles.

At 5:30 A.M. the PRTC attacked troops from the 5th Brigade on the road to San Vicente, and captured five rifles and a large number of dropped packs. The large guerrilla ambushes on every approach route to the dam had surprised the army, as it had not believed that the FMLN could mobilize that many guerrillas.[9]

With all of their forces detained on the land approaches, the Armed Forces High Command (EMCFA) decided to use the Parachute Battalion in an air assault. The paratroopers had been training for just such a mission, and they would now put their training to the test. At 0645 hours, the first wave of paratroopers, supported by attack planes, set down on a landing zone (LZ) below the high ground dominating the northern approach to the dam. A second wave landed on the reverse slope of the hill Cerron Grande, after which the dam was named, to the south. The helicopter assault took the guerrillas by surprise. They had expected a helicopter assault, but had determined that it would take place at a different location where the terrain was more favorable to a helicopter landing. This is where the FPL anti-aircraft teams had set up to cover, and they were not where they were needed when the helicopters arrived. Meanwhile, once on the ground the paratroopers immediately began to attack. Supported by 60 mm mortars and air power, the paratroopers began a two-pronged attack against the guerrillas from the high ground. By 0930, after three hours of fierce combat, the dam was back in government hands. Over 80 guerrilla bodies were discovered and buried in a mass grave.[10]

The objective of the guerrilla attack was partially accomplished, with a well-executed attack by FES units. However, the failure of regular units to stop government defenders from taking up positions on the dam proper had prevented the guerrillas from inflicting all of the damage they had originally planned. The electrical supply was affected, but was quickly repaired and did not have nearly the political impact that had been intended. Heavy casualties had been inflicted on the defending forces and relief forces coming in by land. However, the guerrillas also suffered heavy casualties. In terms of body counts, the outcome was a draw. The political victory went to the government. The armed forces were able to surprise the guerrilla force by vertical envelopment, and inflict heavy casualties on the FMLN before the guerrillas could withdraw. They reacted in enough time to prevent the guerrillas from destroying the electricity-generating equipment, and therefore prevented a major economic and political blow. This action vindicated the armed forces' training program of developing quick-reaction airborne units, and proved once and for all that the armed forces were a competent adversary.

PLANS FOR ATTACKING THE ARTILLERY REGIMENT

Meanwhile, the strategic FES, the F-30 had continued preparations for the attack on the artillery regiment. An operation that could take out most of the Salvadoran artillery assets in one blow would do much to equal the playing field and would be devastating to armed forces morale.

The Salvadoran army was an artillery-heavy army. It had experienced great success with artillery during the war with Honduras in 1969. Immediately following the war it managed to break the international arms embargo and import relatively large numbers of artillery pieces from Yugoslavia. This included M-56 105mm Howitzers, M-55 20mm AA guns, and 120mm mortars. Yugoslavian weapons were cheap in comparison to Western-manufactured weapons, of good quality and compatible with Western ammunition. The M-56 Howitzer fired the same ammunition as the U.S. M-101 105mm Howitzer already in the Salvadoran inventory. The Salvadoran army had used its artillery to great effect against the guerrillas, and it was considered, by the guerrillas, to be one of the most effective weapons against them.

The FMLN had a man infiltrated in the artillery regiment who had reached the rank of sergeant. This man had been providing detailed maps of that installation and equipment so the FPL FES could attack the installation. These maps were delivered to the FPL high command through a guerrilla sympathizer in the Red Cross. Based on these maps and the information provided, the FES calculated that it would take 1,110 blocks of Russian TNT to completely destroy the artillery installations. There were two main objectives. The first objective was to blow up the large ammunition dump there. If there was no ammunition, the guns were as good as useless for some time as it would take time to build up ammunition reserves again. The second FES objective was to use hollow charges to destroy the tubes of the artillery pieces. The idea was that the charges would make the tubes useless by deforming them (bending them or ballooning them).

The FPL plan called for 86 FES commandos to carry out the attack on the objective with no regular forces in accompaniment. Regular forces would play a supporting role. They would attack San Juan Opico, San Pablo Tacachico, and San Isidro Lempa. The regular forces would serve to divert forces away from the artillery regiment and block reinforcements from reaching the base before it was too late.

Once all the planning and reconnaissance was done, the F-30 FES calculated that the attack could take place 30 days from the date they submitted the final plan. This is how long it was expected to take the FMLN to get all of the forces necessary ready and to bring in the required explosives from Nicaragua. This included the approval of the high command, the request to Nicaragua, and the return time to El Salvador. FMLN logistics were highly efficient and fairly advanced for an irregular force.

The planning and reconnaissance were in the final stages. The FES already knew the layout of all the dormitories, the ammo dumps, the pillboxes, locations of the guns, and so on. A tentative date of July 1985 had been set for the attack. However, because of unanticipated changes, there were a few final details to clear up. For example, there had been an unexpected change of command at the artillery regiment (the Salvadoran armed forces usually change command and rotated forces at regular times every year) and the FPL wanted to find out who the new officers at artillery would be. The command change had brought a new security regime. The FPL was trying to figure out the new schedule and numbers of the security company. One important difficulty was that its infiltrated sergeant had been transferred to the artillery battery assigned to the 4th Brigade. The loss of this important source of information meant that the information could only be obtained by infiltrating the base. Although the FES had already done this on many occasions, the new security regime made penetrations more difficult. The security troops were now more disciplined, more alert, and quiet. In addition, the artillery commando platoon began to set up ambushes just outside the perimeter at night, and managed to intercept some of the FES patrols. Because of the difficulties and delays in attacking artillery, the FPL indefinitely postponed the attack against the artillery regiment and assigned the FES to plan and carry out the attack on El Picacho microwave reception station.[11]

PICACHO MICROWAVE ANTENNAE STATION (MARCH 16, 1985)

Picacho hill is on the periphery of San Salvador. The microwave antennae station there was an important communications center for the armed forces and was defended by a reinforced company of National Guard agents. Taking out the communications equipment here would greatly impede military communications with the various units throughout the country and interfere with command, control, and coordination of forces. The attack was a purely military objective with few political externalities, except that, since the station was near San Salvador, it would surely get press coverage.

The plan was for the FES to scale the hill, slip through the perimeter and simultaneously attack the National Guard barracks, the fortified defensive positions, and the microwave antennae. The reconnaissance of the objective and the planning of the operation went smoothly. The National Guard garrison proved to be lax, as there had been no attack on the base or guerrilla activity nearby. The terrain around the installation was very difficult, making it impossible for a large, regular force to attack without being detected in a seriously disadvantageous position. For this reason the FES had been chosen; the FES attack without support from any other forces.

The plan was simple. Part of the FES would pin down and eliminate the defensive garrison and free the way for the rest to fix explosives to the communications equipment and destroy it. The operation started well. The different teams departed on time and began scaling the hill. Good technique was employed, and the FES commandos penetrated the base perimeter easily without being detected. However, for some unknown reason, one team assigned to attack the main barracks moved a little more slowly than the groups assigned to attack the other objectives. The attack began on the fortified positions, the antennae, and the other objectives before this group arrived at its objective. Because of this, the bulk of the garrison, which was in the main barracks, escaped annihilation, were alert, able to organize, and shooting back. This resistance prevented the destruction of some of the antennae that were in the main barracks' line of fire. However, the attacks on the other dormitories and the defensive positions went well. Despite the setback at the barracks the teams assigned to demolish the equipment were able to reach their objectives and place explosives. However, the antennae proved to be more robust than the FES planners had foreseen, and the charges that were placed on the antennae that could be reached were not strong enough to blow them down. Only one antenna was damaged. Furthermore, fire from the surviving garrison prevented the FES from being able to spend the time on the objective to improvise, or modify their charges, and accomplish the mission. The mission would have been a total success had that one dormitory been taken out, even counting the problems with the explosives.

While several of the National Guard bunkers and the barracks were destroyed, only 12 defenders were killed. The FES had estimated in their after-action report that they had killed over 50. One guerrilla was seriously wounded, but not by the defenders. He was accidentally shot by his own men who confused him with government soldiers that were running around in the dark. Since they had been asleep at the time of attack, many of the National Guard were running around naked except for briefs and weapons in their hands; essentially the same uniform worn by the FES. It was very difficult to determine friend from foe. Another man received a light wound but was able to walk off the hill.

After the attack the FES did not withdraw from the area, but rather took refuge in the most difficult terrain and suspended radio communications to avoid detection. They remained in this location until the next night. After darkness they marched to Chapin where they rested one day and then marched to the north of Chalatenango.[12]

EL ROBLAR (1985)

Nearly simultaneously with the El Picacho operation the F-30 had been assigned to plan a special forces attack on the El Roblar military base on the highest point of the Guazapa volcano. The FMLN had long claimed that it had exclusive control of the volcano. The military pointed to El Roblar and claimed that the existence of this base proved the guerrillas' claims were false. El Roblar was a symbolic thorn in the side of the guerrillas. This base was right in the middle of the guerrilla stronghold on Guazapa. The military used it as an observation point, communication station, location for heavy weapons support for military operations against the volcano, and intelligence gathering. Resupply and troop rotation was almost exclusively by heavily escorted helicopter formations.

The base was an ideal target for an FES attack. It was surrounded on all sides by guerrilla-dominated terrain, and was consequently difficult for a reaction force to reach. This meant that in the case of a serious attack, it could not be easily reinforced. Only the air force could save it, and anti-aircraft ambushes would be set up to make this task difficult. In addition, if the attack were rapid enough, the aircraft would arrive too late.

A study was made of the defenses and several penetrations were made of the wire obstacles and minefields. These had to be done very cautiously because El Roblar was known to be heavily mined, precisely to prevent a guerrilla attack. Very careful recons had to be made to mark the exact location of all of the mines and booby traps. The FES reached the stage in preparation where they were making their final recon trips before the attack. During these final penetrations, one of the members of a recon team ran into an unexpected minefield. The army had secretly laid new mines which had not been detected by the FMLN. One of the men activated a mine which exploded. He was only slightly wounded, but the blast seemed to have dazed him and affected his judgement. The army sent a patrol to investigate the blast. If the man had lain still, he might have passed undetected. Small animals, birds, and other natural phenomena sometimes set off mines, especially those attached to sensitive trip wires and booby traps like the one tripped by the FES commando. However, the man panicked and fired on the patrol with the Browning pistol that he was carrying. The patrol killed him and recovered the body. His manner of dress and equipment revealed that an FES attack was being planned. The army laid fresh mines and booby traps. Two more FES men were killed by the new booby traps as they were conducting further reconnaissance. The loss of three FES men caused the FPL to decide to cancel the attack. The new mine system was too complicated to have a good chance of penetrating without conducting further, extensive reconnaissance.[13]

ASSASSINATION OF PILOTS

Meanwhile, the F-30 continued to plan additional operations. After 1984, the United States significantly increased the armed forces helicopter and attack aircraft force. Aircraft delivered included UH-1 transport helicopters, UH1-M helicopter gunships, A-37 tactical bombers, and AC-47 gunships. While the FMLN developed very effective anti-aircraft tactics using small arms, only a few aircraft were ever shot down. A large number were damaged, but a good maintenance shop and special tactics helped the Salvadoran air force keep the majority of its aircraft operational. The FMLN reasoned that in addition to shooting at the aircraft, it would attempt to assassinate the pilots. It took much longer to replace pilots than to replace aircraft. There was a photographer at the Presidente Hotel, one of the best hotels in San Salvador, who collaborated with the guerrillas. This hotel was very close to the armed forces' headquarters, and was partially funded by armed forces' money. As a result, it was frequently used by military personnel for lodging and entertainment. Through this connection with the military, the photographer was a frequent visitor at the various military installations. He took photographs at the Ilopango Air Base of pilots and their vehicles and passed these on to the FPL FES. Slowly, dossiers were made on each man with the intention of using the information to assassinate the pilots when they were off duty, away from the base. The project began in early 1985. However, soon after the first photos were delivered to the FES for their assassination missions, the man was arrested. Someone had gotten curious about why he took pictures of the pilots' vehicles, and he was detained. The mission was to take place in July or August 1985.

The plan was to penetrate the Presidente Hotel with four FES men of the F-30 by way of the front door. They would come in wearing fancy, upscale clothes to allay suspicion, and carry fancy briefcases. Inside the briefcases would be the explosives. An infiltrator or collaborator would then lead them to the rooms of this hotel where the American advisers, pilots, and trainers were staying. They would toss accumulative charges of 1 kilo of TNT into each room, to insure total destruction. As of April 1985 the men chosen for this mission were Edenlison 23, Rene 22, Luis 19, and Amilcar 17. This team was in constant training for the mission at a hamlet known as Cacao, near Cinquera.

Should this plan fail, the F-30 had devised a backup plan. Another team was to make contact with the infiltrated photographer at the Presidente Hotel to point out the cars driven by the advisers. Four kilos of TNT would be placed under the seats and then connected to the motor in such a way that a timing device would be initiated by the starting of the engine and would explode after the engine had been running for the ten minutes. Should this plan fail for any number of reasons, the F-30 team was to find out the routes used by the advisers, pilots, and instructors, to travel between the hotel and the Ilopango air base. Once these routes were known, they were to choose a strategic spot and ambush the vehicles with RPG-2 rocket launchers. The FPL had two additional infiltrators at the Presidente Hotel, both members of the hotel security guards. Both were family members of guerrillas killed in action, and one had served in the army's elite Belloso infantry battalion.

Even though all this elaborate planning was done to attack the Salvadoran air force pilots, the guerrillas did not consider the air force as the greatest cause of their casualties. However, they did notice that air support had a great psychological impact on the troops. Units without air support tended to be much more cautious and reluctant to fight. The units that caused the most guerrilla casualties were, to the FMLN, the Atlacatl battalion, the Parachute squadron, and the PRAL (Long Range Reconnaissance Patrol) units. The Atlacatl was considered to be very aggressive in particular, with a lot of firepower. The parachutists conducted effective air assault operations, and the PRAL penetrated deep into the guerrilla rear and carried out devastating ambushes and assaults. One of the consistent features of these units was that they were generally transported to and supported in battle by aircraft. Any impediment to effective air support would also be an impediment of these units.

While this particular attempt on the pilots' lives was frustrated, the FMLN continually plotted against pilots and officers' lives. Captured manuals and documents continually mentioned pilots as legitimate targets both on duty and off duty. As a consequence there was an endless secret and unknown battle between the FES and the counterintelligence services of the armed forces. This battle lasted through the very last days of the war. For the most part, the armed forces won this struggle, but on occasion the FES would succeed and a few pilots were killed or injured while off duty by the guerrillas.

The defeat suffered by the FMLN at the Cerron Grande dam and the mixed results of subsequent operations ushered in a new era. U.S. aid began to make a real difference in the performance of the Salvadoran military. Enough time had passed so that a significant number of men had been trained, new equipment was standardized, and reserves of ammunition and supplies built up. The army was expanded to around 45,000 men with new battalions thoroughly trained in counterguerrilla and airmobile operations. These began to carry out aggressive offensive operations that reestablished government presence in the guerrilla zones of persistence. Both sides took heavy casualties in conventional combat, but the balance favored the government. The guerrillas could not withstand the high casualty rates suffered in this type of warfare. They changed their tactics in mid-1985, reverting to classical guerrilla warfare. However, they did not abandon the lessons of the previous four years.

Enthusiasm for FES units was higher than ever. The FPL expanded its numbers of special forces. Initially, the only FES units had been the units under the control of the FPL high command. While these troops frequently changed the name and number designation of their unit to confuse government intelligence, they were usually referred to as the F-30. The F-30 was considered a strategic special forces unit, at the disposal of only the FPL high command. However, after the success of the F-30, many guerrillas saw a number of tactical possibilities for FES troops, and regular battalion commanders were making requests to form their own FES units. As a consequence, the FPL began to create tactical FES units that would be attached to the FPL battalions for tactical missions. These units were known as J-28. The J-28 were mostly trained by F-30 combat veterans in FPL schools in Chalatenango. A good example of a J-28 operation is the attack on the Acahuapa coffee mill in December 1985.[14]

FPL FES ATTACK ON THE ACAHUAPA COFFEE MILL (DECEMBER 12, 1985)

The recently formed and trained Lt. Cruz Carabante FES unit (J-28) was assigned the mission of planning and conducting an operation against the Acahuapa coffee mill. This was to be an economic sabotage mission aimed at one of the richest families of El Salvador. The idea was to strike an economic blow, as coffee is one of El Salvador's main exports. In addition, the attack would be a great political blow, because it would demonstrate to the rich that the government couldn't protect even them. The Acahuapa coffee mill was the most important mill in San Vicente and the region known to the FPL as the Para-Central Front. It belonged to the Cristiani family. (Author's note: Alfredo Cristiani was the elected President of El Salvador from June 1989 to June 1994.) Because of FMLN sabotage attacks against the Molinero coffee mill, the enemy began to guard the Acahuapa mill. This was the first economic sabotage operation carried out by FES troops, and the first operation of this new FES unit.

The J-28 took its time to carry out a thorough study of the terrain and the objective. Through numerous reconnaissance incursions, the guerrillas discovered that the 5th Brigade in San Vicente placed a platoon under a lieutenant and three corporals to guard the installation. They carried M-16s, two M-60s, a 60mm mortar, one M-79 grenade launcher, and a PRC-77 radio. This platoon was relieved every two weeks. During the reconnaisance operations the troops' army behaved differently. Some groups had good discipline and were totally quiet, while others made noise and even fired a few shots.

The enemy troops were distributed generally as follows. Fifteen men were in trenches on the edge of an open space. This was the southernmost position. Their fortifications were connected by communication trenches and they lived in tents in between the trenches. A sentry was placed in the south corner of the trench.

The command post was in a brick house in the middle of the area. Near the command post, about 25 meters from the mill, was another guard post. It was believed that four persons occupied this house, including a medical sergeant, a radioman, and the radioman's assistants. A second trench was built near a church to the southeast of the mill. Here it was believed that 15 men or more were stationed. This position was similar to the first. The guard was located right next to the church.

The mill was not guarded internally. However, it was well lit which added to its protection. Around it was a wall of brick and cement. The machinery was located next to the wall in the first gallery. It could be located from the outside because a ventilation pipe was located at this point. During the reconnaissance missions the sappers were able to crawl right up and look inside the trenches, but not the mill. This was largely due to the lights. It proved too risky to cross the wall around the mill without being seen by the soldiers in their fortified positions.

The church had electricity as well as a house on the road to approach the mill.

After a thorough reconnaissance was made, an accurate map drawn, and all of the data compiled, the guerrillas launched the attack. At 1:00 A.M. on December 12, the mission began. All 27 members of the FPL Lt. Cruz Carabante FES unit participated, supported by two squads of the ATS batallion.

Over 60 grenades were used, a mix of industrial, homemade, and rifle grenades. Four 4-kilo explosive charges and two 6-kilo explosive charges were used for sabotage.

The mission began with an RPG-7 attack at 1:00 A.M. on the command post. The shot was fired at a range of 40 meters and hit the target. Immediately upon impact, two FES comrades ran toward the house and threw in grenades. The first man threw in his grenades, while the second man covered him, and then the second man threw in his grenades while the first man covered him. They were there two minutes as planned, and then withdrew. Four bodies were seen in the house. After they had withdrawn, the RPG operator saw some soldiers run up to the house by means of a communication trench that connected the building to a fighting position located 25 meters to the north. The RPG gunner fired another rocket at the house to deal with the new arrivals. The soldiers then retreated from the house, and at 1:10 A.M. the FES team withdrew from this area.

The FES group assigned the attack on the trenches was split into two groups and took up their predesignated positions. When the RPG rocket exploded against the house, each subgroup attacked its respective positions. One advanced from south to north, and the other from east to west. Each group carried 15 grenades. In four minutes all the grenades were thrown. Six grenades proved to be duds. The fuses went off but failed to ignite the explosive in the grenades. After five minutes the comrades withdrew.

Two comrades of the FES guided a squad of the ATS to the trench near the house. The trench was quiet except for a wounded soldier who moaned in pain. An M-60, two M-16s and ammunition were captured. This squad remained in the trench for 20 minutes, until they received the order to assault the command house. As they advanced, they were met by rifle and grenade fire from the trench 25 meters from the house. They retreated because it was already 1:50 A.M., past the hour to retire.

The trench near the church and the guard post were attacked. At first the canvas tents were attacked by an FES subgroup with 30 grenades. All were thrown. Two sappers attacked the flanks and the support position in the middle. Everything was over by 1:10 A.M. However, most of the grenades failed to explode. The guerrillas had to retire without taking the trench, but the enemy suffered a number of dead and wounded. The subgroup attacking the guard post was surprised when it ran into five soldiers instead of one, as was expected. This prevented eliminating the guard post with rifle fire, so the subgroup opted to fire rifle grenades. This killed two soldiers instantly and damaged the houses and the church. After this the comrades withdrew. The reserve squad of the ATS moved up to take the trench but was unable to because their grenades failed to detonate (they were homemade grenades activated with matches and time fuse). This squad retired at 2:00 A.M.

There was the stop group next to the trench and next to the church that wasn't able to join the action. It was between trench #2 and the mill in the coffee field.

There was a group that was acting as security for the sabotage group. It was divided into two groups and was located on the road between San Vicente and Verapaz. The other was located to the west of the mill with two comrades in each subgroup.

The sabotage group of four FES comrades placed a 6-kilo charge on the southern side of the wall surrounding the mill. This charge failed to blow a hole in the wall. Another 4-kilo charge was placed and this charge did blow a hole in the wall through which the sabotage group entered. At 1:15 A.M. the group reached the machinery. A 4-kilo charge was placed but the blasting cap failed to detonate. A 6-kilo charge was then placed on the main machine and destroyed it. After this the team found gasoline and spread it on the coffee sacks and started a fire. At 1:40 A.M. this group retired through the breach they had made for initial penetration. This team withdrew through the position of the security team, who then followed them, and then both withdrew through the position of the trench stop group, who then lifted their position and followed them.

The command post was located 200 meters east of trench #2, in the coffee field from where the ATS squad had come to clean up the trench after the initial attack. The general retreat was made at 2:00 A.M. and was conducted without any setbacks. The enemy reinforcement arrived at 2:30 A.M. coming from the Panamerican highway. They unloaded from their trucks on the highway and reached the mill on foot.

Two M-16s, one M-60, and 4,000 rounds of 5.56 and 7.62 mm were captured in addition to packs, uniforms, and so on. Eighteen casualties were inflicted including nine killed and nine wounded. The guerrillas suffered two men lightly wounded. The central machine of the coffee mill was destroyed.[15]

SECOND ATTACK ON THE 4TH BRIGADE (MARCH 31, 1987)

The sergeant that had been stationed at the artillery regiment was transferred to the 4th Brigade base at El Paraiso. Contact was soon reestablished with the F-30, and he again began to provide information to the FES. The FMLN began making plans to again attack the 4th Brigade. Since the attack in 1983, new measures such as cyclone fencing and lights had been set up to prevent a reccurrence of the 1983 attack. In addition, outposts had been established on the high ground around the base to prevent the FMLN from bringing in artillery to bombard the base as it had previously. In addition, because of the air force and immediate reaction forces, the FMLN would have a difficult time massing the conventional forces for a combined operation, as had occurred before. Nearly two years had gone by since the last attack, and the FMLN had made no repeat attack. The security regime had again grown slack.

The FMLN high command ordered planning to begin for a second attack on the 4th Brigade. The FPL's infiltrated artillery sergeant began providing the FMLN with detailed maps of the brigade installations. In addition, he provided uniforms, boots, insignia, and so on, so the FPL could infiltrate further personnel. The planning suffered a setback in early 1986 when a high-level F-30 commando was captured. He agreed to cooperate with the armed forces and revealed the FPL's plans and the name of the infiltrated sergeant. This man was arrested and security was beefed up for a short period of time.

However, this proved to be only a temporary setback. Believing that the plan of attack had been completely frustrated and that the FMLN would not consider continuing its preparations, security was again relaxed. This showed a serious lack of understanding of FES operations. FMLN FES operations were never cancelled, they were only delayed. The time and effort spent collecting data was considered too valuable to waste. Most base layouts continued the same during the war; they were only modified by adding further security measures. No security measures could stop the FES, but they could make their mission more difficult. The FES had techniques for penetrating and breaching just about any obstacle or security measure. Some security measures could not be breached without using destructive devices or an obvious trail. This made it difficult for the FES to conduct a personal recon of the objectives behind these measures. However, infiltrating FMLN sympathizers into the armed forces was a fairly easy task, and the FES began to increasingly rely on infiltrators to provide information they needed that was difficult to obtain without leaving obvious signs that the FES had been there. The FPL soon had new infiltrators inside the 4th Brigade and after a prudent lull was again probing the base. The following excerpt from a captured FES reconnaissance report illustrates some of challenges faced by the FES as they sought to probe the 4th Brigade defenses.

We carried out three preliminary recon missions. The first was on August 2, 1986. During this mission the men only reconned the perimeter of the base. The second was carried out on August 8, 1986, to find the opening in the perimeter fence. They could not find the breach on the west side of the objective because they ran into a bunker, so instead the men perfected the hole on the south side of the objective. The third recon was carried out on September 9, 1986. This time they penetrated the south side of El Paraiso, crossing the wall that is near the base. They were able to penetrate in to a distance of 30 meters. They did not penetrate any further because they did not know the terrain and had to look for a more adequate breach. They were able to crawl right up next to a sentry post. This is behind the fence and they have a machine gun there, but the soldiers inside were very disciplined and did not talk loud enough to hear very much.

Recon mission of El Paraiso on September 8th and 9th, 1986 carried out by BIRD,

SWEET, and NOSE. They left the base camp at 3:00 P.M. and made the penetration jumping the fence, because they didn't know the location of the breach. After making the penetration they got lost. In part this was because they ran into some strong lighting that forced them to react quickly. The mission was to get a good visual view of the objective inside from the west. An attempt was made, but they couldn't see anything because before they reached the ideal spot, they ran into an enemy soldier. This was on the west side of El Paraiso. Without gathering any information they were forced to withdraw during which NOSE got lost and provoked a lot of barking from dogs. The dogs also barked while the team looked for a new breach. This was the first recon. The team returned to the guerrilla camp in the morning.

The next mission was carried out by BIRD, PEAR, FINGER, and HONEY. The penetration was done without problems by way of the same breach. However, when they were passing the last coil of wire one of the team was passing through a narrow wire coil and set off a trip alarm. There was a moment of panic because they were under the arc of the machine gun on the wall. When this happened, only HONEY had still not passed and he was stuck midway through the wire apron. However, nothing happened and he managed to get through without any problems. The team has a hard time believing they were not detected. This happened about 50–75 meters from where they penetrated. The evaluation is that they consider it necessary to make several breaches to be able to pass the wire apron and this the way avoid detection. At this point the team lost initiative to pass all of the wire entanglements and finish the penetration. All four should have reached the objective, but only two passed. This was because they did not know the terrain, and here they only saw one sentry post and the fence, but they did not see the machine gun because the lights make it very difficult to approach and to see. This recon took place on the south side of El Paraiso. FINGER and HONEY got lost and there was a scandalous barking of dogs, but then they found the breach, and were able to link up.

They ran into another enemy that was standing 30 meters away from the place we were going to pass. In addition, they saw four soldiers. One of them was walking about, apparently without a weapon. The other three soldiers were sentries. The team could not determine whether or not they had a machine gun. This was on the south side of the objective. The unarmed soldier was by the wire entanglement. These sentries and soldiers were seen behind lights. The number of machine guns could not be determined. They have only located one machine gun at the one corner. In this recon the team reached the main fence, but from this point couldn't see inside because it was dark. The fence was maybe two meters tall. It was a double fence structure about a meter from one to the other. The fence was of the common cyclone model. From sentry to sentry there were between 50 and 75 meters, approximately. During this mission, PEAR was about 100 meters behind when an enemy soldier appeared. He went still as the enemy soldier approached. The soldier did not see PEAR and stepped on him. He stood there looking around for a few moments. Meanwhile, PEAR's hand went numb. However, the soldier failed to notice that PEAR was there and moved on. The team returned to the guerrilla camp the next day.

BIRD, PEAR, and FINGER carried out the next mission on September 13, 1986. The penetration through the breach was carried out without any problems. However, once through the breach they ran into an enemy NCO near the exit. Instead of continuing, they silently withdrew to avoid the enemy detecting the opening and sealing it up.

On September 15, 1986 a recon was carried out. BIRD, PEAR, and FINGER carried out this mission. It was to be a recon of the north side of the objective which was believed to be the most narrow part, where the wire entanglements end, leading to the lake. In the trip that was made they observed that on south side the terrain is broken in places with streams that end right next to the objective. The enemy had built a bunker about 6 meters wide by 4 or 3 meters covering the place where the streams end. The streams have cut depressions into the ground here, but they were not good because the enemy has set up lights that shine right into them. The bunkers were covered by short vegetation and the team detected mines. These were in an area with tall vegetation that they had to go through to enter the depressions. There were five mines, but they were not booby trapped. In this sector we saw some soldiers go by as if they were patrolling. The team located four barracks surrounded by a wall. The team took a good look at the roofs, which are made of tin. There was no noise around the barracks, except one in the corner where a radio playing music was on. There were no problems penetrating, but they ran into a heavy weapons position that they hadn't known was there. The team confirmed that it was a heavy weapons position and moved on without problems. The next day they returned to the guerrilla base camp.

During this mission the team noticed that the lights on the west side were not working. On every other mission, all the lights had been on. On the other sides they were working, but were dimmer. The dimmer lights better revealed the inside of the base and the team was better able to see the barracks buildings. They were also able to see other details that the bright lights had prevented them from noticing before. For example, it was noted that each guard tower has three lights on it in the form of a cone.[16]

These notes from one of the several FES platoons from both the FPL and the FAL guerrilla factions that conducted the reconnaissance of El Paraiso provide a small glimpse of what FES recon missions were like. They were largely hit-and-miss affairs that required a lot of patience, discipline, and persistence. It cannot be emphasized enough that despite being detected on occasion, despite their primary infiltrator being arrested and tipping off the enemy that something was up, the FES continued planning the mission until they were ordered otherwise. Some of the greatest FES successes were operations that had been compromised. The surprise was always that the military continually failed to believe that the FMLN would carry out a compromised attack. The FMLN knew that the military could not indefinitely keep its troops at a heightened state of alertness, so the FES continued planning. Eventually, the military would relax the security regime, and this is when the FES would strike.

In October 1986, El Salvador suffered a major earthquake that devastated San Salvador. The military was forced to use its resources to rebuild the damaged infrastructure and conduct rescue operations. While the armed forces' attention was on disaster relief, the FMLN accelerated its plans to attack the 4th Brigade. Plans were finalized in February 1987. The plan was submitted to the FMLN high command and approved. The FES submitted their request for explosives, 1,100 blocks of TNT. Within two weeks all of this material had been delivered from Nicaragua. These reached the FES platoons, who used the TNT to manufacture their charges: 3-to 4-kilo charges for the barracks and bunkers, and 800-and 400-gram charges for follow-up.

The main difference between this attack and the previous attack on the 4th Brigade was that few conventional forces would participate. With the new military situation, any attempt to mass guerrilla forces would be extremely vulnerable to army detection and attack. Only around 50 FES commandos carried out the entire operation. They were divided into attack teams and support teams. The attack teams penetrated the base, while the support teams remained outside the wire to provide heavy weapons support. The regular forces would conduct lighter operations around the base, an ambush on the road, blow up a minor bridge, and so on. This was to impede reinforcements and cover the base attack.

This mission was one of mere destruction. No attempt would be made to occupy the base. The objective was to go in, destroy as much as possible, and get out. On March 30, the FES teams left their camps and began to approach the 4th Brigade base. Infiltrators had informed them that conditions inside the base were favorable. They reached lying-up points and waited for nightfall. After dark they began their approach. When the signal was given around midnight they approached the cyclone fence, opened holes, and penetrated in. Each man in the four-man teams carried a 3-or 4-kilo charge. When they reached their objectives, they waited for the signal. At about 2:00 A.M. RPG rockets, machine guns, and mortars were fired from beyond the fence at the guard towers and other specified targets. As soon as these began to explode, the teams threw two of the large charges into each building or bunker, most of which were less than 50 meters long and 15 meters wide. The effect of the 3-4-kilo explosive inside the closed buildings was tremendous. Anyone that wasn't killed was thrown about and stunned into stupor. Afterwards, without bothering to look, the FES threw in smaller 800-and 400-gram charges. These were designed to clean up any survivors. A total of between 30 and 40 charges (3-4-kilo, 800-gram and 400-gram) were thrown into each objective. This was designed to guarantee total annihilation of the forces within, so that absolutely no resistance could be offered. If this wasn't enough, the FES would put their rifles on automatic and spray the interior of the structure. Amazingly, some men did actually manage to get out of the holocaust alive and even resist. This was the case of Sergeant Fronius, an American Special Forces Adviser.[17]

Sergeant Fronius woke up to the sound of explosions. He was the only American on the base at the time, since the others had gone to San Salvador that night. He grabbed a CAR-15 and left his quarters. The plan was that if an attack occurred, the Americans would try to link up with the brigade special forces company known as GOE. To reach the GOE, Fronius had to leave the main compound and cross the soccer field. As soon as he left his quarters, the adviser was hit in the right shoulder by rifle fire. He quickly bandaged himself and moved forward. At this point he could have gone into the brigade Tactical Operations Center (TOC). After the December 1983 attack, the TOC had been rebuilt to withstand explosive entry for a short period of time. Between Fronius and the GOE was the TOC and a berm that could be crossed by a staircase. On the other side of the berm was the officers' quarters and the soccer field. One of the first FES targets had been the officers' quarters. The FES had successfully attacked this area, and most of those officers that had not been killed or wounded had fled in disarray into the TOC. Fronius began to climb the stairs but was knocked down by an explosion that caused him to roll down the stairs. When he came to rest at the bottom of the stairs he saw an FES team coming over the berm. The FES fired M-16s at Fronius and he fired back with his CAR-15. Fronius was hit several times, but also managed to hit several of his attackers, killing at least one and maybe two. Some Salvadoran soldiers tried to rescue him, but he waved them off. Finally, he was wounded so badly that he could no longer fire. At this point the FES, angered by his stubborn defense, came down the staircase and placed an 800-gram charge under his body. The explosion killed him, ripping his body apart.[18]

By the time Fronius was killed, the officers in the TOC had been able to reorganize themselves and take charge of the survivors of the camp. By 5:30 A.M. the guerrillas withdrew to the hills surrounding the base. By that time gunships were in the air firing on suspected enemy positions outside the base and heliborne relief forces were in the air. When they air-assaulted onto the base they saw a grim scene. The entire compound was in flames with nearly every vital structure either completely destroyed or heavily damaged. Over 120 soldiers had been killed, and several more were missing. The FES had lost only seven dead.[19]

NOTES

1. *Report on the Status of the Final Offensive from Alejandro to Jovel*, dated January 14, 1981. Typed manuscript captured by Salvadoran army at an unknown date.

2. Alfredo Semprun and Mauricio Hernandez, "Sandinismo: La otra cara de ETA," *Blanco y Negro* (January 5, 1992), p. 16.

3. Interrogation Transcript of SSG April 4, 1982; and Guardia Nacional, *Investigation Report of the Circumstances Surrounding the Downing of the Bridge*, October 1981.

4. FPL, *Revista Farabundo Marti: El Pueblo Salvadoreño en su Lucha*, No. 8 (Managua, Nicaragua, 1981), pp. 4–5.

5. The account of the first destruction of the 4th Brigade base is based on information from the interrogation transcripts of JFR, RJH, RAR, and TA.

6. Max G. Manwaring and Court Prisk, *El Salvador at War: An Oral History* (Washington, DC: National Defense University Press, 1988).

7. Interrogation Transcript of AIA, May 25, 1985.

8. Ibid.

9. This account is based on the Interrogation Transcript of JFR, August 24, 1986, and interviews with paratrooper officers who carried out the air assault on the guerrillas at the bridge.

10. Armed Forces of El Salvador, *Report on the Events at Cerron Grande Dam*, July 1984. See also Dale Dye, "Showdown at Cerron Grande: Blooding the Airborne Battalion," *Soldier of Fortune* (November 1984), pp. 51–59.

11. Interrogation Transcript of AIA, May 25, 1985.

12. Ibid.

13. Ibid.

14. Ibid.

15. FPL, *Principales Experiencias Operativas de la D.A. #2 del Año 1985* (San Vicente, El Salvador: Ediciones Chinchontepec Heroico, 1986).

16. Handwritten document entitled *Work Carried out on "Chocoyo"*, dated October 16, 1986, captured by the armed forces at an unknown date.

17. This account is based on several sources: Interrogation Transcript of AIA, May 25, 1985; Marco Antonio Grande, "La Estrategia Del FMLN Parte II: La Guerra Militar," *Analisis* (October 1989), pp. 294–317; "Reportaje de las Americas," *Granma* (April 1987); Interrogation Transcript of TA, August 18, 1987.

18. Greg Walker, "Greg Fronius, Forgotten Warrior," *Behind the Lines* (March/April 1994), pp. 43–47.

19. Ibid.

FES troops practicing the advance on the side, circa 1989. (David E. Spencer collection; photo provided by Ministry of Defense)

A haul of FES equipment captured in a suburb of San Salvador, circa 1986. Note the shorts and shirts with grassy camouflage sewn to them. (David E. Spencer collection; photo provided by Ministry of Defense)

The destroyed Puente de Oro bridge, October 1981. (David E. Spencer collection; photo provided by La Prensa Grafica)

One of the Ouragan jet fighters that was heavily damaged by the January 1982 attack against the Ilopango Air Base. (David E. Spencer collection; photo provided by Ministry of Defense)

Soldiers examining the damage to a Fonseca Battalion dormitory after the conclusion of the CEMFA attack. (David E. Spencer collection; photo provided by COPREFA)

The hole blown in the wall through which the FES team escaped. (David E. Spencer collection; photo provided by COPREFA)

An FES platoon dressed in black uniforms prepares to go into action during the 1989 final offensive. Note the silencers on the AK-47s and the youth of the platoon members. Most pictured here are under age 17. (David E. Spencer collection; photo provided by Ministry of Defense)

A Soviet-made Dragunov sniper rifle, in fairly poor condition, captured from the FMLN by the National Police in 1989. (David E. Spencer collection; photo provided by COPREFA)

CHAPTER 4

ERP Operations

The ERP was an extremely militant faction of the FMLN. It believed that military action more than political action would propel the guerrillas to power. The ERP had strong ties to Cuba and was inspired by other Latin American guerrilla groups such as the Montoneros, Tupamaros, the Chilean MIR, and the Colombian M-19. Its actions and organization often reflected these ties. The FPL, concerned with the idea of prolonged popular war, concentrated more on building long-lasting infrastructure. Its emphasis was more focused on creating units and structures. The ERP was concerned more with action, and its focus was more on organizing for specific operations. While the ERP had special forces cadres, it did not create an official special forces unit until 1982, while the FPL had units as early as 1980. However, the ERP did carry out special forces missions. The ERP planned a mission, and then trained individuals in special techniques to carry out those missions. Later, when the ERP did form special forces units, the specially trained individuals became the core cadres of the special forces units. One of the earlier special missions was the attack on the National Police headquarters.

THE NATIONAL POLICE HEADQUARTERS MOTOR POOL ATTACK

Two separate factors played a part in this operation. First, the ERP had an infiltrator, subsergeant Jose Jacinto Mendoza, in the National Police. Jose's brother Mauricio had been a guerrilla. He had been killed by the security forces in 1978, and ever since then Jose had wanted to avenge his brother's death. Until now he had carried out intelligence missions among the enemy ranks, and had provided valuable information to the ERP. However, his burning desire to avenge his brother threatened to compromise his cover. The ERP began looking for a spectacular way for its man to come out into the open.

In the meantime, soon after the Sandinista revolution, the ERP had made contact with Basque separatist guerrillas from Spain, the ETA, in Nicaragua through the Sandinistas, and arrangements were made for the ETA to train Salvadoran guerrillas in urban guerrilla operations. Of particular interest to the Salvadorans were special explosive techniques used by the ETA. The plan that began to come together was to somehow plant a powerful bomb in the National Police headquarters in San Salvador.

Once the plan was approved, some members of the ERP were selected to go through the ETA explosives course. They travelled on commercial buses to Honduras. From here they crossed the Nicaraguan border without passing through customs or immigration. When they reached Nicaragua, through special codes they made contact with soldiers from the Sandinista army who took their passports without marking them and drove them to a security house controlled by the Sandinista army on the outskirts of Managua, on the highway between Managua and Leon. The course lasted about four weeks and consisted of learning how to calculate and make explosives for different purposes. Because of the mission, the course focused on how to turn a car into an effective bomb and how to detonate it by remote control. Theory was taught at the safe house and then practice was carried out at a remote area designated for that purpose. Once the course ended, the Salvadorans were taken back to the border and given back their unmarked passports. In this way, their presence in Nicaragua was never recorded. In San Salvador, the team made contact with subsergeant Mendoza. Arrangements were made for the guerrillas to turn the sergeant's personal car into a bomb.[1]

On Wednesday, August 12, 1981, Mendoza drove his car into the police headquarters compound with some "friends" and parked his car as usual in the motor pool located on the south side of the headquarters where the police armored vehicles were parked. One hundred pounds of explosive were hidden inside the body of the car. The security elements of the headquarters didn't give a second thought to Mendoza or his "friends," because he often drove his car into work and occasionally brought these friends for different reasons. He parked his car right next to the armored vehicles. The armored cars were targeted because they had been key weapons in ferreting the guerrillas out of urban areas. His friends activated the explosives by inserting the fuses and turning on the radio receiver. In addition, a second 50-pound bomb carried in the car was slipped underneath a homemade armored transport truck, known as a Mazzinger. Mendoza and his friends then walked out of the headquarters a few hours later. At 8:15 P.M. that night they set off the bombs by remote control. The explosion was so powerful that it was heard all over San Salvador, and was so bright that it lit up the city horizon. A German-made UR-416 (essentially an armored UNIMOG truck) was heavily damaged. The Mazzinger was completely demolished. In addition, ten police agents were seriously wounded and the gas pump used to provide fuel to police vehicles caught fire, causing serious damage to the police headquarters and other vehicles parked in the area.[2]

About the same time the police headquarters operation was being planned, the FMLN began looking for other high-profile targets to attack. One of the primary military advantages of the government vis à vis the guerrillas was airpower. The guerrillas had no combat aircraft, while the government, with U.S. help, was increasing its number of assets. At the beginning of the conflict the Salvadoran air forces' main combat aircraft were several French-made Dassault Ouragan and Fouga Magister jets, purchased in anticipation of renewed war with Honduras. In July 1969, the two nations had clashed for three bloody days in which Honduras had gained air superiority, but El Salvador had won the war on the ground. After the war, both El Salvador and Honduras had gone through a mini-arms race in an attempt to assure air superiority. In addition, they had a number Alouette III and Alouette II helicopters, a single Hughes 500 scout helicopter, and even some old P-51 Mustangs in service. Starting in 1981, the U.S. government delivered a number of UH-1 Iroquois helicopters to assist the Salvadoran government in its war against the insurgents. These helicopters had proved their weight in gold for supply, transportation, medical evacuation, and even combat support missions. A blow against the air force would constitute a significant military and moral blow against the armed forces. The Cubans suggested to the ERP that it conduct a special operation to take out the aircraft. In January 1981, the Puerto Rican Machetero guerrillas had successfully blown up several U.S. planes in San Juan (see Chapter 6). If an operation like this could succeed in Puerto Rico, right under the gringos' noses, there should be no reason why it could not succeed in El Salvador. The Cubans saw the operation not only as a military blow, but a political blow as well. At this time, the key to the Reagan administration's Central American policy was El Salvador. Knocking out the aircraft would be a major embarrassment to the United States by making the military look inept, incompetent, and incapable of defending the expensive weapons the United States was giving them. A skeptical Congress would be loathe to vote for military aid to El Salvador if it thought the Salvadoran military was losing the aid as fast as it could get it. Enough congressional resistance could unhinge the Reagan administration's whole Central American policy. This would open the way for the creation of Socialist states through Cuban-sponsored revolution. Seeing a chance to use the Salvadoran guerrillas to strike a political blow against their old nemesis, the Cubans offered to train the men for this mission.

ATTACK ON THE ILOPANGO AIR BASE (JANUARY 27, 1982)

In April 1981, the ERP commander of the San Salvador area, Alejandro Montenegro, received a hand-delivered message from Joaquin Villalobos to select eight of his top people for special training. At the time, Montenegro did not know the reason why this order had been given. Montenegro asked his staff to pick eight people that fit certain criteria: young, physically fit, politically loyal, and tough. Montenegro met with each selected member at different safehouses and locations around San Salvador and personally approved each recruit. In two groups of four, these men were sent to Managua, Nicaragua through Honduras. Here they were given false documents and sent to Cuba, where they underwent rigorous training.

In October 1981, Montenegro received a message ordering him to go to Nicaragua. From Guazapa, where he was stationed, he travelled to San Salvador, took a bus from there to Honduras and then to Managua. In Managua, he met with Joaquin Villalobos who at this time revealed why Montenegro had selected the eight personnel. Villalobos then ordered Montenegro to plan the attack against the Ilopango Air Base. The primary objective of the attack was to destroy the armed forces' helicopters, with a secondary mission of destroying the fixed-wing craft.

Montenegro moved into a safehouse in the town of Santa Tecla, just outside San Salvador. He spent two months, November and December 1981, planning the mission.

The planning of the operation was aided by two infiltrators inside the air force, code named "the twins." They provided Montenegro with the information he needed for the raid, particularly the base layout, dimensions, and guard patterns. One of the twins, the "lesser twin," was a mechanic and was almost captured when the air force became aware of infiltration and arrested people in the shops who were suspected of being members of the FMLN. However, they arrested the wrong men. The "greater twin" was a high-ranking officer, and part of the command staff of the air force. In November, "the twins" provided Montenegro with a detailed map and report on the layout and assets of the air force. Montenegro would verify the information provided by the "twins" by going up the cable car on San Jacinto hill overlooking the base. This hill is one of the popular tourist spots of San Salvador, so it was easy to act like a tourist with binoculars and a camera. From here he could verify the information provided by the infiltrators. Copies of the photos and the maps were sent to Cuba where an exact model of the base was built. The eight men rehearsed the attack over and over again on this model.

A safehouse in Soyapango, just outside the base, became the warehouse for all the equipment needed for the attack. This was gathered gradually. The equipment consisted of seven UZI submachine guns, an RPG-2 rocket launcher, eight pair of dark shorts, eight dark berets, and materials to manufacture explosives. By the time the equipment was collected, the eight team members had returned. Three of them, Sebastian, Rigo, and Samuel made 30 800-gram explosive charges for the operation. Because aircraft are delicate machines, these small explosives were considered large enough for the job. The finished charges were subsequently stored in the safehouse with the rest of the equipment.

As planning progressed, the eight men picked by Montenegro were organized as follows: Sebastian, the leader; Neto, second in command; Samuel, third in command and political commisar; team members included Rigo, Emerson, Heriberto, Cesar, and Henry. Their plan was that the men would penetrate the base at a point on the southwest side of the base, 25 meters from a guard house. The commandos would then have to go 250 meters, passing through the combat and transport planes before reaching the helicopters.

The order of penetration would be the following: Samuel, Henry, and Rigo would go in first with the mission of sabotaging the helicopters. Heriberto and Emerson would sabotage the combat planes. They would be helped by Cesar, whose assignment was to first sabotage the transport planes. Sebastian was to lead and control the mission from a central point on the runway. Neto was to wait outside the fence with his RPG-2 aimed at the base guard house in case the operation was discovered while the commandos were on the tarmac.

On the day of the operation, Montenegro met with the commandos at a predetermined rendezvous point at 7:00 P.M., where he issued them their equipment. An early crisis developed when Neto didn't appear. The men debated whether or not they should continue the mission. The consensus was that they should, despite the security risks, so Heriberto took over Neto's assignment of carrying the RPG-2 launcher. Montenegro then drove from the rendezvous point along a bus route where he had a good view of the base and could watch the whole operation.

At midnight, the commandos approached the base and penetrated the fence. Apparently, the sentries at the guard house were asleep or not alert, as no one challenged the group and they were able to go about their work undisturbed. In one hour and twenty minutes they finished placing all of their explosives, and exited the base at the point of penetration. The explosives had been fitted with one-hour time fuses, so the guerrillas had plenty of time to escape. When the explosives went off, pandemonium erupted at the Ilopango Air Base. Fifteen helicopters and aircraft were destroyed. However, a number of the explosives failed to go off. Thinking they were under attack from guerrillas outside the perimeter using artillery, a helicopter crew managed to take off in one of the untouched helicopters and machine gun the ground around the base perimeter. It was a valiant, but futile effort.[3]

The ERP, enthusiastic over the success of this operation, sent the men who had carried out the Ilopango raid to Morazan. These men were assigned to set up schools and train new recruits. These efforts, and new cadres returning from Cuba, formed the nucleus of a new FES battalion known by the acronym TECMA. The ERP anticipated that a whole battalion of special forces would be needed as the guerrillas attempted to directly challenge the armed forces and carry out large-scale conventional battles with battalion- and brigade-size units. The development of conventional guerrilla forces by the ERP meant that, during 1982 and 1983, combat between the ERP and the armed forces was particularly heavy in eastern El Salvador.

THE FIRST ATTACK ON THE 3RD BRIGADE

In May 1982, the ERP had held a planning meeting in which it discussed the need to carry out bold operations. The possibility of attacking the 3rd Brigade using two 81mm mortars had been discussed. The idea was to drop 60 mortar bombs on the fort. The new special forces units were tasked with conducting reconnaissance to determine the layout of the base and the location of important targets within the base.

In June of that year, the use of conventional tactics by the new ERP battalions began in earnest. In the first battle they massed in excess of 600 guerrillas for a single engagement. These tactics surprised the army, which was now training in small-unit tactics, and severe losses ensued. It was accustomed to combat with 16- to 20-man guerrilla units, and all of a sudden it was being hit by hundreds of guerrillas with support weapons. The guerrillas laid siege to an army company in the town of San Fernando. The army sent reinforcements to break the siege and the guerrillas set up a plan to trap and destroy these reinforcements. The ERP calls this battle the battle of Moscarron Hill. This was the first time that the guerrillas used massed forces against an army unit. Three 81mm mortars were captured from the army in that battle. While the line companies were held at bay by guerrilla-blocking forces, the guerrillas surrounded and destroyed the heavy weapons and support company.

On November 7, 1982, an army company was ambushed on the road between Corinto and San Francisco Gotera, Morazan. The guerrillas decided to mass to see if they could destroy the army unit trapped on the road. After an all-day battle they forced the soldiers to retreat. In the withdrawal the army abandoned two 120mm mortars and two .50 calibre machine guns. This gave the guerrillas an enormous increase in firepower. Fortunately for the guerrillas, they also had trained personnel to operate the weapons. In January 1981, two army officers had defected and joined the guerrillas; one of them was Captain Francisco Mena Sandoval, who had extensive training in the use of mortars.

The capture of 81mm mortars in June and 120mm mortars in November gave the guerrillas considerably more firepower than they had originally contemplated. Furthermore, the successes of the guerrillas in recent months made them more confident that they could launch a more spectacular operation against San Miguel.

They began to expand the plan. Not only would it be a harassment attack, but a major operation combining support weapons, regular guerrillas, and special forces. The idea was to simultaneously bombard the base, and under cover of the bombardment, attack other targets around the city to include three access bridges and economic targets. The regular forces would set up ambushes along the likely routes of reinforcement and attempt to annihilate the rescue forces. The attack was christened "Operation Pedrero."

In May 1983, the guerrillas overran an army communications and intelligence base at the top of Cacahuatique hill. In June 1983, while the FES conducted reconnaissance, 1,000 combatants of the Rafael Arce Zablah Brigade (BRAZ) marched to Cacahuatique hill and set up positions on and around the hill. At this stage in the war, the guerrillas enjoyed enough freedom that they planned to move the heavy mortars to Cacahuatique by truck. However, it was the rainy season and the trucks became stuck. The mortars had to be broken down and carried on muleback. From here the guerrillas made their final preparations to attack the fort. The defector Mena Sandoval was in charge of coordinating the action of the artillery and the special forces. Using FES techniques, he personally participated in reconnaissance missions as a member of three-man teams to locate the objectives. They also reconnoitered sites for the location of the mortars and other heavy weapons to be used in the attack. One of the innovations developed for this operation was special aiming stakes for night firing. The FMLN technicians of Radio Venceremos, the guerrilla radio station, designed stakes that consisted of hollow metal poles with a series of tiny lights, like those used to indicate that a radio is on, on one side. The side with the lights was set up facing the gunners, and the side without the lights was directed toward the enemy. This allowed the guerrillas to aim their weapons at night, without using candles or fire that would reveal their position.

A large force from the ERP's Commander Clelia, a northern group of the Rafael Arce Zablah Brigade (BRAZ) based to the north of the Torola river in Morazan, would be responsible for the lion's share of the operation. They would strike from Cacahuatique hill. An FES group would blow down the three bridges connecting San Miguel to the north. The artillery would attack the fort and the regular forces would attack several economic targets including coffee mills and power stations. A much smaller force totalling 140 of the BRAZ's southern group, Commander Gonzalo, would come up from the swamps of Jucuaran in Usulutan Department. They would serve as a distraction force and launch a direct attack on the 3rd Brigade base with a 60mm mortar and a .50 calibre machine gun. Among them was the 4th section of special forces. The harassment attack would divert the army's attention while the special forces would penetrate the base perimeter and blow the ammunition bunkers. During the evening of September 3, the guerrillas worked feverishly to set up their weapons and move into position. For the attack on the base the ERP would employ four mortars, one 120mm and three 81mm. These were located 1,500 meters from the brigade base on an elevation known as Mayucaquin. They were given the call sign Bravo 1. At 500 meters from the base the guerrillas set up a 75mm recoilless rifle. This weapon had the call sign Bravo 2. One hundred meters closer was a battery of .50 calibre and M-60 machine guns. This was call sign Bravo 3. On the south side of the fort was the .50 calibre machine gun and the 60mm mortar of the southern group. Mena Sandoval was at the fire control center with a PRC-77 radio located 800 meters from the base. Through the radio he synchronized watches with his call signs and then waited for the command to commence firing. At 2300 hours he told each of his call signs to open fire. While the recoilless rifle and the machine guns hit specific bunkers and guard towers, the first mortar salvo hit the front guard house. From here the mortars began to work their way inward, walking their rounds on to the barracks and buildings.[4]

Meanwhile, the FES troops from the fourth section were making their way through the wire. Still in the midst of the wire entanglements, they were detected and fired on by alert troops. Their leader, Guadalupe, was killed and several others were wounded. Because of this the mission to blow the ammo dump and arms room failed. However, at the bridges the FES sappers under Sanchez were able to reach their objectives. One by one they methodically blew the bridges down. Flying overhead was Col. Joseph S. Stringham, the commander of the American advisers, known collectively as Milgroup. The charges used on the bridges were so large that as each went off, it shook his aircraft. He knew this marked the beginning of a very low time for the Salvadoran government forces.[5]

DEMOLITION OF THE CUSCATLAN BRIDGE (DECEMBER 31, 1983)

In conjuction with the El Paraiso attack described in the chapter on the FPL, the ERP forces of the FMLN attacked the Cuscatlan bridge. The FMLN had destroyed the Puente de Oro Bridge in 1981 in an attempt to cut off the northeastern part of the country from the center and west. While its destruction did cause a lot of damage, and cut off communications, this was only temporary. The army soon built a smaller Baily bridge over the Lempa river, and communications were restored. It also beefed up security around its remaining bridge, the Puente de Cuscatlan. This bridge connected the southeastern part of the country with the center, and was an important economic link. Since it was in its area of influence, the ERP was assigned to destroy the bridge. The assigned date of the operation was to coincide with the attack on the El Paraiso base and the Colima bridge. The combined attacks against the 4th Brigade, Chalatenango, the Colima bridge, and the Cuscatlan bridge were to be the most devastating FMLN offensive of the war. The operation was planned over a long period of time, as the bridge had long been considered a vital target. After the destruction of the Puente de Oro bridge, destruction of the Cuscatlan bridge meant that the country would again be physically divided.

Due to the importance of the Cuscatlan bridge, several FES commandos of the ERP were sent to Nicaragua to again undergo a special demolitions course conducted by Spanish ETA terrorists. This course was coordinated with the ETA and Sandinistas by one of the ERP's top commanders, Ana Guadalupe Martinez. While most of the course was refresher training for the ERP commandos, the novelty of the course was in the use of remote control devices.[6]

However, even with the ETA course, the Cuscatlan bridge would not be as easy to destroy as the Puente de Oro. Aware that the bridge was a target, the government had placed a garrison of 250 men, a reinforced company, to guard it. Furthermore, it was now aware of the demolition techniques used by combat swimmers, and watched the river carefully for saboteurs. This was aided by the fact that the river was fairly shallow.

The only solution seemed to be to attack the bridge frontally and attempt to overcome the defenders. Across open ground this could be extremely costly. The calculated losses would take a long time to replace, and there could be no guarantee of success. Furthermore, even if the attack were successful, the losses sustained might offset the strategic effect of blowing down the bridge. The ERP planners wrestled with the problem. They decided to use the FES troops for the mission. However, the open terrain around the bridge and the limited avenues of approach made even this difficult. The ERP decided to use its heavy artillery that had been so devastating against the garrison on Cacahuatique hill, and the 3rd Brigade base in San Miguel. At Cacahuatique hill, the position had been manned by a Cazador unit. The Cazador units were elite troops that had been trained by the Americans and had a fearsome reputation. An unsupported FMLN infantry attack initially failed against the stubborn defense of the army troops. The guerrillas then brought out their mortars and laid a concentrated barrage on the army trenches. Not used to being shelled, and out of ammunition, the army troops broke quickly and were driven off the hill. The lesson was that even elite forces could not stand up to being shelled. This was confirmed by the success of the attack on San Miguel. This lesson was applied to the problem of the Cuscatlan bridge. The ERP decided to use massed artillery to help the special forces men get to the bridge. Based on the experience of the Cacahuatique hill attack, the ERP calculated that the massed artillery would adequately destroy or neutralize the defenders while the FES made their approach, set up the explosives, and brought down the bridge. They were not disappointed.

Mortars and their ammunition were brought in secretly and set up. The attack opened with a devastating artillery barrage on the positions of the defenders. This was carried out by the massed concentration of firepower of two 120mm and a half dozen 81mm mortars. These were all of the mortars the ERP posessed. In addition to high angle weapons, direct fire was provided by 90mm, 75mm, and 57mm recoilless rifles. This was the most devastating and concentrated barrage ever experienced by government troops. The fire was extremely accurate as the positions had been thoroughly reconoitered and marked by FES teams. Firing tables, ranges, and other data had been compiled for weeks before the attack. Initially, the soldiers stayed calm and attempted to resist. However, the accurate artillery fire began to take its toll, killing and wounding many men. By this time FES sappers had advanced. Part of the commandos attacked the defenders' positions while the rest moved toward the bridge. Those attacking the soldiers began to hurl in satchel charges and spray the positions with concentrated automatic fire. However, the army still resisted. The FES continued hurling charges. Finally, all of the officers were killed, or severely wounded. Disoriented, terrified, and leaderless, those soldiers that could, fled. The remaining resisters were dislodged in short order. Meanwhile, the FES bridge teams clambered onto the pylons of the bridge and calmly set up their demolition charges according to previously and carefully made plans. The TNT was carried in broken-down packages of 50 sticks each. From these packages, the charges were constructed to blow down the bridge.

According to the subsequently captured plans and technical drawings, charges were placed on the main pylon, and on the pylons on each end of the bridge. Further charges were placed on the pylon on each end that serves to anchor the cables. The charges for the principal pylons and pillars consisted of 500 sticks of TNT. Complementary charges of 100 sticks of TNT were placed on the concrete block where the support cables were anchored. Each charge was primed with multiple blasting caps connected to det cord, and the charges were reinforced. Equal lengths of time fuse were connected to the det cord with their appropriate strikers. All the strikers were initiated simultaneously.[7]

After the defenders were subdued, the FES had all the time they needed to set up the charges and blow down the bridge. The operation was completed without any delays.

MINING OF THE OBRAJUELO AIR STRIP (MARCH 23, 1984)

In early 1984, an ERP FES unit received an order to carry out a coup de main against enemy aircraft in the San Miguel area. The military effect of this attack would not be significant, but the psychological and propaganda effect would be great. The FES noticed that, periodically, supplies were flown into a small airstrip outside of San Miguel at a place called Obrajuelo. The airstrip was small, resting on high ground. The terrain was bare with only knee-high grass all around it. The dirt strip doubled as both a civilian and military airport. On one end of the runway was a large shed where a small plane could be stored, as well as a small brick house. Further exploration showed that the airstrip was lightly defended by a reinforced, platoon-size element of soldiers. Part rested in the shed while the other part watched from inside the house. Little patrolling was made of the perimeter, and because of the boredom, many of the guards were found to be asleep. The soldiers were rotated every few days.

The only time security was heightened was when a cargo plane landed. The normal arrangement was that the plane would call in to the brigade headquarters, which in turn would call over to the airstrip security to inform the leader about the estimated time of arrival. The soldiers would then come to life, setting up advanced positions around the strip, and aggressively patrolling the perimeter. This was to prevent the guerrillas from penetrating the perimeter and sabotaging or firing on the aircraft during landing or takeoff. Furthermore, additional troops were then sent from the brigade in trucks to pick up the cargo and provide added security. The recon elements noted that cargo planes only landed during daylight hours, and they rarely were on the strip for more than an hour. Between the landings and takeoffs of the planes, the security element was generally inactive. If night deliveries needed to be made, helicopters were sent which landed directly inside the 3rd Brigade perimeter. It would require a major operation to destroy the aircraft during the hours they were on the strip.

The solution to attacking the planes was probably inspired by an Argentine terrorist operation in 1975. Argentine guerrillas had placed a large, command-detonated mine in a drainage pipe underneath an airstrip in Tucuman Province, and blown up a C-130 taking off with a load of Argentine troops.

However, conditions here were slightly different. There was no drainage pipe, so a hole would have to be dug into the surface of the runway and covered up to avoid detection. However, the runway was dirt, so this would be fairly easy. The approach to the airstrip would be through essentially open terrain, but since security was almost nonexistent when the airstrip was empty, the approach would be no problem since it would not be expected.

At midnight on March 23, 1984, a three-man team snuck onto the airstrip, dressed only in briefs and covered entirely with a mixture of mud and water. This mud application was to allow the men to blend in with the strip. However, before they reached the landing strip, they had to crawl through grass. Each man had a grass cape to wear while he crawled up to the edge of the runway. Once here, they left their grass capes and continued on in their mud camouflage. While one man trained an RPG on the house and shed, the other two crawled out on the runway and planted the mine. They carefully made a hole in the runway. Digging silently with a small spade, they set the top layer of earth aside carefully. This layer was drier, more compact and lighter in color than the soil underneath. They then excavated the rest of the hole and set that dirt in a separate pile and placed the explosive in the excavated hole. They activated the device and then carefully replaced the dirt. All excess dirt from the interior of the hole was placed in the bags carried by the commandos. They left enough room in the hole to replace the top soil. This was replaced carefully, and then tamped down quietly to match the undisturbed portion of the runway surface. Finally, when everything was completed, the men silently crawled back to their waiting team member. The whole process of crawling out, planting the mine, and withdrawing lasted two hours. They had been completely undetected. Later on that morning, one of the two C-123s that the government had received from the United States came in with a load of cargo. As it landed, the plane detonated the mine. Pieces of the plane flew up into the air amid smoke and dust. The plane veered crazily and crashed. The FES suffered no losses to themselves and scored an important psychological victory. Soon afterward, this runway was paved.[8]

The 3rd Brigade base at San Miguel was a major target for the FMLN throughout the war. The 3rd Brigade was the army unit with jurisdiction over the entire northeast portion of El Salvador. Morazan and San Miguel, Salvadoran departments within the jurisdiction of the 3rd Brigade, were the principal areas of persistence of the ERP. This was the most hotly contested terrain of the war. The base at San Miguel served as the command, support, and logistical nerve center for this region, and attacks against the 3rd Brigade base always had an effect on military operations in this important region.

SECOND ATTACK AGAINST THE 3RD BRIGADE

On May 6, 1984, the ERP made another attack against the 3rd Brigade base. This attack mimicked the FPL attack on El Paraiso. It was a combined attack employing FES, regular guerrilla, and artillery units. Guerrilla infiltrators within the base had aided in planning, and the attack took place when the majority of the base personnel were either on leave or on operations.

About 1,000 guerrillas from the ERP's Rafael Arce Zablah Brigade are calculated to have participated in the operation. When the attack started, members of Detachment 7, B Company 3/7th Special Forces Group (Airborne) helped stave it off. An EC-130 flying out of Soto Cano air base in Honduras arrived overhead. The special forces detachment was able to establish radio communication with the EC-130. The EC-130 is a cousin of the AC-130 but is not armed. Instead it carries sophisticated communications and camera gear. It is used for observation and surveillance as well as conduction and coordination of missions.

The Green Berets on the ground had several old Browning .30 calibre machine guns that they had found in the 3rd Brigade armory and just recently repaired. They had also gathered plenty of ammunition for the guns. These weapons were no longer in front-line service, and the advisers decided to have fun with them. They had planned to go out to the range, have a barbecue, and shoot them for kicks. God was on the Green Berets' side that night as the equipment for their diversion excursion was now playing a key role in saving their lives. In addition, they had some M-60 machine guns and M-16/203 grenade launchers. From the top of their living quarters they fired all night at the attacking guerrillas. The men had filled a number of cans with motor oil that they would periodically pour over the guns to cool them down. When the oil ran out, the men urinated in the cans and then poured this over the guns. This expedient method kept the guns from overheating. With the support of the EC-130 the Green Berets set up a lethal system. The aircraft would use its 2-kilowatt infrared searchlight to illuminate concentrations of guerrilla forces. The Green Berets used night vision goggles to observe the searchlight beams, then they would shoot an azimuth to the beam and the gunners would line their guns up on the azimuth and fire. Using this method the Green Berets, along with Salvadoran personnel, beat off the guerrilla assault. Large numbers of FES and regular force guerrilla bodies littered the ground in front of Detachment 7. Local civilians reported that the guerrillas retreated with truckloads of dead and wounded.[9]

One of the FES units that participated in this attack on San Miguel was a unit known as the "Samuelitos," in English, "Little Samuels." The Samuelitos were all between 10 and 15 years old. About 70 of them had been recruited into the unit in 1983. The unit was named after Samuel, the political commissar who had participated in the 1982 attack on the Ilopango air base. A number of the bodies now littering the ground around the U.S. Special Forces detachment were the corpses of the children from the Samuelitos. According to a Salvadoran government report, the children's bodies were dressed only in dark briefs, painted black, with explosives strapped to them.[10] It was surmised that they had been assigned to blow themselves up once they reached their objectives.[11] The heavy casualties suffered by the Samuelitos in this attack and the subsequent attack on the CEMFA caused this unit to be disbanded, but not the recruiting and training of children as FES commandos. Children were found to be useful FES candidates because they were small, and could get through many obstacles better than adults. In addition, children could be more easily manipulated in terms of ideological commitment and fanaticism for the cause.

ATTACK ON THE CEMFA (OCTOBER 10, 1985)

As part of the assistance package, the United States helped the Salvadorans build a new centralized training base. This was a basic training facility for all new recruits entering the Salvadoran army. In addition, it was a center for providing specialized training in certain subjects. For example, a generic commando course was offered that gave basic special forces training to most of the brigade and detachment special forces/recon companies. This central training facility greatly enhanced the army's expansion from 15,000 to 60,000 troops. Before, units had to be trained in the United States, Panama, or neighboring Honduras. Political and economic problems with these three options had made the building of the CEMFA necessary.

Because of the role it played in expanding and improving the army's capability, it became a primary target of the FES. An additional target was the Green Beret advisers at the facility. Since 1984, the U.S. soldiers stationed in country had taken a greater and greater combat role in El Salvador. In addition, the U.S. special forces air wing began flying combat support missions out of Soto Cano air base in Honduras. U.S. military personnel became targets, and the advisers at the CEMFA became an objective for the ERP special troops of the TECMA. The TECMA began to conduct reconnaissance of the CEMFA in 1984. In addition, some members of the ERP intelligence service had been infiltrated onto the base posing as recruits. The infiltrators were part of the highly clandestine intelligence sections of the various FMLN factions. The intelligence sections were separate from the FES, as their mission was the collection of intelligence and the infiltration of the armed forces. However, the intelligence sections cooperated closely with the FES and supported them with information, infiltrators, and so on. The army had detected guerrilla activity in the area and, fearing an attack, had put up a cyclone fence. These had been found to be much more effective barriers than rolls of concertina. However, this only made the FES mission of penetration more difficult, not impossible. In addition, a huge command bunker (TOC), designed to resist attack, had been built in the center of the installation. All of the command and communication equipment was located in this bunker. Again, this made the FES mission more difficult, but did not stop them.

By September 1985, all of the preparations for the attack were ready. The entire TECMA battalion of around 150 men was to participate. They would penetrate the base with the support of approximately 350 members of the BRAZ.

The following document is the operations order for one platoon of the TECMA that was assigned to attack a company of the Fonseca battalion, assigned to provide security for the base. It must be remembered that this order was for one platoon of 11 men out of a total of 150 FES personnel that attacked the base. This order was later captured by the armed forces in San Miguel. The order only provides a narrow window on the entire operation, but is extremely useful because of its detailed description of objectives, organization, tactics, and equipment.

Platoon Mission

Mission for platoon #2 of the first company of Special Troops is the assault and annihilation of the CEMFA command post located in La Union Department.

Secondary objectives include the destruction of the Fonseca Battalion barracks where the 2/4 Company is located as well as the arms room of the Fonseca Battalion.

To carry out this operation we have one platoon of FES of 11 men that have a high level of technical skill and some combat experience with high morale. We also have a squad from the BRAZ with seven combatants with some technical skills and high combat morale. We have the weapons assigned to the force. Among these, automatic rifles such as M-16, G-3 and Galil.

Team Missions

The mission assigned to team #1 of platoon #2 is the following. Annihilate the command post and if there is opportunity to capture it, this would be better.

This team has the following comrades:

Chamorro

Julio

Alejo

Tito

This team has the following weapons:

6 large charges of 6 sticks

8 charges of 800 grams

1 rifle for each combatant with

175 rounds, and

4 magazines for each rifle

Individual Missions

Chamorro, the team leader will kill the sentry at the command post and will be the one who will support the explosives man, *Alejo*, while he throws his charges into the building.

After having thrown the large explosives, Chamorro will finish the job off with rifle fire. If there is any resistance, Chamorro will throw the small 800-gram charges to end this. While Chamorro throws the explosives, Alejo will cover.

Tito's mission will be to wipe out the soldiers that are in the trench next to the command post. Tito will open fire with his rifle and provide support so Julio can drop an 800-gram explosive into the trench.

Julio's mission will be to drop the explosive into the trench, and at the same time carry out the mission of communications.

Team Communications System

All of the team leaders will, when the mission is completed, send a comrade to inform the platoon commander on the mission status, if the mission has been completed, or there are problems. At this point, depending on the situation, higher command will give new orders as to what should be done.

Mission for Team #2 of Platoon #2

The mission for this team is to attack and annihilate the barracks of the Fonseca Battalion's 2/4 company.

This team is composed of the following comrades:

Rommel

Yovani

Yimi (Jimmy)

Daniel

This team has the following weapons:

3 large charges of 6 sticks

6 small 800-gram charges

1 RPG-7 with 4 rockets

1 9mm pistol with 18 rounds and 2 magazines

1 Galil rifle with 175 rounds and 4 magazines

1 M-16 rifle with 175 rounds and 4 magazines

Individual Missions

Rommel, the team leader will annihilate the guard that is at this barracks and will support *Yovani*, who will throw explosives through the doors. At this barracks, the explosives will be thrown through the back doors and Rommel will support from the main door with his rifle.

Daniel, as he is not carrying large charges, will use his rifle to provide automatic fire at the doors so no one will come out through them. After the large charges are thrown, he will move up to finish off with small charges.

Yimi (Jimmy) will be the man that will carry the RPG-7. From this place he will fire at the barracks housing company one-third of the Fonseca Battalion. He will fire the first two rockets and then, depending on the reaction of the enemy, fire a third rocket, keeping the last one in reserve.

Subgroup Mission

This will be *Rene*. The mission of this comrade is to kill any group of soldiers in the first barracks. The mission of this comrade is to occupy this position until ordered otherwise. It is assumed that this barracks is empty.

Order of March

Will be as follows: Team #1, Chamorro's team, will be responsible for opening a hole so the rest of the force can enter.

After them, the BRAZ squad will march. This squad has the assignment to fire on the trenches from outside the perimeter and cover Chamorro's team so that they can break through the outer fences.

Following will be team #2, Rommel's team. This team will penetrate deep into the enemy position.

Each rifle will be issued 175 rounds and 4 magazines per rifle.

Tactics

Approach secretly to the edge of the fence to guarantee opening the breach without being detected. Once the opening is made, wait at this place until the hour of attack.

The comrades from the BRAZ will open fire against their two assigned trenches. This will be their mission.

The fence will be breached at the front so that from here the teams assigned to attack the already mentioned objectives can enter violently.[12]

As mentioned above, the military had detected increased activity around the CEMFA, but other indicators suggested that most of the guerrillas' resources were going to operations in San Miguel, not La Union. Still, the U.S. advisers decided to split their forces so that all would not be caught at one time on the base in the case of attack. Half would stay in nearby La Union, while the other half remained on the base.

On the night of October 10, 1985, the 150 men of the TECMA reached the outer perimeter fence at two points by 11 P.M. Meanwhile, the infiltrators within the base took up their positions. Their mission was to go to the adviser quarters and wait with weapons at the ready. When the FES attack on the perimeter began, these men were to kill the advisers in the following confusion. However, events were to conspire against them. Three advisers were in the TOC monitoring communications, while two remained in their quarters. The base commander had gotten wind of the attack so he had ordered the entire 1st Company of the Fonseca Battalion up to man the perimeter. The rest of the companies were unavailable. It was not known that the American advisers were the ultimate target, so no extra precautions were taken. Unfortunately, the men of the 1st Company had been kept in the trenches all day long, and many had fallen asleep from exhaustion. Only a young lieutenant and his aide were alert in the commander's post. They guarded 1,200 sleeping recruits.

Meanwhile, the FES troops began approaching the base from the north and south. In the north they moved along a draw which provided them cover from observation on that side of the base. At the same time, a large force from the ERP Rafael Arce Zablah Brigade (BRAZ) set up a base of support on the west side of the base, across the road running north and south here. By the time they were in place, the FES men had reached their final positions to wait for the signal to attack. When the BRAZ opened fire on the western defensive positions of the base, the FES men sprang forward to attack their objectives. Many of the sleeping sentries were dispatched with knives or sharpened stakes shoved into their throats. However, some positions were alert and resisted. The FES were determined to break through the outer perimeter. They brought up rocket launchers. Under their cover fire they attacked the offending army bunkers and knocked them out of action. The 1st Company lieutenant was forced out of his post by an RPG rocket. He was shot in the back of the head by his aide, a BRAZ infiltrator. This attack opened up a breach through which the FES rushed. They managed to reach the barracks of some of the basic training recruits. With ruthless efficiency they bombed and strafed the barracks. Meanwhile, the infiltrators attacked as they had been assigned. Most attacked empty targets. Having been compromised, they were subsequently killed by army troops. The FES cut the base in two along a north-south axis. Two Green Berets were trapped in their quarters. The FES ran from building to building throwing in their charges. One 3-kilo charge was thrown into the building where the two advisers were trapped. However, the FES suffered a stroke of bad luck as a large number of these explosives failed to go off, including the charge thrown into the building where the Americans were trapped. About this time, the army soldiers recovered from their surprise and the FES troops were checked and driven out of the compound. Around 15 FES members were killed. However, problems were just starting for the guerrillas. In the interim, the base commander had called for air support. Before the BRAZ units could withdraw, two helicopter gunships began to strafe the guerrilla positions to the west of the base. Soon afterward, the airborne battalion was air-assaulted in and further reinforcement units arrived and began to roll up the guerrilla flank from the south. On October 11, a column of the retreating BRAZ was caught in a box canyon on the Conchagua volcano. Air force paratroopers on the high ground poured down fire while helicopter gunships and attack planes made run after run against the trapped column. By the end of the battle, guerrilla dead and wounded numbered in the hundreds. The army suffered 63 dead and had a large number of wounded. Around 50 soldiers were taken prisoner. In addition, the guerrillas made off with 68 M-16 rifles, three M-79 grenade launchers, two M-60 machine guns, and a 90mm recoilless rifle.[13]

The heavy losses suffered by the BRAZ in this combined attack ushered in tactical changes already being discussed and implemented among the FMLN in 1985. Essentially, U.S. aid, and the new capabilities displayed by the Salvadoran armed forces, made the guerrillas' conventional tactics of directly challenging large army units with large guerrilla units untenable. The guerrillas were forced to abandon large unit tactics and revert to small unit guerrilla warfare. However, they did not want to lose the capability to carry out large-scale attacks if needed. The FMLN became expert at coordinating the massing and operation of numerous, scattered small units. It could mass these units on a target and then just as easily disperse them. The FMLN called this method concentration and deconcentration. In addition, it expanded the concept of layered attacks. This was essentially the simultaneous attack of many objectives. One or several of the many attacks was the real objective, while the other attacks were designed to confuse and delay military reinforcements. The following is an operations order for a TECMA FES attack on the town of San Luis de la Reina. It is not known if this attack was carried out, but the order is useful because it illustrates the integration of the new methods with FES tactics.

Combat Order #5

Main Objective

Wednesday March 20, 1985

On Wednesday March 12, our high command, Commander Raul, gave the 1st FES company the mission of attacking the enemy positions located at the cemetery of San Luis de la Reina, in the north of San Miguel Department.

The mission's objective is to totally annihilate the enemy forces and capture his weapons and some prisoners at the position. Also, the mission objective is to totally consolidate the enemy positions and this is our responsibility. The date to carry out this mission will be either the 22nd to 23rd or 23rd to 24th of this month.

General Context

At a time when Yankee Imperialism is promoting the elections maneuver as the answer, we need to inflict a heavy military blow against the enemy, especially against these demoralized troops, as they are troops that have received special training from the gringos. Furthermore, they are troops that have already been bested by our special troops. We also seek to raise the morale of the masses in this zone with this action. The masses have only seen two (guerrilla) military victories in this zone. We also seek to raise the morale of the local structures of our party and to sharpen the contradictions between the (non-FMLN) political parties, especially ARENA and the Christian Democrats. Also with this action, we hope to break the morale of this highly trusted battalion of the dictatorship in the eastern zone, as this battalion has the responsibility for all of the northern part of the Department of San Miguel. IN THE FACE OF THE ELECTORAL FARCE, POPULAR STRUGGLE!!

Particular Context

The positions belong to the Cuscatlan Battalion. At the moment, the positions are maintained to protect the elections in this town. With this action, the masses will no longer trust the enemy to protect the elections. The masses will believe that we will attack again. The nature of the terrain is bare, burned, there are trenches made of rocks, and the positions are located on the high ground of the cemetery.

The Enemy Situation

The enemy is very demoralized and furthermore, they are troops that our Special Troops have already fought twice, and we know how they behave in combat. Furthermore, with this action we want to unmask the statements made by Col. Estaben, who said that in the east we had lost the war, and this was why we had gone to the west.

Own Forces

They are forces that have already gone through the second phase of training combined with the combat experience that we have obtained. They are troops who are also at a good tactical and technical level, high combat morale, and with great disposition to carry out the missions assigned to them. It is important to point out that this would be the first combined action of the three platoons of the 1st Company of special troops. It also is very important for us because we will achieve the consolidation of our special troops as we annihilate, for the first time, enemy positions with our special troops. At the same time we will obtain the trust of the comrades of the 4th Platoon that are currently at the school. When we obtain the victory we will obtain the consolidation of this platoon. They will acquire confidence in training and we will also expand our forces through our military triumphs.

Leader: Luis.

Operational Force: Three platoons of Special Troops.

Area of Operations: San Luis de la Reina.

Mission: Annihilation or surrender of an enemy company that is providing security to the people of San Luis.

Attack Mode: Penetrate deep into the enemy position to carry out annihilation.

Contingencies: If on the objective are only found two enemy sections and the other two are outside of our objective, only annihilate the forces at the objective.

Support: So that you can carry out the mission, you will receive the following support: Comrade Nelson in command of two regular platoons and one local guerrilla platoon will operate in the area to the south and southeast of the objective. Comrade Cornelio with his guerrilla unit reinforced by a regular squad will operate to the east of the objective on the road from San Luis to Llano el Angel. A regular platoon will set up an annihilation ambush on the eastern side of the town, under Comrade Calixtro. A regular platoon under Comrade Nasser will be the reserve for the operation which can be called for if enemy positions are located to the west of the objective.

Equipment: Three platoons with automatic weapons, with 120 rounds of ammunition each. One RPG-7 rocket launcher with 4 rockets; 94 explosive charges of the offensive, defensive, and 800-gram types. 4 model 208 radios with their respective code books.

Tactics: Infiltration and silent approach to the enemy positions, guaranteeing the factor of surprise and the total annihilation of the combat forces using our techniques to perfection to guarantee the success of the operation and the total occupation of the positions.

Directions of attack are the following: Three teams attack from east to west, these teams will be 1, 2, and 4. The 3rd team will attack from south to north and the independent team will attack from west to east.

Unit Mission

The 2nd Platoon of the 1st Special Troops Company will attack the enemy positions located at the cemetery of the town of San Luis de la Reina, northern San Miguel Department.

Team Missions

Team #1 will attack the positions at the fountain, Chamorro will kill the sentry, Julio will throw explosives, and Alejo will throw explosives.

Team #2 will attack the positions at the rocky little hill, *Leonso*, the squad leader, will kill the sentry, *Aparicio* will throw explosives, and *Fernando* will throw explosives.

Team #3 will attack the positions at the gate (door). *Milton*, the squad leader will kill the sentry. *Yobany* will throw explosives and *Balta* will throw explosives.

Team #4 will attack the positions at the dark tree. *Alfredo*, the squad leader, will kill the sentry. *Ever* will throw explosives and *Pancho* will throw explosives.

Team #5 will be the independent team that will attack the position in the poor people's cemetery. *Ruben* will kill the sentry. *Tito* will throw explosives, *Lito* will throw explosives, and *Adonys* will throw explosives.

Contingencies

In the case that Alfredo (team #4) encounters no enemy he will reinforce Alonso (team #2). If Milton's team (team #3) encounters no enemy he will reinforce Chamorro (team #1). In the case that there are enemy in the cemetery house, Milton's team (team #3) will attack this position and these two teams have the responsibility to first make sure if there are enemy or not. And if Milton's team (team #3) fails to find enemy in this position he will seek to close in toward Chamorro (team #1) and pay attention to the cemetery house (in case the enemy moves to occupy it during the battle?).

In case we have wounded, evacuate them to that place of the cemetery, as the first aid post will be there.

Order of Withdrawal

First Ruben's team (#5) will withdraw to the concentration point that will be the small elevation of the fountain and the other teams will withdraw together to the concentration point where the independent team will be (covering?). Together from this point we will march to the retreat zone, depending on the existing conditions.

Communications

By team through runner if there is a problem or once the situation is under control. The runners of Milton (team #3) and Alfredo (team #4) will first go to the position of Leonso and he will send them to Chamorro (team #1). Communication between the different individual combatants of the various teams will be through password which will be RED LIGHT, and this will be used during the battle and in case the teams are scattered. The password during the withdrawal will be PINEAPPLE.

Radio Communications

The first place of communication will be the fountain to find out what the enemy situation is. The next place of communication will be the camouflage place where two squelches will be sent and received. From this place we will be an hour from the objective and the independent team will be two hours from its objective. When we are ready to attack three squelches will be sent, and if a team is lost it will communicate. The location of the command post will be the fountain.

Calculation and Distribution of Time

From Portillo de San Geronimo to the old man's house is four hours. From this house to the fountain is an hour and a half. From the fountain to the camouflage place is 45 minutes. From the camouflage place to the point to initiate the attack (PIA) is one hour.

Order of March

To the fountain the entire platoon will march in the order team #1, #2, #3, #4, and #5. From the fountain the independent team will go ahead. The other four teams will march together to the camouflage point and will march in the order #1, #2, #3, and #4.

Weapons and Resources to Be Used

We need very good rifles. The platoon will use 16 rifles, 64 explosive charges, 4 issued to each man. These charges will all contain shrapnel. The quantity of ammunition to be drawn will be 2,400, 150 issued to each man. One radio and two watches will be issued to each team.

Equipment Issued to Each Team

Team #1

Chamorro Galil 150 rounds 4 explosives

Julio G-3 150 rounds 4 explosives

Alejo G-3 150 rounds 4 explosives

Team #2

Leonso Galil 150 rounds 4 explosives

Fernando M-16 150 rounds 4 explosives

Aparicio MP-5 150 rounds 4 explosives

Team #3

Milton Galil 150 rounds 4 explosives

Yovany G-3 150 rounds 4 explosives

Balta G-3 150 rounds 4 explosives

Team #4

Alfredo G-3 150 rounds 4 explosives

Pancho G-3 150 rounds 4 explosives

Ever FAL 150 rounds 4 explosives

Team #5

Ruben Galil 150 rounds 4 explosives

Tito G-3 150 rounds 4 explosives

Lito G-3 150 rounds 4 explosives

Adony M-16 150 rounds 4 explosives

CARRYING OUT OUR MISSION WE MAKE EACH BATTLE A VICTORY!!
IN OUR COMBAT UNIT THE COMBAT ORDER IS ALWAYS GIVEN!!
WE LIVE TO FIGHT! WE FIGHT TO WIN!!

Northern San Miguel
Chamorro, 2nd Platoon leader.

(Support Mission 1)

Leader: Nelson

Operational Force: Two regular force platoons and one guerrilla platoon.

Area of Operations: El Tablon, Cerro Belen, San Cristobal.

Missions: (1) Annihilation ambush at El Tablon. (2) Mining and blocking force on Cerro Belen. (3) Concentrated attack against San Cristobal.

Contingencies: If the enemy stays covering the general areas of Ciudad Barrios, Sesori, San Luis, and Llano el Angel with a company at each objective, the plan made initially will be implemented. If when the operation begins the enemy maintains positions at the turnoff to San Cristobal, variant one—consisting of a concentrated attack against that position with the objective of dislodging the enemy and taking that position, tie them down, or stop them from offering aid to the attacked units at the main objective. The first variant applies if the enemy is located at El Tamarindo. If at the moment of attack the enemy is not at Sesori, the force will not carry out the blockage of El Tablon and will have to become a reserve force of the main objective locating themselves around the bridge on the road from San Luis to Sesori near the Tamarindo River.

Equipment: All of the force armed with rifles and 150 rounds per weapon. 1 M-60 machine gun with 300 rounds of ammunition. 4 model 208 radios with their code books. 10 pressure-activated mines.

(Support Mission 2)

Leader: Nasser

Operational Force: One regular force platoon.

Area of Operations: West of San Luis.

Mission: Reserve Force.

Contingencies: Will be in charge of attacking to dislodge or tie down, any enemy position that at the time of the attack is found outside our objective and this if the position is oriented to the west of the objective. If the enemy is concentrated at San Luis will cooperate with the force attacking the position, with the only reservation that as a reserve force it will not get involved in the fighting unless it is necessary. It will act in any capacity that the command of the mission orders.

Support: Contemplated in the contingencies.

Equipment: All of the unit armed with rifles with 150 rounds per weapon. One model 208 radio with code book.

(Support Mission 3)

Leader: Calixtro

Operational Force: A platoon of regular forces.

Area of Operations: East of San Luis de la Reina on the road out of town.

Mission: Annihilation ambush against the enemy that retreats from the objective on this route.

Contingencies: If the enemy retreats dispersed and by other routes, you should persecute these forces. If the position is not taken by the special forces and they need support, you will attack the enemy position from the east to the west. If the enemy reinforcement is near and the position is not taken, you will have to move to support the force of Cornelio or Nelson. If the enemy advances from Carolina toward the objective you will have to move to cover the area of Santa Clara to establish a blocking position while the position is taken.

Support: In the contingencies.

Equipment: All of the force armed with rifles with 150 rounds per weapon. One model 208 radio with code book. 6 offensive charges. 4 pressure-activated mines.[14]

The complexity of this operations order is somewhat mind-boggling. There are missions and contingencies for each platoon, and in some cases team size elements. The order above is the overall plan used by the overall commander of the operation. Each platoon and team would only receive an order containing their portion of the plan. However, each of these platoons would have been stationed in a different base camp. These base camps changed at least every 15 days for security reasons. The commander would have to contact and brief each commander at each camp separately for this mission. Then he would have to make sure that each of the disparate elements reached their objective at the appointed time and place. This was assured through strict and sometimes brutal discipline. The FMLN became expert at conducting this type of operation. The complexity of the order described here was fairly routine. One of the FMLN secrets of success was a highly developed radio communications system. Starting as early as 1982, the FMLN learned the value of good communications and was almost entirely dependent on its radio net. In this light, it is curious that FES teams did not normally carry radios, at least during attacks (this attack being an exception), but communicated through runners that were sent back and forth between commanders and the teams (see the CEMFA operations order).

Even though the majority of FES operations from late 1985 on were of this layered type, the FES could still mass against a single target on occasion and deliver a devastating attack at the army's weakest point.

OVERRUN OF 3RD BRIGADE BASE AT SAN MIGUEL (JUNE 19, 1986)

The saying, "the third time's the charm" applied to FES attempts to penetrate the 3rd Brigade at San Miguel. The two previous attacks had caused significant damage from the outside, but had failed to successfully penetrate the base.

Starting in 1985 and continuing through 1987, the armed forces launched a series of operations known by the code name "Fenix." The Fenix operations consisted of using regular and special forces units to drive guerrilla units into predetermined kill zones where artillery and airpower could be used to destroy the insurgents. Initially, they were very effective and the guerrillas suffered heavy casualties. Army pressure on the guerrillas in Morazan from Fenix operations was so great that the ERP command decided it needed to carry out a major attack to force the army to halt operations against Morazan. The ERP needed space and time to reorganize its forces and develop new methods to deal with the new army tactics. The

ERP decided to attack the key command and control center for the Fenix operations in Morazan. This was the 3rd Brigade base at San Miguel. It was where the armed forces would least be expecting an attack, especially since they knew that the FMLN was suffering heavily in Morazan.

The intense army pressure and the need to devote every resource possible to resisting the army offensive in Morazan dictated that only a small number of troops could be spared for this operation. Only a platoon of PRTC, a company of regular ERP troops, and a company of TECMA personnel would participate in the operation. The objective of the attack was not to overrun the base. The guerrillas simply did not have the numbers for that. Rather, the main objective was to cause as much damage as possible and force the army to halt operations in Morazan. While the FES penetrated into the base, the other forces would attempt to distract the defenders on the base perimeter with supporting fire. The FES would attempt to penetrate into the heart of the installations and then carve paths of systematic destruction back out to the perimeter along their original routes of penetration. Once this was accomplished the FES would rendezvous with the forces outside the perimeter and withdraw.

San Miguel was El Salvador's third largest city, and because of its location, there was an abundance of guerrilla sympathizers within the city limits. After the first successful attack on the 4th Brigade headquarters at El Paraiso, the FMLN had decided that it could at any moment decide to attack any installation. It mobilized its informants near all of the military installations to regularly conduct reconnaissance and submit intelligence reports on the installations and troop movements in their area. This did two things. First, it forced the armed forces to always stay on its toes, knowing that every base was being probed. Second, when the opportunity arose, there was a ready and thorough source of information on any permanent installation the FMLN might choose to attack.

Taking advantage of this readily available information, the FES were able to plan the mission in a short time. Being thorough however, they still conducted their own reconnaissance patrols of the installations. This was facilitated, as the 3rd Brigade base was located in the middle of San Miguel, and was surrounded on all sides by urban developments. This made it possible to approach the base without having to traverse large open spaces. The suburbs around the base would also provide ample cover for the supporting forces to make their approach on the base.

Another element that was closely watched by the FES planners was the troop level within the base and the city. Based on reports provided by informers infiltrated within the military, June 19 was chosen because most of the brigade troops were heavily committed to the offensive in Morazan. Only around 200 soldiers besides normal service personnel would be on duty at the brigade headquarters, about a reinforced company. However, the key troop commitment to Morazan was the entire elite Arce Immediate

Reaction Battalion, which was based at a separate installation in San Miguel near the brigade headquarters. The presence of Arce battalion troops in San Miguel could have posed a major threat to the success of the entire operation, as the Arce troops could be expected to attempt to outflank the attacking force and trap the guerrillas between themselves and the brigade perimeter. To contain the Arce battalion would have required a major operation by itself, and one with a high risk of failure. The Arce battalion was known for its aggressiveness and tenacity in battle. The officers and troops were highly motivated, and unexpected and innovative tactics were the norm with these troops. For this reason, they were feared. Not having to deal with even a small number of Arce troops was a major concern for the FES planners.

The FES troops and their supporting units conducted several intense rehearsals against mock positions before the attack. The FES calculated the amount of explosives they would need for their operation. A rush order was relayed through the ERP high command back to Nicaragua. The transfers were made from Sandinista army stocks to the FMLN, which then shipped the yellow Russian TNT, det cord, and blasting caps hidden in the false bottoms of moving vans and semi-trucks filled with the regular merchandise that traversed the roads of Central America. These explosives were stored, along with the necessary weapons, in some of the many safehouses around San Miguel, close to the objective. The FES always attempted to set up weapons deposits near their objectives so they wouldn't be burdened during their approach marches.

Some of the trucks from Nicaragua pulled right into San Miguel, dropping off their secret cargo, under the pretense of making a normal pit stop for maintenance, fuel, or so the drivers could rest. As San Miguel lay along the major trucking route through El Salvador, unloading cargo here was a completely normal activity that aroused no suspicion.

During the day of June 18, the various components of the attacking force made their final preparations. About 9:00 P.M. they were aroused and the various components of the force were concentrated. Ammunition was distributed, final questions asked, answers given, along with a motivational harangue by one of the guerrilla commanders. After a few ceremonial cheers, the force left. Guided by FES soldiers dressed as ordinary guerrillas, the force made a careful approach march along a preselected route to a farm on the outskirts of San Miguel. They arrived just before dawn. The guerrillas set up security and rested. They laid up all day while the commanders verified last minute intelligence reports and made last minute clarifications and modifications of the plans. Early in the morning, after only a little rest, the FES troops changed into civilian clothes and slipped one by one into town. Some of them made a last minute visual inspection of the objective. Others went to the safehouses to make sure that their explosives and equipment were in proper order. At dusk, the other FES members began to slowly trickle in. They completely stripped and put on black or dark jogging shorts. They then began the slow process of completely painting their bodies with charcoal paint. Finally, each man checked his individual equipment. This consisted of a rifle, a black or dark bag full of various types of explosive charges, depending on the mission assigned to the individual, and rifle magazines. One out of every team of four carried an RPG-2 or RPG-7 rocket launcher with four rockets. About midnight the various FES teams began to make their approach to their assigned jumping-off points. They were careful to stay in the shadows and avoid detection by people or army patrols.

When it was time, each team began its advance through the base perimeter. The man with the RPG launcher set up with his weapon aimed to cover his teammates' withdrawal, if they were discovered. Under the watch of the RPG man, the rest of the team continued their advance. In less than 10 minutes the FES teams made their way through the wire and the minefields without being detected. However, their rapid progress was brought to a sudden halt by an unexpected obstacle. Powerful base lights mounted on machine gun towers illuminated the rest of the way into the base. If even one team was discovered, the rest of the teams could be trapped and slaughtered by the machine gun towers, and the operation would be a total failure. While the FES were trained in overcoming lights, operationally, they avoided having to use this training. Runners were sent carefully back through the cleared paths to consult with the team leaders, who then consulted with the overall FES commander. The commander ordered that they continue, instead of turning back. He reminded them of the principle that where there was light, there was also shadow, and they should move through the shadows. The teams dutifully obeyed. The guerrillas inched their way past the machine gun towers. Meanwhile, the RPG gunners trained their rockets on these towers, nervously fingering their triggers. The teams' daring was rewarded by the sound of silence. Once the FES were past the lights, there was an abundance of darkness. The teams had to stop for a minute to regain their night vision. However, they rapidly adjusted and used the newfound darkness to quickly penetrate to their jumping-off points, just outside the inner bunker line deep within the base. While the lights had held them up, they arrived just within the established timetable to begin the attack. They didn't have long to wait for the preestablished signal.

The combined support group of PRTC and ERP had left their lying-up point just before midnight and had marched down the back streets toward their assigned positions. Taking advantage of the shadows, they made their way cautiously toward the brigade complex. There were no army patrols or other holdups. It was obvious that they were completely unexpected. As rehearsed, they quietly took up their positions across the street from the brigade. As soon as they were ready, they waited for the right time and opened fire. The support group began to fire on previously identified outer bunkers. They were joined by the FES RPG gunners who were finally allowed to fire at the machine gun towers and take out the menacing lights. Pandemonium broke out on the base itself. Most of the army troops were asleep, and those that weren't hesitated a few moments, confused about the direction and nature of the firing they were hearing. These few moments of hesitation were always fatal. The FES teams rushed past the mostly unmanned inner bunker perimeter, into where most of the buildings were located. Their first targets were the troop barracks of the Ponce and Leon battalions. The objective was to eliminate them while they were vulnerable and concentrated. Speed was essential to carry out their mission before the enemy had time to react. Once the troops were eliminated, the other objectives would be easier to destroy.

Not all of the soldiers had been in the barracks, and those that had been more fortunate had made their way to the bunker line to resist the guerrilla attack. Unfortunately for them, they concentrated on the fire coming from outside the base. As the FES withdrew back out to the perimeter they used their remaining explosives and ammunition to attack the bunker line from behind. These had to be taken out to prevent FES casualties as they made their withdrawal through the perimeter obstacles. Particularly troublesome points of resistance were taken out or silenced by the RPG gunners along the perimeter.

Part of the base at San Miguel is a large helicopter port located just outside the inner bunker line. Several craft were at the base on call for use in the Morazan offensive. While the attack was in progress, three helicopter crews made a mad dash in the hopes that they could take off, save the craft, and strafe the attacking force. However, an FES team assigned to take out the helicopters reached the area first. One by one, the valiant crews were slaughtered in their craft by an FES team assigned to sabotage the machines. All three helicopters were then destroyed with small explosive charges. The ERP FES knew exactly where to place the charges for the greatest effect, due to their training and preparation for the successful Ilopango air base raid of January 1982.

Another FES team had been assigned to kill the U.S. advisers at the base. However, the advisers had saved themselves by escaping out of their dormitories, still in their underwear, through an underground tunnel. The FES team only found empty rooms. It took less than a half hour from the time the attack began to the time the last FES team exited back out of the perimeter. However, outside the base the battle raged all night. The support group battled the base defenders and other security forces units long after the FES had made their escape. The guerrillas claimed to have captured 50 weapons and destroyed many of the installations of the 3rd Brigade to include part of the armory. The dormitories of the Ponce and Leon barracks were completely destroyed. The FES estimated that 120 soldiers were killed, mostly the men in these barracks. In addition, the Cuscatlan battalion and Arce battalion installations suffered some damage. The FES lost approximately five men inside the base. Most of these men were killed by remaining too close to their own explosives after they had been thrown. It is unknown how many killed and wounded were suffered by the support force.

The army claimed that it won the battle because it had prevented the guerrillas from overrunning the base, as had occurred at the 4th Brigade base at El Paraiso. However, this was not the FMLN objective. The guerrillas considered the attack a total success because, after this attack, the army pulled back its troops from Morazan to rebuild and reorganize in San Miguel.[15] The pressure was off the guerrillas in Morazan, and they could now rest and recover. This objective had been achieved at a very low cost to the attacking guerrilla force, and had inflicted a considerable amount of damage on the enemy.

NOTES

1. Alfredo Semprun and Mauricio Hernandez, "Sandinismo: La otra cara de ETA," *Blanco y Negro* (January 5, 1992), pp. 14–18.

2. ERP, *Informe a Alcatraz*, 1981.

3. Interrogation Transcript of Alejandro Montenegro, who defected from the FMLN in 1983. Montenegro's name can be revealed because he made several public statements concerning his activity in the ERP after his capture.

4. This account is based largely on: Capitan Francisco Emilio Mena Sandoval, *Del Ejercito Nacional al Ejercito Guerrillero* (San Salvador: Ediciones Arcoiris, 1992), pp. 307–319; Carlos Henriquez Consalvi (Santiago), *La Terquedad del Izote* (Mexico: Editorial Diana, 1992), pp. 187–191; and Jose Ignacio Lopez Vigil, *Las Mil y Una Historias de Radio Venceremos* (San Salvador: UCA Editores, 1992), pp. 248–255.

5. Max G. Manwaring and Court Prisk, *El Salvador at War: An Oral History* (Washington, DC: National Defense University Press, 1988), p. 148.

6. Semprun and Hernandez, "Sandinismo," pp. 14–18.

7. Account based on the Interrogation Transcript of JFR, August 24, 1986; Interrogation Transcript of RAC, May 12, 1987; and on the technical drawings and instructions of the bridge and how the explosives were to be placed, which were later captured by the armed forces.

8. FPL-FMLN, *Experiences of the Conduct of Anti-Aircraft Defense.*

9. Greg Walker, "Sapper Attack!", *Behind the Lines* (July/August 1993), p. 9. See also Greg Walker, "Blue Badges of Honor," *Soldier of Fortune* (February 1992), p. 36.

10. Armed Forces of El Salvador, *Activities in Which Terrorist Special Forces Have Participated*, March 1990.

11. The reporting of explosives strapped to bodies, and the interpretation of this as being for suicide missions may just be a bit of government propaganda or a sign of prejudiced interpretation.

12. ERP, *Mission for Team 2 of Platoon 2*, handwritten order on lined notebook paper, captured by the armed forces in Morazan on March 31, 1986.

13. This account was based on three sources: ERP, *Mission for Team 2 of Platoon 2*; an interview with a Salvadoran officer stationed at the CEMFA during the attack; and Walker, "Sapper Attack!", pp. 9–11.

14. ERP, *Combat Order #5*, typed manuscript document on white letter paper, captured by the armed forces in Morazan on May 13, 1986.

15. Interrogation Transcript of JAFA, April 19, 1990.

CHAPTER 5

Special Forces of the FAL

The first FAL special forces unit was known as the U-24 formed in mid-1982 at Palo Grande, Suchitoto. It was originally made up of 24 men trained in Cuba. Besides the U-24, two other special operations units were formed. A special forces platoon called commandos of the BRAC or COB-RAC was formed to give the FAL's maneuver battalion its own organic FES capability, rather than always being dependent on the U-24 units under the command of the FAL high command. The final unit was the "Panteras" (Panthers), organized at the beginning of 1985. This unit was formed after the COBRAC and U-24 were fused and transferred to high command control. The Panthers were a unit consisting of a couple of FES-type squads. They were part of the Jacobo Campos Valle column, one of the company-size units of the BRAC. With the loss of the COBRAC, the formation of the Panthers again gave the BRAC its own, organic FES capability. All the FAL special forces units were based on the range of hills between Guazapa and the San Salvador volcano, some of the main strongholds of the FMLN guerrillas, particularly of the FAL and the RN factions.

The U-24 participated alongside the FPL FES in the attack on the 4th Brigade in December of 1983. Little is known about their other operations prior to 1985. However, because of the nearness of these units to El Salvador's cities, the U-24 often conducted urban operations or operations in conjunction with urban units.

MARIONA PRISON BREAK (JULY 14, 1985)

On August 3, 1984, some members of the U-24 carried out an unauthorized assault on a bank in Soyapango to gain funds for their platoon. The robbery failed, and the bank was surrounded by the Treasury police.

Realizing their situation was hopeless, they negotiated for three days and finally gave themselves up to the Red Cross. Salvadoran justice assigned them to Mariona prison. Here they languished until July 14, 1985.

Although upset with the U-24 for the botched operation, the FAL high command considered the prisoners too valuable to remain in prison. Because of this, the order was given to liberate the prisoners in the shortest time possible. The operation would require the active participation of the men on the inside, as well as the force that would act from the outside. The units on the outside studied the external situation, and those in Mariona studied the internal situation. The information was passed back and forth every visiting day until the operation was carried out on July 12, 1985 at 5:30 P.M.

To allay suspicion, the information was carried back and forth by representatives of various organizations who visited with Captain Victor Manuel, the leader on the inside. The visiting organizations carrying messages included the following: COMADRES, CODEFAN, International Red Cross, Doctors of the World, U.S. Congressional aides, among others. Through these messengers, an explosive charge was smuggled piece by piece into the prisoners.

The attack on the Mariona prison was planned by Lt. Junior and Sgt. Augusto. These two men planned everything regarding the attack on the outside of the prison. The person who planned it on the inside was "Ramon." To carry out this work there was excellent coordination because there was constant communication between the exterior and the interior.

Because of the U-24's reduced size, the unit had to be reinforced by a team from the Rafael Aguiñada Carranza Battalion (BRAC). The members of the special forces who took part were Junior, Augusto, Paco, Juancito, Chema, and Lucho, a total of six members of the special forces. There were also three members from the BRAC, making a total of nine members from the FAL who carried out the attack on the prison. The operation was under the command of Lt. Junior.

The final message was passed on Thursday, July 11. The attack would be carried out at 5:30 P.M. the next day. The attack signal would be the explosion of an RPG-2 rocket, fired at a guard tower at the southeast corner of the prison. If the unit was discovered on the outside of the prison by an enemy patrol, or suffered some other mishap, the operation would be suspended. Once the signal was heard, the men on the inside were to use their explosive to make a hole in the prison wall. If the charge placed on the inside failed, the team on the outside carried another charge in reserve which they would place from outside. This action would be coordinated by yelling over the wall.

The escape route would be up the San Salvador volcano, and the unit would try to reach Guazapa during the night. The signal for retreat after the objectives had been accomplished would be ten blows on a soccer whistle.

The teams were organized as follows: Team 1 would attack the guard tower at the extreme southeast corner of the prison. It would be composed of two people, Paco and Sgt. Augusto. Team #2 would attack the southwestern guard tower, and would consist of Chema and Lecho. Team #3 would be the command group, and would take up a position 100 meters south of the prison. Lt. Junior and Sgt. Juancito made up this team. Team #4 would be composed of the three members of the BRAC, Jose, Alcides, and Quique. This team would be located 200 meters south of the prison covering the road going to Mejicanos.

The attack was led by Lt. Junior. In five minutes it had concluded, and the prisoners and their liberators were speedily making their way up the San Salvador volcano. The guard tower on the southeast corner was blown apart, and the explosive placed on the inside worked perfectly, blowing a neat hole in the brick wall of the prison. The prison guards, armed with old Mauser bolt action rifles, were hardly a match for the better-armed guerrillas.

To carry out the attack, the following weapons were used: 8 M-16 rifles, an M-60 machine gun, 2 RPG-2s, 2 400-gram explosive charges, a 9mm pistol, 5 American-made offensive grenades, and a YAESU radio.[1]

KIDNAPPING OF INES GUADALUPE (SEPTEMBER 10, 1985)

The kidnapping of Ines Guadalupe, President Napoleon Duarte's daughter, was a complex and multiunit operation. A team of four men participated from the U-24. These were Augusto, Junior, Melkin, and Chema. The rest of the people were urban commandos and the plan was organized by people from the metropolitan area. The urban commandos approached Ines's car, and shot her bodyguards dead. They then grabbed Ines and took her aboard a stolen Hiace van. A short distance away, they abandoned that vehicle and split up into five separate cars to confuse any chase forces. When the car carrying Ines reached San Laureano in Ciudad Delgado, they switched to a Jeep Cherokee belonging to the FAL. A squad of expansion troops in San Laureano under Rene Armando provided security. This squad accompanied them to the Las Cañas river where the U-24 team met the Cherokee. From here the FES troops took Ines to Guazapa volcano. This unit was made up of six men under the command of Sgt. Raymundo. In their path, a unit of the BRAC provided security along the detour from the road which leads to San Jose Las Flores in the jurisdiction of Tonacatepeque. From here they went directly to the Los Lirios hill where the U-24 FES camp was located. The leader of this camp was Captain Arnulfo.

The weapons used in the operation were a Czech Skorpion submachine gun, a Galil rifle, .45 calibre and 9mm pistols, as well as stun grenades.[2]

DESTRUCTION OF THE FINCA EL PINAR CIVIL DEFENSE POST (AUGUST 22, 1985)

On August 10, 1985, a mission was received by group #1 of the U-24 FES commandos to attack the Civil Defense positions at the Pinar and Granadillas farms located on the San Salvador volcano. The mission was to be carried out on August 20, 1985. The order included detailed information on the strength, composition, and position of the government forces. This mission was to be the main focus of a series of coordinated attacks against army posts at El Matazano hamlet, jurisdiction of San Juan Opico, Department of La Libertad, and San Juan de Los Planes. The latter objectives would be attacked simultaneously by forces of other organizations, the ERP at El Matazano and the FPL at San Juan de Los Planes.

The objective of attacking the two positions at the Pinar and Granadillas farms was to annihilate the members of the Civil Defense and to recover war materiel. The strategic objective of this attack was to support expansion activities on the San Salvador volcano because the government positions here were an obstacle to political proselytizing in this area. The chief of expansion had only been able to move with great difficulty to carry out his work.

The same day the order was received, four special forces troops of the U-24 were sent to the San Salvador volcano to reconnoiter the objectives and confirm the information that had been included in the original order. Old information was confirmed, and new information added to the target dossier. A total of ten FES members and ten members of COBRAC (commandos of the Rafael Aguiñada Carranza Battalion), supported logistically by expansion units in this sector, were assigned to make the attack. This group reached the San Salvador volcano on August 12, and set up camp at the Mirasol farm. This group carried out its own recon on August 15, and another on August 18. When all the preparations were finalized, a message was sent on August 18 to the FAL commander, Ramon Suarez, on Guazapa hill containing the following information: (1) The operation was confirmed for August 22, 1985 at midnight; (2) It was requested that the remainder of the personnel and their weapons be sent for the attack; (3) A request was made for a medic to be sent with this personnel.

The overall commander of the operation was Lt. Manuelon who was the BRAC 1st Company leader. The remainder of the personnel that were to participate in the operation arrived on August 21, 1985. Four members of U-24 and eight of COBRAC would attack the Pinar Finca. The Granadillas farm would be attacked by four U-24 commandos and nine COBRAC guerrillas. The total number of combatants was 25. The attack was to start at midnight of August 22, and last no longer than two hours.

The result of these attacks was the destruction and burning of the local command post at Pinar farm as well as the death of three Civil Defense members. Two G-3 rifles were recovered. The attack on the Granadillas farm failed. The attackers met stiff resistance from the defenders who holed themselves up in an impregnable bunker. When the attacking force had not been able to dislodge the defenders by 0200 hours, they withdrew. One guerrilla was killed at Granadillas farm, and one wounded at Pinar farm. The dead guerrilla's M-16 was lost at Granadillas.

At the other objectives, El Matazano and San Juan de Los Planes, the attacks were carried out at 10:00 P.M. on August 22 and finalized by midnight, the battles lasting around two hours.[3]

THE KIDNAPPING OF COLONEL OMAR NAPOLEON AVALOS LOPEZ (OCTOBER 26, 1985)

The FAL saw an opportunity to kidnap an army colonel, Colonel Avalos. This kidnapping operation took place after the Ines Duarte Guadalupe kidnapping and it was thought that a similar prisoner exchange could be carried out. Two guerrillas had recognized the colonel as he travelled to a farm he had in Cojutepeque. He did not take many security precautions, and as a result was a tempting target. This information was passed on to Camilo, the head of the FAL special forces over that area. Camilo chose Remberto to plan and lead the mission. Remberto planned to use deception to be able to gain the advantage of surprise and use it to subdue the colonel. Eight new army uniforms and jungle boots were obtained. Seven guerrillas would wear privates' uniforms, while Remberto would wear the uniform of an army lieutenant. Obtaining weapons was no problem, since all but one of the guerrillas involved in the operation were already armed with M-16 rifles, the standard army issue rifle. The plan was to pose as a standard army patrol from a nearby base. The only problem was that between the colonel's farm and the guerrillas was a small village named San Ramon with a Civil Defense post. If the men at this post saw the guerrillas they might fire on them despite their army uniforms, since they were normally advised of regular army patrols. Furthermore, if there was a struggle at the farm, this might alert the Civil Defense post, which could either make an attack on the guerrillas, or more likely, set up positions that would effectively block the kidnapping party's route of escape. Therefore, the uniforms were largely to fool any civilian informers the security forces might have in the area, as well as to cause enough hesitation on the part of the targeted colonel and his bodyguards to allow the kidnappers to gain the upper hand.

The operation began at dusk on the day before the kidnapping. The eight guerrillas, dressed from head to toe in army uniforms, equipment, and weapons, started out from San Juan Buenavista of Verapaz. They walked to the highway between Verapaz and Cojutepeque and marched all night until they came to San Ramon, which was along the highway. They skirted the town to avoid the Civil Defense. This was done by using a shallow riverbed that ran in the general direction of the farm. Once they skirted the town they left the riverbed and emerged onto the dirt road that led to the farm from San Ramon. Just before sunrise they came to their predesignated lie-up point just outside the farm. This was an elevation from which they had a good view of the farm as well as of the approaches from San Ramon. Here the guerrillas got some sleep before the operation the next day. In the morning the guerrillas laid up in their position observing the movement on the farm. They were very patient. They watched until they were satisfied that there were no additional bodyguards or weapons on the farm, and that the colonel was completely unaware that he was a target. Finally, they saw the colonel go into the farm stable with his children, his bodyguards, and a couple of workers. This was the opportunity they were waiting for. Half of the guerrilla team was assigned to set up a blocking and covering position pointed toward San Ramon, while Remberto and the other three guerrillas walked down to the farm. They walked boldly, trying to give an air of authority as if they were really members of the army. Unhindered, they walked right into the stable and told everyone to put their hands up and then lie face down on the ground. Without protest everyone complied. While his three companions covered the others with their M-16s, one of Remberto's guerrillas went up to the colonel, jerked him up roughly and tied his hands behind his back. This finally brought a word of protest from Colonel Avalos who, in a puzzled tone of voice, asked why he, a lieutenant, would order his men to tie up an army colonel. Remberto replied curtly that he was only obeying his orders without specifying what they were. He also reiterated that his men were from the army, that the colonel shouldn't worry, and that everything would be sorted out. This apparently satisfied Colonel Avalos who made no further issue of his treatment. One of the other members of the guerrilla team then searched the remaining captives lying on the floor. He relieved Colonel Avalos' bodyguards of a Galil rifle, three 9mm Browning automatic pistols, and three .38 calibre revolvers. He then took these captives and hustled them into a room which he locked from the outside so they couldn't warn anyone else on the farm of what was going on, and see in which direction they took the colonel. When the colonel saw that they were taking his children away he expressed the fear that his children would be physically or sexually harmed in some way. Again, Remberto, in his lieutenant's uniform assured the colonel that nothing would happen and that he should not worry. The colonel again accepted this and became silent. Once the people were locked up, the four guerrillas put the colonel into his own white Toyota sedan and drove calmly away from the farm. Covered by the other four-man team they drove nonchalantly up to the main road and turned toward Verapaz. As they passed through San Ramon, they drove at high speed to avoid being stopped. They passed right through a group of army soldiers posted along the road. The soldiers noticed the zooming car, and recognized it as the colonel's. Not wanting to have an unpleasant confrontation with an irate colonel in a hurry, they didn't even bother to look up to see who was in the car. They just waved it on through. After they had gone through, Colonel Avalos commented on what idiots they were to not even notice who was in the car. Units in El Salvador are fairly small, and everyone is known to everyone else. Had they even bothered to look up, they would have noticed that the four other "soldiers" in the car with the colonel were strangers. This would have raised immediate alarm, but the soldiers didn't even bother to look up; just recognizing the colonel's car was sufficient. They drove to just outside of Buena Vista and pulled off the road in a concealed grove just off the highway. Now totally suspicious, the colonel asked them if they were really army personnel or if they were guerrillas. Remberto told them they were guerrillas and told him that his life was not in danger. Colonel Avalos told Remberto that he was very impressed with the execution of the operation and congratulated him on his efficiency and professionalism. He then asked permission to sing softly. Remberto said that he had no problems as long as it was not too loud. Colonel Avalos explained that it was to let out his pent-up emotions and to calm himself.

After about an hour and a half, Camilo and other leaders of the U-24 showed up. They abandoned the Toyota sedan and made for the San Pedro Hills by following the course of the Jiboa river. Camilo and the other U-24 leaders led the way while Remberto and his men brought up the rear. Colonel Avalos was handed over to the higher command of the FAL here. Because of army movements in the area, Colonel Avalos was handed over to the local PRTC unit who took him to their stronghold in Morazan.[4]

ATTACK ON ARTILLERY SUPPORTING OPERATION FENIX (JANUARY 13, 1986)

In 1985, large amounts of U.S. aid began to make a visible difference to the Salvadoran armed forces, and the army began to gain the upper hand. New army tactics began to do serious damage to the FMLN. This was especially true of the Fenix operations. "Fenix" (meaning Phoenix) essentially consisted of army units using saturation patrols to take control of an area, separate the guerrillas from their civilian support, and then drive the guerrilla units into prearranged kill zones, where the armed forces could bring to bear their advantage in artillery and air power. The operations were very successful. The heavy artillery barrages and air bombardment caused particularly heavy casualties. In an effort to reverse this situation, the guerrillas tried to take pressure off the guerrilla forces by neutralizing the armed forces' support weapons.

The U-24 FES platoon of the FAL received the mission to destroy the artillery pieces that were supporting a Fenix operation from the San Jose

Guayabal soccer field, Cuscatlan Department. They were causing a lot of casualties, and making it very uncomfortable for the FMLN units in the area. The guerrillas wanted the guns silenced. The FAL U-24 FES platoon was assigned this mission, and carried it out on the night of January 13, 1986.

Because of the urgency of the mission, there was limited time to carry out reconnaissance. However, the guerrillas had a good idea of the layout of the town and the terrain because of collaborators and the limited reconnaissance they were able to conduct.

The ten FES members of the platoon were divided into two teams. Team #1 would attack the pieces, while team #2 would take the high ground, 200 meters to the north of the soccer field. Team #2's mission was to assault an army machine gun position at this location, which dominated the terrain, to prevent it from firing on team #1. They were then to turn the weapon on its former owners, and provide fire support for team #1 from the high ground against army forces that would surely resist the main attack.

At midnight the two teams approached their objectives in silence. Team #2 stealthily approached the foxholes at the top of the hill. They were trying to get in close to take the position as quietly as possible. They were even hoping to be able to slit the soldiers' throats with knives to avoid the sound of gunfire. When the first man reached the lip of the trench, he peered in and saw it was empty. This was fortunate, because the commandos took the high ground easily. However, it was unfortunate, because they couldn't capture the machine gun, which would have provided a high volume of suppressing fire to assist team #1 in destroying the artillery pieces. They set up facing the artillery pieces in the soccer field down below.

Team #1 was not as fortunate. One man was left on the edge of the field with an RPG-7 rocket launcher to provide support. The remainder of the team crawled stealthily across the field to attach explosives to the artillery tubes. If they were spotted on the field, it was hoped that they would be close enough to rush the pieces, and while under the cover of team #2 on the high ground, and the RPG man, be able to destroy the pieces. However, almost immediately they were detected by an alert sentry as they were approaching the guns. Heavy firing broke out from the soldiers' positions. Team #2 attempted to support from the dominating heights, but their lack of heavy firepower failed to suppress the soldiers enough for the commandos to reach the guns. In the firefight, one of the exposed commandos on the soccer field was killed. The rest made a mad dash back to a position of relative safety. Because of the intensity of the firing, the FES could not go out on the field and recover their fallen comrade. They were forced to abandon his body and the M-16 rifle he was carrying. The leader of team #1 decided that he had one more chance to destroy the guns. He told the RPG gunner not to fire his rockets at the soldiers, but at the artillery pieces which were perfectly silhouetted by the glow of the tracer fire and the flash of the grenades. Before they were forced to withdraw, the RPG man scored a direct hit on one of the guns. It was damaged, but the three remaining guns of the battery were still intact. The mission was only a partial success, and did not silence the guns. The Fenix operations continued unhindered against the FMLN on Guazapa hill, and in the process, the U-24 unit suffered heavy casualties from the guns they had failed to destroy.[5]

THE TAKING OF THE TOWN OF JERUSALEN, SAN VICENTE (MAY 1986)

The FAL in San Vicente was feeling the pinch from Operation Fenix. Large numbers of guerrillas and masses had fled from Guazapa to the San Pedro hills of San Vicente. Furthermore, the new aggressiveness of the army had interrupted the logistics flow and the FAL in San Vicente was running short of weapons. The commanders in this region began thinking of a way to capture weapons from the army. Attacking a regular army unit was possible, but could result in heavy casualties for the attackers. The most vulnerable part of the army's defensive network was the civil defense posts at most of the major farms and towns in the region. A good size civil defense post was located at Jerusalen, and it was reputed to have a large arsenal of weapons.

The next problem was to determine how to attack the post. Although civil defense troops were not as well equipped as the regular army troops, they could often defend their positions very stubbornly and inflict heavy casualties (Granadillas farm, for example). They were usually led by tough ex-army NCOs that had spent several years in combat. It was thought that if the guerrillas could get up close to the post, they could take it in a quick rush that would catch the defenders by surprise and not permit them to mobilize their forces. Drawing on previous experience (such as the kidnapping of Colonel Avalos), the FAL decided that a select force would attack the post. The men would be completely dressed in army uniforms and equipment and would pose as an army patrol from the 5th Brigade. The uniforms were obtained from captured stocks and from infiltrators in the Brigade.

On the date of the operation, the guerrillas put on their army uniforms and marched silently to the road into Jerusalen. At 5:00 P.M. they began marching into town. This was not a usual time for guerrilla operations, but it was common for army patrols to be seen at this time. Led by "Remberto," the 15 guerrillas came out on the road and then lined up in army fashion and marched down the road toward Jerusalen. Remberto marched at the head of the group. He wore a tailored uniform and metal lieutenant's bars on his hat that had been shined so they stood out and could be seen from a distance. Putting on the air of being an arrogant, confident first lieutenant, Remberto led his men up to the door of the post and called for the sergeant in charge. So far, no one suspected anything. Meanwhile Remberto's men casually took up positions from which they could cover all of the possible points of resistance.

The sergeant came out of the post, snapped to attention, and gave the lieutenant a smart salute. In his best command voice, Remberto calmly informed the civil defense sergeant that he and his men were FMLN guerrillas and that he was the leader of the group. He ordered the sergeant and his men not to put up any resistance and to turn over all the weapons to the guerrillas. The sergeant looked around and saw that he and his men were surrounded and that they would be killed and overwhelmed if they resisted, so he surrendered.

The guerrillas entered the post and quickly rounded up all of the defenders which they tied up and kept inside the post. Then they gathered up all of the weapons and equipment, 50 M-1 carbines, 1 G-3 rifle, 2 PRC-77 radios, ammunition, uniforms, and so on. They took the sergeant and another civil defense soldier prisoner and quickly withdrew into the afternoon. Under cover of night, they made their way back up into the hills and buried the weapons in a secret cache.[6]

DESTRUCTION OF THE LA LIBERTAD ELECTRICITY SUBSTATION

At the beginning of July 1986, an FES team led by Isaac, and including Dario, Santos, and Diego was sent from Guazapa to La Libertad Department via the San Salvador volcano. Here they made contact with the expansion group of the FAL in this region. The expansion group was trying to build up the guerrilla organization in this area. To support the expansion effort, there had to be a spectacular increase in terrorist effort. It was decided that Isaac's team would attack the electrical energy substation at the hamlet of Ateos in La Libertad. The expansion group in La Libertad had a clandestine camp in the Lourdes area of the department. La Libertad was enemy territory, and the army had most of its strategic forces in this Department including the Cavalry Regiment, the Artillery Regiment, and both the Atlacatl and Bracamonte immediate reaction battalions. The guerrillas did not have the freedom of movement here that they had in Chalatenango, Morazan, or Jucuaran. The FAL high command communicated with the expansion group and set up a contact date for the FES team to arrive and set up operations in La Libertad. They were to meet on the Ponderosa farm at the extreme southern end of the San Salvador volcano. When the FES team showed up, the expansion group did not. After waiting for 24 hours, the FES team returned to the main guerrilla camp at the Mirasol farm on the San Salvador volcano. A second contact was set up by Ramon Suarez at the same farm for July 12. This time, three additional guerrillas escorted the FES team for backup and security reasons.

The instructions said that they were to meet at a large tree by a storage shed on the farm. The FES team and its escort moved carefully through rows of coffee bushes. About 100 meters from the shed they stopped where they still had cover behind the coffee bushes and also had a clear view of the tree and the storage shed. They set up an overwatch position and waited. The failure of the previous contact had put everyone on edge. They were being extra cautious to avoid a trap. At the appointed time, 10:00 A.M., they saw their two contact men walk up to the tree. Leaving the escort group in the overwatch position, they moved up. After some pre-arranged signs, countersigns, and verifications, the escort was motioned forward. They stayed put until 5:00 P.M. to avoid moving in broad daylight. At that time the escort group returned to the Mirasol camp up on the volcano, while the FES team followed its new guides to La Libertad. They marched through the night until they reached the expansion group's camp at 5:00 A.M. Between July 13 and July 15, the FES team rested and discussed the information that was already known about the objective. This information was largely from local collaborators that had been recently recruited by the expansion group. That night, the entire FES team and two members of the expansion group went out to conduct a reconnaissance of the objective. It was essentially a rehersal for the attack, as the two expansion guerrillas had been designated to participate in the operation as guides and as security outside the objective while the FES penetrated. They reached the objective at 1:00 A.M. Using their special techniques the FES slowly explored the terrain around the substation. They found three bunkers, but they were empty. Finding no security detail around the structure, they looked for a way to penetrate the station itself. They found this was surrounded on all sides by a three-meter-high wall, topped by two meters of cyclone fencing. This presented a difficult obstacle to overcome. Isaac ordered that a further search be made to see if there was a way to get past the wall without crossing over it. They found a drainage ditch running underneath the wall which led directly to the interior of the installation. Through this ditch they were able to penetrate the installation and locate their primary objectives of destruction, the station computer and the main transformer which was about four meters square. The FES team was able to finish reconnaissance and return to the expansion camp by 6:00 A.M. on July 16. The lack of security around the facility and the excellent route of penetration discovered caused Isaac to decide that no further reconnaissance was necessary. The FES team now made out its request for equipment and waited for the explosives and the orders to arrive.

On July 21 the six men, two expansionists and the four FES team members, left their camp at dusk. They carried a 5-kilo charge for the transformer and a 3-kilo charge of TNT for the computer. In addition, each man carried an M-16 and a U.S.-made M-26 grenade. They reached the objective at 10:30 P.M. The expansion group set up security outside the installation, and the FES team went into the objective, penetrating rapidly by way of the drainage ditch. The explosives were placed on the computer and the transformer, the time fuse lit, and the FES team exited back out the drainage ditch, the same way it had come in. At 11:00 P.M. the explosives went off with a large boom. The guerrillas did not, however, get to see their handiwork as they were already moving to their rendezvous point. This was back at the Ponderosa farm. Their guides returned to the expansion camp, and the FES team laid up all day waiting for its escort. At 5:00 P.M. the same three escorts arrived and led them back to the Mirasol camp up on the volcano. Finally, back at the camp they learned the results of their mission. There was much celebration, and they were met by a member of the FAL high command who informed them that the explosion had knocked out the lights of an important farming and agro-industry area that included coffee mills, farms, and ranches.[7]

CONSOLIDATION OF THE U-24 AND THE COBRAC

On August 3, 1986, a meeting was held on Guazapa hill of all of the special forces of the FAL, the U-24, and the COBRAC. Chepon informed the men of both units that the FAL high command had made a decision to combine the two units into one. The unit would be divided into two platoons under the political command of Chepon. The second in command and commader of the 1st platoon would be Ramon, formerly of the U-24. Odir of the COBRAC would be the leader of the 2nd platoon. Each platoon would have twelve men divided into three squads of four men. The combined unit left Guazapa hill on August 10, and marched for three days until it reached the El Jicaro camp in Chalatenango. Here it set up a training school for refresher training. The course lasted six weeks and consisted largely of perfecting infiltration and the assault techniques of different types of objectives. It was designed to meld the two units into one and standardize their operating procedures so that the men from both units would operate smoothly together. The course ran from 5:00 A.M. to 9:00 P.M. The course ended on October 5, and on October 6, the unit began its march back to Guazapa hill.

They remained on Guazapa hill together until November 10, when the 1st platoon was sent to San Jose Las Flores, Chalatenango to support expansion operations in this area. Here they carried out reconnaissance of various objectives, two fruitless night ambushes of military vehicles on the Main Northern Road, and a reconnaissance and attack on March 1, 1987 of an army position of the 1st Brigade's San Carlos battalion on a hill overlooking the Guaycume bridge. They inflicted an estimated ten casualties including wounded and dead, captured five uniforms, eight rucksacks, and five 90mm projectiles. After this attack, the 1st platoon was recalled to Guazapa hill for a time of rest. On April 5, they were assigned to the south side of Guazapa hill to reconnoiter army positions along the Main Northern Road.[8]

FES DURING 1989 FINAL OFFENSIVE (NOVEMBER 11, 1989)

FES units of the FMLN played an active role in the November 11 offensive. Prior to the offensive, FES units had been actively carrying out reconnaissance of the key objectives. The high command also assigned the FES the mission of coordinating the mobilization of the guerrilla forces. Since 1985, the FMLN had split up into small squad- and platoon-size elements; 10 to 30 combatants in camps dispersed all over the combat zone. The commanders were able to maintain control over these elements through the excellent radio net that they had developed. They also developed the ability to amass a large force, attack, and disperse with amazing speed and coordination. While this was good practice, the mobilization of guerrilla forces for the 1989 offensive was on a scale not seen before. Virtually all of the FMLN was to take part, and a group to coordinate all of this movement had to be set up. In addition to the coordination of troops, there was a massive infusion of weapons into El Salvador for the offensive. These weapons had to be prepositioned and then distributed. Both of these activities had to be kept very secret, as any leak would tip off the armed forces and spoil the plan. It was not that the army didn't know that the offensive was coming. The FMLN had been announcing it since 1986. In fact, army intelligence even knew that it would happen on November 11. What was vital was that it not know the scale of the impending attack. The FES was chosen to participate in these efforts. They were ideal; small, already compartmented from other FMLN guerrillas, highly trained, and highly motivated. During the five days preceding the offensive the FMLN began its mass mobilization. The FES were sent in small teams to guide far-flung guerrilla units to their assigned positions. The FES teams sent runners to the units in their jurisdiction and told them to meet them at specific locations on certain dates. Usually, this would be at locations where the FES had earlier built secret caches of weapons. As the various units arrived, the FES distributed the weapons and ammunition to the arrivals. In some cases, the FES would meet their assigned units and then lead them to the cache location. Once the guerrillas had received their new weapons, equipment, and ammunition, the FES would march their charges to their objectives. All of this took place at night and, depending on the location, could take several days to complete. In San Salvador and other cities such as San Miguel, FES units led the guerrilla units in. Once in position the FES regrouped and attacked various predetermined objectives. They attacked stubborn army posts, and key strategic objectives such as bridges, road-blocks, and so on. Unsuccessful attempts were made to kill or kidnap President Alfredo Cristiani and his family.

The FES could be distinguished because they exclusively wore black uniforms and jungle boots. They were almost completely outfitted with Communist bloc weapons: AK-47s, M-16s, Dragunov, RPG-7 rocket launchers, RPK machine guns, PPK pistols, Russian hand grenades, PKM machine guns, and explosives. Some of the men had Yugoslavian-made silencers on their weapons. The FMLN turned the neighborhoods they occupied into virtual fortresses. All the streets' entrances were blocked with barricades and trenches. Corner houses were occupied and turned into centers of resistance with machine guns, rocket launchers, and automatic rifles. Holes were knocked between the walls of the houses along the block to allow rapid and protected communication and movement between the whole block. The middle houses and multistory buildings were used as sniper nests. The FES occupied some critical corner positions, but were usually assigned as snipers in the middle houses. When the army began its counterattack, it was usually first greeted by accurate sniper fire. This took a high toll on the advancing troops. According to a combat medic of the Salvadoran army, the majority of the army dead were killed by snipers with bullet wounds to the head, a testament to the effectiveness of the FES sniper fire. The FES teams assigned the defense of strategic buildings were fanatical. They delayed the army for hours, but paid dearly with their lives. An entire FES platoon of the FAL was wiped out in a store belonging to the "Despensa de Don Juan" grocery chain in Soyapango.[9] The fanaticism of the FES is amply demonstrated by an example of the fighting around the Ilopango air base. The advance of the paratroopers was stopped cold by some guerrillas in a corner position that could not be routed out with infantry weapons. All of the good positions to fire on were swept by guerrilla automatic weapons fire, rockets, and rifle grenades. Soldier after soldier that made the attempt was hit and had to be rescued by his comrades. People were being lost in the rescue attempts as well. The guerrillas used one soldier in particular as bait for the others. No one could reach the wounded man without being hit. The attack bogged down. The officer in charge was irate at the guerrillas' stubbornness; it was holding up his whole advance. He was able to contact an overflying Hughes 500 helicopter and call it down to assist. He asked the pilot to hover at street level with the blades whipping around just above the rooftop of some single-story dwellings. Under fire from the guerrillas, this helicopter then hosed down all of the windows and doors with sustained bursts from its 7.62mm General Electric multibarrelled minigun. The paratroopers advanced, rescued the wounded man, and as soon as the helicopter broke its attack, assaulted the position. They were stopped cold. The guerrillas popped back up and laid down withering fire on the advancing troops, forcing them back. The officer, now completely angered, called upon his 81mm mortars. Earlier in the day he had ordered the mortars brought out just in case he found a use for them. His men had muttered under their breath for having to lug the extra weight, but his premonition would now be proved to have been a correct one. He had the mortars set up in a playground less than 200 meters away from the guerrillas' position. The mortars were elevated until the tubes were aimed nearly vertical. The mortars then fired salvo after salvo, nearly 100 bombs, dangerously close to his own men taking refuge in the houses only a few meters away from the target. While this may have seemed excessive, the commander wanted to take no chances. When the smoke and dust had cleared, the paratroopers again advanced. There was no resistance. Inside the position they found the remains of 17 guerrilla defenders.[10]

In Soyapango the army did not have the forces to take back each house and each block. Instead it tried to envelop the guerrilla forces by taking key positions and major routes of advance and withdrawal. It was successful in this attempt and by the end of the first day had trapped a large number of guerrilla combatants, and more importantly, several key guerrilla leaders within the zone it had outflanked. Because of the dangers of shooting their own men at night in built-up areas, the soldiers established defensive positions at the places they'd reached and waited for daylight. What was left of the FES was given the mission to help the guerrilla forces, particularly the leaders, trapped within the army ring to break out. Some FES were assigned to personally escort the leaders out while other teams conducted distraction attacks. At various locations the FES advanced along the rooftops until they were overlooking the army defensive positions. From these positions they launched a rain of explosives down on the surprised soldiers. These were followed by bursts of automatic fire. Confused fighting raged for several hours. In some places these rooftop explosives attacks were to distract government troops, and in others the objective was to open corridors through the government trap to allow the guerrillas within it to escape. While the attacks were eventually beaten back, the FES were successful in getting all of the leadership out of the trap and many guerrillas as well. The army did not realize what the objective of the attacks had been until several subsequently captured guerrillas revealed this in their interrogations.[11]

The FMLN first employed surface-to-air missiles during this offensive. In 1985, a training diagram of an SA-7 was captured from Nidia Diaz, one of the top commanders of the PRTC. Because the Cubans and Nicaraguans feared a U.S. invasion, none were delivered to the FMLN, to avoid giving the United States an excuse. In 1987, Humberto Ortega, defense minister of Nicaragua, promised that missiles would be given to the FMLN guerrillas, although none were given at the time.[12] Sometime after this promise was made, the first FES teams were sent to Nicaragua for training on the missile systems.[13] An entire SA-7 operating manual captured on Cerro Tigre in early 1988 provided evidence of this training. The missile business was a highly clandestine activity. It is not exactly clear how early the Nicaraguans began supplying the missiles to the FMLN, but it is probable that it had the missiles in its inventory in Nicaragua prior to the offensive. The FMLN was just waiting for the right political moment to import these weapons into El Salvador without jeopardizing the Nicaraguan Sandinista government's survival. On November 16, 1989, the outrage expressed by the international community over the FMLN offensive was now channelled at the government. Six Jesuit priests were murdered by renegade elements of the military, and now the world community was holding the entire institution responsible for the acts of an irresponsible few. This provided the right political opening, and several planeloads of missiles were sent. In one highly embarrassing incident, a plane carrying 18 missiles crashed, killing its Nicaraguan air force crew and providing new evidence of Nicaragua's deep involvement in the arming and support of the Salvadoran guerrillas. Soon after this incident, the first SA-7s were employed in combat. Several were fired at aircraft being used in mopping-up operations against guerrillas that had retreated from around Ilopango toward Zacatecoluca. However, these missiles were fired individually, and the relatively antiquated missiles were easily dodged by Salvadoran air force pilots that had been training in anti-missile tactics since the discovery of the operations manual. The FES had been more successful employing machine guns and rifles against aircraft. A small number of planes were downed, and many were damaged by machine gun and sniper fire.

FES ACTIVITY AFTER 1989

In 1990 and 1991 the FES received SA-16 shoulder-launched missiles vastly superior to the obsolete SA-7. The Sandinistas also delivered several Redeye missiles captured from the Contras. These weapons proved deadly. Several planes and helicopters were shot down with them. When the army would launch an operation, the guerrillas used newly developed tactics to bait aircraft into a trap.

Once the direction of the army movement was known, the missile teams set up on strategic high ground. A fierce guerrilla attack would be launched against the army unit with the intention of driving the army unit into the area surrounded by the high ground occupied by the missile teams. The guerrillas would then attempt to inflict enough damage on the unit to force it to call for air support. The guerrillas would wait patiently until the aircraft appeared in the area and then multiple missiles would be fired in a deadly ambush.

Just such an ambush forced a company of the elite Bracamonte battalion to seek asylum in Honduras during mid-1991. The company blundered into low ground amidst a guerrilla attack. The guerrillas struck from the path leading out of the area, cutting off their escape. The guerrillas began inflicting casualties from the high ground. Over a dozen soldiers were wounded after several minutes of fighting. When the company commander called for air support and medical evacuation, multiple rockets were fired at the aircraft making attempts to reach the beleaguered company. The only route of escape, short of destruction, was to flee across the river into Honduras. Faced with the alternatives, the company commander opted for sanctuary in Honduras. Some in the international press speculated that this incident was an example of low army morale and outright cowardice. It was not a matter of cowardice; it was a matter of being completely outclassed and stuck in a hole. The officer's mistake was blundering into the guerrilla trap in the first place. However, once this mistake was made, the company commander made the right decision, and saved his men to fight another day on more equal footing.

NOTES

1. Interrogation Transcript of RAR, April 27, 1987.

2. Ibid.

3. David Spencer, *FMLN FES: Fight Much With Little* (Provo, Utah, 1990), unpublished manuscript.

4. Interrogation Transcript of AIA, May 25, 1985.

5. Interrogation Transcript of RAR, April 27, 1987.

6. Interrogation Transcript of SAJR, June 18, 1986.

7. Interrogation Transcript of RAR, April 27, 1987.

8. Ibid.

9. Interrogation Transcript of JFFC, January 24, 1990.

10. Interview with paratrooper officers, March 1990.

11. Ibid.

12. Roger Miranda and William Ratliff, *The Civil War in Nicaragua: Inside the Sandinistas* (New Brunswick, NJ: Transaction Publishers, 1993), pp. 40–41.

13. Interrogation Transcript of JAFA, April 19, 1990.

CHAPTER 6

Guerrilla Special Forces in Latin America

The story of the Salvadoran FES would not be complete without reference to the special forces groups of other Latin American revolutions. Because of the constant contact between Latin American revolutionary groups, the guerrilla special forces units, prior to the Salvadoran struggle, influenced operations carried out by the Salvadoran FES. During and after the Salvadoran war, the success of the FES influenced the creation and operations of guerrilla special forces units in other Latin American struggles. There is now some unconfirmed evidence that suggests the possibility that FES principles and concepts have been spread beyond the borders of Latin America, appearing in Africa and Asia.

SPECIAL FORCES OF THE CUBAN REVOLUTION

The first guerrilla special forces were developed in the Cuban Revolution, during 1959. By this time, Castro's guerrilla columns were essentially conventional forces that were directly challenging equal size and greater units of the armed forces of the Batista regime. Special units were created to carry out dangerous missions during these battles. Often, the special units would be employed to revive a battle that had bogged down into deadlock. This consisted of destroying or neutralizing an enemy strong point or heavy weapons position. A good example of this type of unit was Che Guevara's column "suicide platoon." The suicide platoon was composed of combat-proven volunteers. It received the toughest assignments during combat, but also received the best equipment, food, and an assured place in history. Every time one of its members died, a new candidate was chosen. This happened after nearly every battle, as one or more of the members of this platoon were almost always killed or severely wounded. It was considered such a great honor to be chosen, that those who volunteered and were not chosen had difficulty not showing their disappointment or holding back tears. The suicide platoon always led the guerrillas in combat.[1]

The suicide platoon was formed in November 1958, at Che Guevara's guerrilla base of Caballete. Here, Che was preparing his forces for the planned campaign in Las Villas province. The suicide platoon was seen as an elite assault force to take army barracks and forts. All of the men were volunteers and those chosen were those who in combat had proven to be the greatest risk takers. Command of the suicide platoon was given to the short, 23-year-old Roberto Rodriguez, known by the guerrillas as "El Vaquerito" (the little cowboy).

The first battle in which the newly created suicide platoon participated was the capture of Fomento. The guerrillas attacked the town on December 15, 1958, and by the night of December 18 all of the town but the main barracks with 121 Batista soldiers had surrendered. Lieutenant Perez Valencia had orders to resist and wait for reinforcements. What he didn't know was that his men outnumbered the guerrillas by a fourth and the guerrillas were down to about 40 rounds of ammunition per man. The guerrillas were desperate to take the barracks to capture ammunition from the garrison. Four guerrilla platoons surrounded the barracks and kept up harassing fire. The guerrillas were able to set up in surrounding buildings only 25–30 meters away. The Batista officer, Perez Valencia, called for air strikes that he personally guided to guerrilla targets that he could see because of their proximity. However, this did not deter the guerrillas because they could clearly see that no troops were coming up the road to aid the barracks. It was only a matter of time before the garrison gave up. However, if they did not hurry, they would run out of ammunition and be unable to take the barracks. The barracks was of cement construction surrounded by walls on all sides. These walls had firing loops all around them, so that any approach to the barracks was difficult. The suicide platoon tried to rush the walls. First some guerrillas got on the roof of a clinic that overlooked the barracks to set up a base of fire, and then others tried to close in by using the garden walls of houses near the installation. In a few seconds, the suicide platoon lost one killed and one wounded, with no visible losses suffered by the enemy. "El Vaquerito" came up with the idea of setting fire to the fort. They would find some gas tanks and tubing and with a pump squirt gasoline all over the fort and then squirt gasoline with the pump and light it at the end so it would set fire to the barracks. In other words, Vaquerito was trying to figure out how to make an improvised flamethrower. This plan came to an end when the equipment needed to carry it out could not be found. Fortunately for the rebels, the garrison surrendered when they realized that reinforcements weren't coming.

For his actions at Fomento, "El Vaquerito" was promoted to Captain. On December 21, 1958, the suicide platoon participated in the taking of

Cabaiguan. At 5:00 A.M. four platoons under the personal command of Che Guevara were dropped off by trucks outside the town and began to silently advance. The suicide platoon was on point, reconnoitering the terrain. The guerrillas first took a tobacco warehouse, the squad of soldiers inside surrendering easily. Che then ordered an advance on the microwave station and its garrison of ten men. By this time a Batista B-26 was strafing the troops. When one of his men was killed, El Vaquerito became angry and ordered his platoon to assault the microwave station, which was on the top of a bare hill devoid of cover. One of his men suggested that first they try to see if the garrison would surrender before risking the platoon that way. El Vaquerito took his man's advice, and called on the soldiers to surrender. To everyone's surprise, the microwave station immediately surrendered. By nightfall, the guerrillas surrounded the army barracks, which quickly gave up without much of a fight.

On December 23, 1958, the suicide platoon participated in the attack on the town of Placetas. This was the last Batista position blocking the rebel advance on Santa Clara, the provincial capital and main objective of Che Guevara's campaign. The garrison of Placetas consisted of 150 soldiers and police distributed at different places around the town: the barracks, town hall, the police station, the school, high ground overlooking the Central Highway, the Spain neighborhood, and the Caridad movie theater. The attack began at 4:30 A.M. with the suicide platoon attacking the soldiers at the movie theater. By 6:30 A.M. the theater was taken, and after taking the microwave station unopposed, Vaquerito's platoon was fighting the enemy on the high ground above town. There were about a dozen rural guards with a .30 calibre machine gun in a dominating position. The gun was limiting guerrilla movement and had to be taken out to continue operations. Vaquerito led his men in an exposed charge, but despite the risks it had the right effect, and the guards withdrew, leaving the machine gun and its ammunition behind. When all of the other positions had fallen, the guerrillas concentrated on the garrison. The suicide platoon attacked from behind the compound, while other platoons attacked from the other directions, surrounding the garrison. After a few hours of firing, the guerrillas called on the garrison to surrender. After short negotiations with Che Guevara, the barracks fell. The way was now open to attack Santa Clara.

Before launching his attack against Santa Clara, Che decided to consolidate his hold on the countryside to protect his flanks. A number of small towns in the vicinity were subsequently taken by Che's troops. On December 25, 1958, the suicide platoon participated with four others in the attack on the town of Remedios. The suicide platoon launched the first attack, taking the polling station after a short fight with the demoralized rural guardsmen that occupied it. The suicide platoon then attacked the police station which was in the town hall complex. Here the police resisted fiercely. The suicide platoon cut off the policemen's water supply and then at night attacked the building with Molotov cocktails. When the building became a raging inferno, the policemen's fire died and the survivors surrendered. While other platoons surrounded and took the barracks, the suicide platoon was taken by truck to assist the taking of Caibarien. This battle had started just before 11:00 P.M. on the night of December 25. The suicide platoon arrived on the morning of December 26. This was just in time to assist another platoon in laying siege to the barracks. They cut off the soldiers' water supply and maintained such a steady fire that no soldier could show his head without being killed. Still, the garrison refused to surrender. They tried to set the building on fire by rolling down rubber tires that had been set alight, but this failed. Finally, Vaquerito found a pumper fire truck. He ordered the tanks filled with gasoline. His plan was to squirt gasoline on the fort and then set it on fire. Once the truck was brought forward, he got a loudspeaker and told the garrison what he planned to do. A white banner was quickly raised, and Caibarien fell to the revolution. After these and several other small towns fell, Che Guevara ordered his forces to march on Santa Clara.

For the attack on Santa Clara, the suicide platoon had a strength of 24 men. On the morning of December 28, Che Guevara's forces began taking up positions around Santa Clara to block reinforcements, and to penetrate into the city itself. They were stopped by large Batista forces supported by aircraft after making small gains. That night under cover of darkness, Che decided to infiltrate his men into the city and instead of attacking one part of the enemy at a time, attack all his positions simultaneously to divide his forces and conquer. Under this plan, the suicide platoon was given the mission of attacking the police headquarters. In its movement, the platoon had a skirmish with soldiers at a mobile electric generator, who surrendered after inflicting a few wounds on the suicide platoon. After the fight, the suicide platoon moved toward the train station where it spent the night. The morning of December 29, the suicide platoon advanced toward the police station. It was joined by other guerrilla units, increasing the number of guerrillas for this attack to 70. The police station had a garrison of 500 men with armored cars and machine guns. Despite the odds, the guerrillas attacked. It was a tough battle. All of the approaches to the building were swept by withering fire from positions inside the police headquarters and on top of the roof. The Del Carmen park in front of the compound was full of policemen while the armored cars patrolled the streets. Vaquerito found it impossible for his force to advance in the open, and after several men were wounded pulled back to design a new attack. He ordered part of his forces to advance to the church in front of the police station by breaking holes in the walls of the homes and advancing under the cover of walls to their objective. In this manner several invisible corridors were made to positions that dominated the police station. Meanwhile, another group, including Vaquerito, advanced toward the station by jumping from rooftop to rooftop. On a rooftop, 50 meters from the police station on Garofalo Street, the men of the suicide platoon attacked a group of rural guards running through the park in front of the station. However, this revealed the suicide platoon's position and it was spotted and attacked by the .30 calibre machine guns of two staghound armored cars down in the street. The rest of the platoon dove for cover, but Vaquerito did not take cover and was hit in the head and killed. Leonardo Tamayo, only 17 years old, was given command of the suicide platoon.

The next day, December 30, the suicide platoon used its hidden corridors to take the Del Carmen Church. From its towers and roof they rained down harassment fire on the police station. In one instance, an armored car driver decided to take a stretch and lifted his hatch. It was a fatal mistake; he was shot in the head, and his vehicle was effectively put out of action. On December 31, Che Guevara sent more reinforcements to the suicide platoon, the total now reaching 130 men. It had slowly surrounded the station with positions on the rooftops, dominating all movement. Finally, late in the afternoon, the police garrison of 396 men surrendered. This action effectively ended the war for the suicide platoon.[2]

THE GUERRILLA SPECIAL FORCES OF ARGENTINA

Montoneros

After the assassination of Arturo Mor Roig on June 14, 1974 the leadership of the Montoneros created what was known as Special Combat Groups (GECs). During the assassination one guerrilla was killed and another captured. The leadership attributed this failure to the lack of training and experience. The expansion of the combat organization had been made at the sacrifice of training and experience. Because of this the GECs were created. Their mission was to carry out special tasks assigned by the top leadership. They became the elite of the Montoneros.[3]

THE ASSASSINATION OF COMMISSIONER VILLAR

One of the missions subsequently assigned to the GECs was the assassination of General Villar, head of the Federal Police. Since the days of President Lanusse, he had been one of the principal enemies of the Montoneros.

Intelligence operatives were assigned to watch Villar's movements and find a weak link in his security. The original plan was to place a bomb in his car, but security was too tight. Another suggestion was to set up a roadblock and machine gun his caravan. However, it was decided that the operation could cost a lot of Montonero lives and there was a good chance that the general would emerge unscathed. After a long and patient waiting period the Montoneros got an intelligence break. Members of the Juventud Tradajadora Peconista (JTP) informed the Montoneros that General Villar's boat was being repaired at the Astarsa repair docks at El Tigre in Buenos Aires. While this news was not very significant, the people who had dropped the boat off had asked that the boat be repaired quickly as the general wished to use it on the next holiday.

Attempts by the Montoneros to find out the exact date bore fruit. Through informants at the repair dock they discovered, on October 25, that the general was planning on sailing on November 1. It was decided that the best way to assassinate Villar was to place an explosive charge on his boat and set it off while he was sailing. The bomb would be placed on the boat the day before the general was to use it, without informing the collaborators at the repair dock.

In a planning meeting, the GEC chose two platoons of five men each which would be directed by "El Vasco." Members of the group were "El Gordo Alfredo," "Nacho," "Pipo," "Frances," two drivers, the wife of Gordo Alfredo, and another lady comrade as complements. "Beto" coordinated the operation.

Gordo Alfredo was a first-rate, certified diver and also sold diving gear to earn a living. In the wee hours of November 1, he and Pipo put on complete diving gear on the edge of the canal and slipped into the water without being seen, as the canals were not watched. The swimmers carried 20 kilos of trotyl. Trotyl was chosen because it only needs 360 degrees of heat to explode.

Meanwhile, the remainder of the group set up security in the area to make sure there were no accidental encounters with the swimmers. If there were, they were to help the swimmers make a quick getaway. Frances was chosen for this job because of his intimate knowledge of Buenos Aires. Frances carried an Ithaca shotgun, El Vasco a submachine gun, and the rest carried rifles.

The two frogmen found Villar's boat anchored alone at the dock. They climbed aboard stealthily, making sure that nobody noticed their presence. When they were sure that no one had noticed, they planted the explosive under the driver's seat of the boat and slipped back into the water. The bomb had been equipped with a radio command detonation device. Once the frogmen returned, the group set up an observation post among some trees, 300 meters from the dock. Here the guerrillas had the remote control detonator and a telescope to watch for the arrival of General Villar.

Gordo Alfredo, his wife, Pipo, and the other female comrade pretended to be a pair of couples on holiday, fishing from a little boat. They even brought sleeping bags to complete the charade. The one oversight was that none of them had any idea about how to fish, so they faked it and mixed in with the other fishermen. This was good enough as none of the real fishermen seemed to notice the lack of skill on the part of the guerrillas. The rest of the team set up security in a back street near the canal.

When Villar approached, the Montonero unit that was responsible for the area, the Northern Column, sent a runner to advise the team. They were coming in two green Ford Falcons and a cream-colored truck with a cover. When the guerrillas saw that the wife of the general was also getting on board, they almost called off the mission. However, they decided that it was more important to eliminate the general, as they might not get another good chance for a long time.

As the general got in his boat, his entourage sat on the edge and watched him. The guerrillas counted 12 policemen standing around the dock. It was tempting to blow him up right there. With 20 kilos of trotyl, the explosion would surely reach his entourage. A general and his 12-man escort would be a good day's work. However, the presence of civilians that could get hurt prevented the guerrillas from setting off the bomb.

The boat was started and the motor heated up for a long time before the craft got underway. When it had gone about 10 meters up the river, the guerrillas gave the signal and the bomb was detonated. The explosion was so great that it lifted the whole boat out of the water and scattered bits and pieces over several hundred yards. General Villar's body was cut to shreds in the driver's seat. His wife's body was thrown from the boat onto the bank of the canal. Nobody else was killed. In the midst of the explosion, the members of the GEC team quietly withdrew and made their escape. The Argentine military and police never did figure out exactly how this mission was accomplished.[4]

OTHER GEC MISSIONS

The most spectacular operation carried out by the GEC occurred on August 22, 1975. This date was chosen to commemorate the third anniversary of the Trelew massacre. In 1972, members of the Montoneros had staged a jailbreak. Several of the escapees were reportedly shot, once they were recaptured. This day of infamy became an important date to the Montoneros. The Montoneros blamed the Argentine navy as the group most responsible for the massacre. The plan was to commemorate the date by striking deep at the heart of the navy.

The target chosen was the new frigate, the Santisima Trinidad. This frigate, with British technical advice, was being built at the Rio Santiago de Enseñada shipyard as part of an Anglo-Argentine agreement. It was the pride of the navy because of its national construction. The Montoneros felt that the construction of the Santisima Trinidad was a doublecross. Instead of forging ties with the British, who still occupied the Falkland Islands, which Argentina claimed, the Montoneros felt that the navy should use its ships to retake the islands from the British.

Planning for the operation began in November 1974. The Montoneros were inspired by the British commando raid on Bordeaux in December 1942, using kayaks to stealthily carry their explosives into the harbor and quietly attach them to German shipping before slipping away undetected. They acquired a foldable, camouflaged kayak that they used to carry 170 kilos of explosives into the shipyard. The Montonero swimmers got close enough to the unwary navy security personnel to hear their conversations. They reached the ship's hull undetected as it sat lashed to its mooring. Over the next three hours, the GEC attached all of the explosives to the previously determined positions on the hull. When they were finished, they withdrew as silently and undetected as they had arrived. The explosion rocked the dock and lifted the ship out of the water. The Santisima Trinidad failed to sink, but the explosion did knock out all of the ship's computers and electronic equipment. It also caused some serious damage to the hull, and delayed the ship's construction by another year.

A final GEC operation took place on December 14, 1975. Using the same techniques that had brought them success against the Santisima Trinidad, GEC swimmers placed explosives on the yacht Itati. This yacht was the property of the high command, but generally used by Admiral Massera, the head of the navy. While Massera was not injured, the yacht was badly damaged by the explosives.[5]

The Montoneros were a well-funded and well-organized guerrilla group. Most of their leadership came from the educated and moneyed middle class of Argentina. As a consequence, everything they did was always very elaborate. The GEC was no exception. The Montoneros had time to sit back and develop uniform regulations for their cadres. They had different uniforms for their political militias, combat units, and special forces. The special forces' uniform consisted of navy blue slacks, a sky blue long-sleeve shirt, and a black leather jacket with two breast and two hip pockets. Black shoes and a black beret completed the uniform. On the left breast pocket they wore the metal GEC shield, half black and half red. On their lapels they wore the gold metal crossed rifle and lance insignia of the Montonero combat units. Rank was worn on the sleeve.

Members of the GEC would continue their activities after the revolution in Argentina was crushed. During the 1980s a captured Sandinista special forces assassin, who had been given the mission of infiltrating the Contras and killing the top military commander, revealed that Montonero guerrillas were training Sandinista frogmen and conducting gun runs across the Gulf of Fonseca to the Salvadoran guerrillas.[6] This was done in speedboats equipped with explosives, so the boats could be blown up if captured. Also, during the Falklands war, Montoneros in Spain helped the Argentine navy set up an operation to infiltrate Gibraltar and attach limpet mines to British shipping. This plan was foiled when an Argentine naval officer was visited by police for his riotous behavior, and promptly declared himself a prisoner of war.[7]

ERP

The ERP was not as successful with special forces as the Montoneros. In August 1975, the Central Committee of the PRT-ERP held a meeting in which it discussed the international and national state of the revolution. Representatives of the MLN Tupamaros, Chilean MIR, and Bolivian PRTB were present as invited guests. They were optimistic primarily because of the "liberation" of Vietnam from U.S. domination. This optimism carried over into the national situation. It appeared that the ERP was making advances by long strides. Plans were made for an expansion of forces.

It was proposed that the "Montaña" or Jungle company be expanded to a battalion, and that a rural front be established in northern Tucuman with the idea of eventual expansion into Salta and Jujuy. Furthermore, it was proposed that a "Buenos Aires Battalion" be established, and finally that an "elite squadron" be formed. This squadron would be attached to the Political Bureau and would have the mission to carry out special operations, to provide the Bureau's security, and to obtain extraordinary resources for the Bureau's functioning.[8] The Special Squad was made up of a small number of guerrillas who were chosen for their experience in combat and their audacity under fire. There was no formal training. The euphoria and expansion of the ERP in 1975 was short-lived. The Argentine army took a direct role in the fighting at the end of the year, and it proved to be ruthlessly efficient in destroying the guerrilla organization.

By early 1976, the situation for the guerrillas was going very badly. The ERP was in a difficult situation. The attempt to take the Monte Chingolo arsenal had been an unmitigated disaster. Over 60 guerrillas had been killed, and a large quantity of weapons lost along with them. This was a very heavy blow. Not only had the Monte Chingolo operation gone poorly, but the Jungle company had taken heavy losses in its attempt to develop a rural front. Furthermore, the economic situation of the ERP was very bad. The only way operations were maintained was through the generosity of the Montoneros, who bailed the ERP out.[9]

To alleviate the ERP's poor economic situation, the Special Squad was ordered to dedicate itself wholly to the task of "recuperating" money.[10] Recuperation was a euphemism for bank robberies and kidnappings for ransom. It conducted several operations, but this drew enemy attention to the squad. In mid-1976, the Argentine army completely destroyed the Special Squad in two violent assaults.[11]

SANDINISTA SPECIAL FORCES

Like the Cubans and Argentines, the Sandinista guerrillas of Nicaragua began creating special forces units once they began to rapidly expand and conduct open warfare, taking on the Nicaraguan National Guard units in face-to-face combat. Conventional fighting took place on the famous

Southern Front. Here, several efforts were made to create special forces units. The following are a few examples. There was a group of elite sappers under the command of El Suizo, a Swiss international.[12] El Suizo was obsessed with the elimination of the strong Nicaraguan National Guard position on Hill 50, just north of the Ostallo river. The hill dominated the Pan American highway at the point where a bridge crossed over the previously mentioned river. This position was the key to the National Guard defense on the Southern Front. In June 1979, the Sandinista guerrillas under Eden Pastora had taken Peñas Blancas and Sapoa in a lightning strike. However, Guard forces on Hill 50 had stopped the guerrillas dead in their tracks just south of this hill. The guerrillas had been forced to halt, and a war of attrition with trenches and artillery developed. The Guard had dug in on the north of the Ostallo river, and the Sandinistas had dug a trench line on the south side of the river. Guard artillery on the back slope of Hill 50 harassed the Sandinista trench line daily. In addition, the Guard launched daily air strikes against Sandinista positions from the trench line back to Peñas Blancas. The Sandinistas replied with artillery and mortars of their own. Since Somoza's forces were under an arms embargo, they improvised weapons to use against the Sandinistas. One greatly feared weapon was oil barrels filled with TNT or homemade napalm and dropped on guerrilla positions from great altitude by helicopters, out of range of the Sandinistas' heavy machine guns. These barrels were detonated by Argentine grenades inside the barrels that were set up in such a way as to detonate on impact. These devices didn't always go off, or the grenade explosion sometimes failed to ignite the bomb. Unexploded barrels littered the Sandinista side of the battlefield. El Suizo was obsessed with eliminating the Guard on Hill 50. The unexploded barrels that littered the battlefield gave him an idea. If he could recover enough TNT from the barrels, his special forces group would attempt to dig a tunnel underneath Hill 50 and blow it up. El Suizo could be seen around the Sandinista front lines on a daily basis scavenging TNT from the unexploded bombs. El Suizo never was able to carry out his plan as the Guard collapsed and withdrew from Hill 50 before the tunnel could be dug. There were many technical problems with the kind of attack that El Suizo was planning. Time was a factor. How he was going to dig under the Ostallo river would present serious engineering problems. A much better plan would have been to make hand-held bombs out of the recovered TNT and conduct a stealthy raid against the artillery position using the destructive power of the explosives.

Such a raid was planned by a Peruvian special forces officer that had joined the Sandinistas through the Peruvian Partido Socialista Revolucionario (Marxista-Leninista) PSR-ML. Luis Varesse, of the National Secretariat of the PSR-ML, had enjoyed close ties with the Sandinistas for some time. In 1978 Ernesto Cardenal and another Sandinista, Commander "Mauricio," travelled to Lima to ask for solidarity for the Sandinista Revolution. At a meeting at the headquarters of the party, the PSR-ML offered its unconditional and total support to the Sandinistas.[13]

At the end of May 1979, a request came from the Sandinistas for volunteers to be sent to fight in Nicaragua. Many Peruvian officers who belonged to the party offered their services to the FSLN; however, because of financial problems, only two were chosen by the PSR-ML. One of these was a 45-year-old infantry officer who had taken courses in intelligence, and had graduated from the general staff school. The second was 37-year-old Eloy Villacrez Riquelme, who was an engineering officer who had specialized training as a commando.[14] Villacrez chose the pseudonym "Eloy."[15]

The day they arrived at the front at Peñas Blancas they were met by commander Marvin, the front Chief of Staff, and Federico, in charge of personnel. Because of his commando training Eloy volunteered to form a commando unit to carry out operations to infiltrate behind the enemy lines and put the Nicaraguan National Guard artillery out of action. Eloy organized a special forces unit with commander Victor and immediately began planning the operation. Reconnaissance was carried out, but the operation was suspended at the last minute. Why Eloy's commandos were never allowed to attack the Guard artillery is not known.

Despite the cancellation of this mission, Eloy's unit continued to operate and carried out a number of penetration missions in the National Guard's rear. On one occasion, Eloy's unit received information that there was a squad of ten Guards holding a hill. Eloy decided to launch a raid and destroy the Guard forces on that hill. The plan was made and the unit set out. However, when they began their assault they found that the information had been given to them to draw them into a trap. There were not just ten men, there were near 100 enemy soldiers that were set up in an ambush waiting for them. Through Eloy's leadership he was able to get his men out without a single loss and inflict losses on the enemy, who were members of Somoza's elite EEBI. When the ambush opened, he quickly found refuge for his men in some dead space, a bit of terrain where the direct fire weapons of the guards could not hit. Leaving his men here he conducted a personal reconnaissance and located the weakest point in the enemy line, where the firing was light. He returned to his men, made a hasty plan and led an assault at this point. The attack inflicted a number of casualties, at least six, and broke through the EEBI trap.[16] Other activities of Eloy's group have not yet been revealed.

A third example of the attempt to create a Sandinista special forces unit was a proposal by Commander Wachan to Tauro, an Ecuadoran internationalist, and Joaquin, a Venezuelan internationalist, that they form a sapper squad. Tauro was an older man, over 30, who was what could be described as a leftist mercenary. He went and fought with leftist forces all over the world. He had plans to go to El Salvador or Rhodesia after the end of the war in Nicaragua. Joaquin had some revolutionary experience in Venezuela. He and Tauro had been assigned together in a Sandinista squad and had become close friends.

Tauro worked on Commander Wachan's proposal. He envisioned this group as a select unit that during the final offensive, the drive on Managua, would advance ahead of the guerrilla columns to capture key terrain features such as bridges, making sure they weren't mined. The unit would also capture key hills and positions, conduct reconnaissance and other special activities. The unit would consist of between 10 and 14 comrades under Tauro and Joaquin.[17] Tauro gave Wachan the following list of required equipment for his unit: tools, detonators, demolition charges, walkie-talkies, batteries, binoculars, one rifle with a telescope, camouflage uniforms, UZI submachine guns. He thought that at least half the men should carry submachine guns instead of the much heavier FN FAL rifles.[18] The plans were never finalized and the order was cancelled, probably for lack of men and equipment.[19] Instead, Tauro and Joaquin were assigned to form two separate heavy machine gun squads when heavy machine guns arrived in an arms shipment.

THE PUERTO RICAN FALN MACHETEROS

The Macheteros are a small group that have long plagued the United States over the issue of Puerto Rican independence. It is known that this group has had long-term ties with Fidel Castro, who has been willing to support the group, albeit its small size, because it is a major irritant to the United States, Fidel's principal adversary. Interestingly, Cuban support also included FES-type training, probably in 1980, the same time that the first groups from the FPL were being trained in the FES sapper techniques. In a way, the first FES operation of the Salvadoran revolution may have been carried out, not by Salvadorans, but by the Puerto Rican Macheteros.

At midnight on January 12, 1981, Machetero guerrillas penetrated the Muñiz Air National Guard base that is adjacent to the San Juan International Airport in San Juan, Puerto Rico. The compound was surrounded by an eight-foot-high chain-link fence. The northern perimeter bordered the San Juan International Airport. The south and east of the compound were surrounded by a lagoon and swampland. The main gate was on the west end. There were only two contract civilian security guards on duty, one at the front gate and one walking the perimeter. Otherwise, the compound was unguarded. The guerrillas watched the perimeter guard do his rounds. When he went up to the front gate to make the change of guard, the guerrillas made a breach in the northeast corner of the fence. At the change of the guard, the two civilians talked for a while, exchanging impressions, small talk, a cigarette, coffee, and so on. It was an old routine, and because nothing usually happened, the guards were in no hurry. To them, the main threat was possible thieves, stealing expensive tools and aircraft parts. The attack took advantage of this routine and complacency, and had to be completed during this time lapse, before the new guard could come out to walk the perimeter. The guerrillas silently made their way to where 11 A-7 Corsair attack planes were parked on the tarmac out in the open. They did not bother with two A-7s and a cargo plane parked further away, or three planes in the hangars. Their plan did not allow them to spend more time. They worked quickly, placing explosives in the air intakes, the wheel wells, and exhaust pipes of each aircraft. Each explosive charge was attached to a one-hour time fuse. In addition to the Corsairs, there was an F-104 Starfighter without an engine that had been brought to the base for an upcoming open house. Ignorant of its derelict condition, the guerillas placed explosives in the wheel well of this aircraft as well. The guerrillas pulled the time fuses and withdrew, making their way out, the same way they had come in. At 1:30 A.M., the charges began to go off. The charges in the wheel wells set fire to the fuel tanks which sent flames 60 feet into the sky. Ammunition, in the Corsairs' gatling guns, cooked off all night. The F-104 was broken in two, but did not burn like the others. Eight Corsairs were destroyed, but the explosives in three planes failed to go off. Two of these planes, however, were damaged. The fires also destroyed rescue equipment and a pickup truck nearby. The fires were so fierce that they were still being put out well into daylight hours. Although the loss of the planes incurred nearly $45 million worth of damage and was a great propaganda blow for the Macheteros, the attack was hardly noticed in the United States. Although the loss of the aircraft crippled the Puerto Rican Air National Guard, the equipment was second line, not front line. In addition, there had been a lot of debate about closing the Muñiz base and transferring the squadron to the much more important and secure Ramey airfield. This attack merely confirmed the arguments for closing the base, and the whole affair was swept under the rug. Later, on January 12, the Macheteros published an announcement that the attack had been made to repudiate American intervention in Central America, and to show solidarity with the Salvadoran revolution, which had just launched its Final Offensive two days before. It was also the anniversary of the birth of Eugenio Maria de Hostos, a nineteenth-century patriot who fought for independence from Spain. Anti-U.S. protests were regularly carried out on his birthday.[20]

While it is purely speculation, it may have been the success of this attack that served as a model for the uncannily similar January 1982 operation against the Ilopango Air Base in El Salvador.

THE COLOMBIAN M-19 GUERRILLA SPECIAL FORCES

Like the Puerto Ricans, the Colombian M-19 also formed a special forces unit that used tactics remarkably similar to the FES. The M-19 special forces were undoubtedly trained by foreigners in these techniques. However, it is not known if they were trained by the FMLN, or if they received their training, like the FMLN, from Cuba. It is known that the M-19 were a favorite of Fidel Castro's between 1979 and 1981, immediately after the attack on the embassy of the Dominican Republic. Fidel Castro arranged a deal with the drug cartels to offer them protection in Cuban waters and air space if they would in turn transport arms and money to the M-19. Furthermore, several hundred M-19 guerrillas were trained in Cuba during this same time period. In 1980 they attempted an invasion of Colombia through landings on the Pacific coast in the north and south of the country. This operation failed, but many of the participants survived.

Captured FMLN FES commandos who received their initial training in Cuba in the early 1980s stated that there were other nationalities in the same camps undergoing similar types of training. None of them specifically mentioned Colombians. However, this does not mean that Colombians did not receive FES training in Cuba.

It is also known that the M-19 maintained good relations with the FMLN and the Nicaraguan Sandinistas. In 1984, the Colombian army captured documents in the Cauca valley indicating strong ties between the M-19 and the FMLN. This included the sharing of technical and tactical information. It is not known what type of information was shared. When the M-19 special forces units appeared, the M-19's relations with Fidel Castro had cooled somewhat. However, the M-19's relations with the FMLN and the Sandinistas at that time were very good. It is just as likely that M-19 cadres were trained in FES tactics and techniques either in El Salvador proper or by Salvadoran commandos in Nicaragua.

Wherever and by whomever they were trained, the M-19 special forces using FES techniques made their debut in 1985. The unit was assigned to attack an army base in western Colombia.[21] The tactics they used in this attack were strikingly similar to those used by the FES in El Salvador. This attack is described below.

ATTACK ON THE CISNEROS ENGINEER BATTALION (OCTOBER 19, 1985)

In 1984, the M-19 and the Colombian government signed a cease-fire with the intention of coming to some type of peaceful agreement with the insurgents. However, neither the military nor the guerrillas really seemed sincere in their intentions. Terrorist acts continued, and in December there was a major battle at Corinto in the Cauca valley. By April, there was open warfare between the guerrillas and the army in the northern part of the valley. It was apparent that during this time the M-19 had acquired new equipment and weapons, and they were fighting better than ever. Furthermore, the M-19 had made alliances with the other Colombian guerrilla groups to fight the government with one single, unified front (similar to the FMLN in El Salvador).

However, unlike the Salvadoran army, who had to learn through the school of hard knocks, the Colombian army had been fighting insurgents since 1948. Some of the lessons the Colombian military had learned were even studied and employed by the United States in Vietnam. The fighting did not always go well for the guerrillas, and they suffered heavy losses in men, weapons, and equipment. The M-19, with an affinity for spectacular operations, began looking for an opportunity to strike back. They were especially anxious to test their new special forces unit in action.

The special forces reconnaissance reports indicated that the Engineer Battalion in Armenia was vulnerable. The battalion was not involved in counterinsurgency operations. Its mission was more to build roads, bridges, and so on. This meant that the troops had little, if no, combat experience. The base was on the slope of a hill next to a main road. The hill was covered with high grass, which had not been cut down around the fence. Furthermore, at night there were few sentries. The largest contingent of guards covered the main entrance. Only a few were scattered to guard the officers' and enlisted men's dormitories, the armory, and a helicopter on the parade ground between the dormitories. Some of the dormitories were empty. The total number of soldiers and cadres at the base was 400. Near the base was a soccer stadium. From the top of the stadium, one could easily look down onto the base. The Cisneros Battalion was an inviting target.

The M-19 plan was simple. About 20 guerrillas would penetrate the base and sabotage the dormitories, the helicopter, and the armory. They would start from the center and attack outward. Another group of 50 guerrillas, wearing army uniforms, would take the stadium and provide fire support to the special forces assault group with rockets (M72A2 LAWs) and machine gun fire. In addition, an undetermined number of guerrillas would infiltrate the city of Armenia to block relief forces from the 8th Brigade (located in Armenia) and the national police. This was a textbook FES attack, a la FMLN. The final reconnaissance was made before noon on October 18. All was in order; the attack plan was given the green light.

Unknown to the M-19, after the go-ahead had been given, two sections, about 80 men, of elite counterinsurgency troops arrived at the base just after the M-19 finished their last reconnaissance patrol. The troops had been operating in forested and mountainous terrain near Armenia for several days and were in bad need of a rest. That afternoon they arrived at the Cisneros Battalion to take a well-deserved break. They were housed in an empty barracks across from the parade ground. Having been in combat, weapons and ammunition were left ready by their bunks, and they posted their own guards.

Around midnight, the guerrillas began to deploy. By 0100 hours, the support elements had set up their roadblocks and snipers' nests in the town to block reinforcements. The occupation of the stadium went without a hitch. Because they looked like an army unit, no one bothered them. Meanwhile, the M-19 special forces were already crawling slowly through the grass toward the fences of the base. They each wore overalls and caps, to which had been sewn fresh clumps of grass on the back side. Each guerrilla carried a submachine gun and a bag of explosives.

By 0130 hours they were crawling slowly uphill through the tall grass on the far side of the base. They reached the fence undetected and quickly breached it. From there, they fanned out to carry out their individual assignments. Some slipped off their camouflaged suits to reveal military uniforms underneath. The suits were left near the breach in the fence. Two sentries making their rounds were dispatched quietly with knives, as well as a corporal and a sergeant who happened to be walking about. Some took up positions near the battalion's dormitories. Explosives were thrown in. The first explosive went off, shaking the entire city. LAW rockets and machine gun fire then began raining down on the base from the stadium. In a few minutes, sniper fire could be heard coming from downtown as the first soldiers and policemen began to move toward the battalion.

Meanwhile, inside the base, not all was going as the guerrillas planned. When the first explosion went off, other guerrilla commandos began running toward their objectives. A team of three, two women and a man, had not yet reached their objectives: the helicopter and the armory. To their surprise, they received concentrated fire from the "empty" barracks now occupied by the counterinsurgency troops. The man was killed instantly. The two women were wounded. One of them pulled out an explosive charge, activated it and attempted to throw it. She failed and blew the two of them up instead. Fire from the counterinsurgency troops also forced other M-19 commandos to abandon their objectives. The counterinsurgency troops then began to assault through the machine gun and rocket fire toward the guerrillas inside the compound. The remaining members beat a hasty retreat back through the wire, taking their casualties with them. Between the commando explosives and the rockets, most of the battalion's buildings were on fire; however, key targets like the helicopter and the armory were untouched. There were reportedly over 20 army dead, and many wounded.

The guerrilla force in the stadium kept up their fire until 0245 hours. At this time they withdrew, running down a street. Because they were dressed in army uniforms, no one attempted to stop them.[22]

FURTHER M-19 SPECIAL FORCES OPERATIONS

In November of 1985, members of the M-19 special forces were assigned to participate in the attack on the Justice Palace in Bogota. Their assignment was to defend the roof against helicopter landings with a .50 calibre machine gun. When the M-19 carried out their initial assault on the building, some of the M-19 guerrillas acted too early, so other guerrillas were not in place when the attack began. Also, there was more resistance than initially expected, and because of this, part of the guerrilla force never made it into the building. This included the special forces team and their precious machine gun.[23]

In 1986, the M-19 attempted to strike a blow similar to the FMLN's El Paraiso operation, against the 3rd Brigade installations on the southern edge of the city of Cali. The objective was to demonstrate the power of their Americas Battalion. This battalion was a composite force of members from six different Colombian guerrilla groups and other Latin American organizations. It was reported that there were Peruvians, Venezuelans, Ecuadorans, and others. The attack met with mixed results, but details are not known because the Colombian military censored all press reports on this operation. Because of the outward similarities, it is likely that FES-type special forces led the attack on the 3rd Brigade at Cali. FES tactics in Colombia are a subject for further study.

GUATEMALA AND MEXICO

While there are no details of FES-style attacks having occurred in Guatemala, in late 1994 the author recorded a video shown on the U.S. Spanish-language television station Univision, showing Guatemalan guerrillas practicing FES movement techniques. Press coverage of the guerrilla war in Guatemala has been heavily censored, and the Guatemalan military is not traditionally as open as the Salvadorans. However, it is likely that some FES-type activity has occurred or will occur if the war doesn't end first.

In January 1994, the Mexican EZLN Zapatistas made their debut in Chiapas, Mexico, taking a number of towns and carrying out a well-orchestrated and long-planned public relations campaign. The military and political actions of the Zapatistas strongly resembled those of the Salvadoran FMLN. While the FMLN has now desisted its official revolutionary activities, there are probably many FMLN veterans who have marketed or volunteered their skills to groups like the EZLN. However, even if this is not the case, Mexico was an important ally of the FMLN during the war in El Salvador. Mexico gave sanctuary, allowed fund-raising, and provided political aid to the Salvadoran guerrillas. Mexico may even have clandestinely allowed the FMLN to ship weapons and supplies for the guerrilla forces through its territory. FMLN guerrillas who shipped commercially acquired M-16 ammunition to El Salvador through Mexico, in secret compartments built into trucks, say they were never bothered by the Mexican authorities. Some official collusion and bribe-taking were probably involved. Whether this was on a local level or on a more general level is not known. What is clear is that throughout Mexico there was much sympathy for the Salvadoran guerrillas.

The official tolerance of the Mexican government toward the Salvadoran FMLN may have backfired on it, as Salvadoran guerrillas may have provided training and other aid during the years they operated in Mexico to the guerrillas of the Mexican EZLN. This may have included the teaching of FES techniques, and should the guerrilla war heat up in Mexico again, it would not be at all surprising if a number of operations employing FES techniques were attempted.

The spread of the techniques and tactics of the Latin American guerrilla special forces may not be limited only to the American continent. For reasons of scope and space, this book will not go into detail about other parts of the world. However, suffice it to say that recent operations by the Tamil Tigers of Sri Lanka bear a strong resemblance to Salvadoran FES attacks. Actions in Somalia against the United States and the United Nations were also based on Latin American guerrilla techniques. Warfare is an evolutionary profession. Successful warriors economize their resources by keeping up with and learning from past and present conflicts. Because of this, it should not be surprising that guerrilla and low-technology forces around the world would employ tactics that proved successful in El Salvador and elsewhere in Latin America.

In the United States and the West we often look down on these primitive methods because we have a tendency to rely on our superior technology. In Vietnam, El Salvador and elsewhere, this has often proved a fatal and costly mistake.

NOTES

1. Che Guevara, *Reminiscences of the Cuban Revolutionary War* (New York: MR Press, 1968), pp. 252–253.

2. The source for most of the accounts of the suicide platoon is Paco Ignacio Taibo II, *La Batalla del Che* (Mexico: Editorial Planeta, 1989).

3. Eugenio Mendez, *Confesiones de un Montonero* (Buenos Aires: Editorial Sudamericana Planeta, 1985), p. 116.

4. Ibid., pp. 116–120.

5. Richard Gillespie, *Soldados de Peron* (Buenos Aires: Grijalbo, 1987), pp. 241–242.

6. Gene Scroft, "Battle Zone Bocay," *Soldier of Fortune* (September 1987), p. 67.

7. Lawrence Brown, "Special Operations in the Falklands War," *Special Forces* (August 1988), pp. 40–43, 62.

8. Luis Mattini, *Hombres y Mujeres del PRT-ERP* (Buenos Aires: Editorial Contrapunto, 1990), pp. 450–461.

9. Ibid., pp. 488–489.

10. Ibid., p. 503.

11. Ibid., p. 506.

12. Alvaro Carrera, *Nicaragua: Frente Sur* (Caracas: Fondo Editorial Carlos Aponte, 1987), p. 21.

13. Jose Antonio Fernandez Savatteci, *El Soldado y El Guerrillero* (Lima), p. 103.

14. Ibid.

15. Ibid.

16. Ibid., pp. 111–112.

17. Carrera, *Nicaragua*, p. 52.

18. Ibid.

19. Ibid., p. 53.

20. *New York Times*, January 13, 1981; *Washington Post*, January 13, 1981.

21. Olga Behar, *Noches de Humo* (Bogota, Colombia: Editorial Planeta, 1988), p. 51.

22. Pedro Claver Tellez, "Que Paso Realmente en el Batallon Cisneros de Armenia?" *Cromos* (October 1985), pp. 26–28.

23. Behar, *Noches de Humo*, p. 138.

CHAPTER 7

Conclusions and Analysis

This book is a historical and technical study of the relatively unknown phenomenon of guerrilla special forces, particularly those in El Salvador, with some discussion of other Latin American cases to show the development and continuity of the ideas. Guerrilla special forces are not a new or unique phenomenon. As discussed in the chapter preceding this, most of the important Latin American guerrilla organizations created special forces units of one type or another. Some were more effective than others, and some were more special than others (by special we imply trained in "special" skills). Almost all were created at a moment in history when guerrilla forces were rapidly expanding and developing semiconventional and conventional capabilities. Special units were created to retain and expand unconventional and irregular warfare capabilities and to enhance the operations of the new conventional units. The development of guerrilla special forces reached its zenith during the Salvadoran revolution of 1979–1992. During this time, guerrilla special forces carried out the most spectacularly successful special operations that had ever been carried out on the continent.

The dynamics that made this possible were the accumulation of experience from the Cuban Revolution down to El Salvador, and more important, the infusion of Vietnamese sapper/commando techniques that had been developed and honed over the long years of war against the French, South Vietnamese, and the United States. This aspect of the Vietnam War must have been seriously overlooked by the U.S. advisers in El Salvador, as it was not until late in the war in El Salvador that special forces attacks using Vietnamese techniques became less effective against the Salvadoran army. However, they remained sufficiently effective to be transferred to Guatemala, and probably Mexico, where only time will tell if the Guatemalan and Mexican guerrillas are capable of repeating the successes that the Salvadoran guerrillas were able to attain using the Vietnamese techniques.

Although each of the special forces of the major organizations of the FMLN developed its own unique tendencies, the basic techniques remained remarkably unchanged from the original techniques taught to the Salvadorans by the Vietnamese and Cuban instructors. The ERP developed a flair for the spectacular and high-profile attack. The FPL usually employed the special forces in combined attacks, preferring to use its special forces as a spearhead for its maneuver battalions. While not always as spectacular, its operations were often more destructive in the long term. The FAL, because of lack of resources and numbers, were never as effective as either the FPL or the ERP special forces, and were employed in much more tactical functions. However, the FAL special forces became adept at conducting kidnappings, bank robberies, urban operations, and other operations involving deception. Despite these differences, the fundamental techniques and tactics remained those handed down to them from Vietnam. The special forces tactics employed against the Americans, French, and South Vietnamese were never adequately countered in Vietnam. Because of this, they were handed down to the Salvadoran guerrillas, who combined the techniques with their own operational heritage and scourged the armed forces of their country. Although partially countered, the FMLN FES were never completely understood or foiled. As a consequence, the lessons learned by the FMLN are now being handed down to other guerrilla forces around the world. The Vietnamese special forces techniques as employed by the Salvadoran FMLN may always be difficult to counter, but they will never be adequately countered unless they are understood. This book is a serious attempt to describe, analyze, and understand these forces. It is a first step.

Latin American guerrilla special forces, with special emphasis on the case of El Salvador, hold some very important lessons for modern armies contemplating scenarios of low-intensity conflict. In today's world, special forces are often popularly thought of as "high-tech troops." By this we mean a select group of highly trained men that have access to a variety of sophisticated gadgetry that gives them an edge over the human element of their opponents. The more gadgetry they possess, the better.

The FMLN FES were created as a special force for exactly the opposite reason. The core raison d'être of the FES was to have a unit of select men who, through their complete mastery of human soldiering skills, would overcome the technology of their enemies. While conventional special forces are supersoldiers, the FES special forces were superguerrillas.

While over time the FES acquired some of their own "high-tech gadgetry" (ground-to-air missiles, sniper rifles, etc.), it was very modest in comparison to other forces. Furthermore, their major successes continued to be mostly attained through the use of low-tech methods. One of the most striking things about the FES techniques, described in Chapter 2 of this book, is how simple their methods really were. There are special skills described, such as the techniques for overcoming lights, movement techniques, and some of the information on explosives. However, even these are essentially commonsense skills, and not as exotic as one might expect. What set the FES apart from other guerrilla units of the FMLN is not so much the techniques or the equipment, but rather the discipline and individual élan with which the FES practiced these techniques in comparison with other guerrilla units. FES units were literally "superguerrillas," able to employ guerrilla warfare techniques like no other guerrilla force.

However, this begs the question: Why did guerrilla forces have a need to create superguerrilla units? It is interesting that throughout Latin America, not even excluding Argentina, guerrilla special forces were created at a time in the revolution when the guerrilla forces were making a transition from low-level guerrilla warfare and terrorism to regular or semiregular warfare. This is always the stage when the guerrillas experience an influx of large numbers of recruits from the civilian population. While these recruits swell the ranks, they do not have the know-how, dedication, or experience to adequately carry out some types of missions. When this occurred in Latin America, the revolutionaries responded by forming special units to maintain the capability to carry out those missions. In addition, the new regular and semiregular forces gave the guerrillas capabilities they did not enjoy before, such as the ability to fight an army unit one-on-one, or overrun an army base. The guerrilla special forces units were given the mission to enhance and assist these capabilities through the "super application" of irregular warfare principles and methods. Prior to this stage of guerrilla expansion, guerrilla units were small, clandestine, and compact. All the members of a guerrilla unit or cell have to be highly motivated, trained, and fit in order to survive. Guerrilla units at this stage operate in a hostile environment, deep in the heart of enemy territory, constantly hunted by army and police. Every operation has to be carefully planned and carried out, and because the numbers are small, they have to be spectacular and daring. In essence, during this stage just being a guerrilla combatant is to be part of a special force.

However, when the transition is made to more conventional warfare, things change. Conventional forces cannot survive without some form of control over territory and sufficient logistics to equip and feed a relatively large force. This effectively creates a rear area where forces can relax and train without fear of attack. As a consequence, standards are relaxed, as the constant need to battle for survival is reduced. Furthermore, to maintain such large forces, guerrillas are forced to accept recruits with lower ideological commitment and military training/capability than before. If the revolutionaries want to retain the capability to conduct guerrilla operations, they must create special units to maintain those capabilities.

In El Salvador, semiconventional and conventional warfare dominated between 1982 and 1986. The most spectacular and successful FES operations were also mostly carried out during this time period. When the FMLN abandoned conventional tactics in favor of attrition warfare and a reversion to irregular tactics, FES operations continued, but were hard to distinguish from the operations of other units.

The dynamics in El Salvador were echoed in other revolutions as well. In Cuba, the suicide platoon was formed in the last year of the Cuban Revolution, when Castro's columns had become large units capable of taking the Batista army on directly. The special forces of the Sandinistas were largely creations of the Southern Front, where regular warfare was taking place between the Somoza National Guard and the Sandinistas. In Colombia, the M-19s' use of special forces coincided with a large increase in guerrilla forces and semiconventional operations between 1984 and 1987. During this time, the M-19, imitating the experience of Nicaragua and El Salvador, formed a united front with their fellow guerrilla groups and created conventional guerrilla units. The exception is in Argentina, where neither the ERP nor the Montoneros had developed the kind of conventional units present in the other revolutions. However, in the case of the Montoneros, when the GEC was created, the guerrillas had recently incorporated a number of new recruits from their supporting political movements into their combat cells. There was a relatively major expansion of forces. Operations carried out by these new recruits produced mediocre results at best. The mixed results of some of their operations motivated the high command to form a unit that it knew would be more reliable for certain types of missions. So while one might think that Argentina is the exception, there were common dynamics shared with the cases of Cuba, Nicaragua, El Salvador, and Colombia. The enigma is Puerto Rico, where guerrillas seem to have used the FES techniques, but not necessarily formed special units. However, this is all speculation, as little is known about this case.

In El Salvador, the most spectacular results were obtained when the FES operated in conjunction or in support of the larger conventional forces. As the FMLN was forced to reduce and scatter its conventional forces, FES operations and outcomes were reduced in direct proportion to the reduction of conventional force capacity. In addition, as the war continued, the armed forces developed some relatively simple countermeasures to FES units. The key to countering any tactic or method was to discover the pattern and develop countermeasures to those specific patterns. Some FES tactics were fairly intuitive and simple to counter, given a sufficient budget. Other techniques were much more difficult to detect and were never adequately countered. Fortunately for the armed forces, they were able to inflict heavy attrition on the FES units. This was perhaps the armed forces' most successful countermeasure: to find and attack the FES before the FES attacked them. Between the dead, wounded, and captured, the small units were devastated. The FES were never able to adequately make up their losses with equal quality replacements. As a consequence, the quality and results of the operations continually declined. The attrition combined with the reversion to unconventional warfare and armed forces' countermeasures reduced the number of FES attacks on major military installations to virtually zero during the last two years of the war.

FES PATTERNS

Before the Attack

What were the FES patterns? FES operations, like all methods, displayed several common characteristics. Perhaps one of the most important of these was the meticulous planning and preparation at all levels. Almost all of the FES operations originated with directives from the FMLN or organizational high commands. The high command structures seem to have been very careful about which orders they gave, and always seemed to have issued the orders on the basis of thorough intelligence (often gathered by the FES themselves). In the case of El Salvador, the guerrilla high command exercised a great degree of control over the operations carried out by the special forces. However, the high command was careful not to excessively micromanage after it had issued its general order to the FES unit. The latter was by and large given wide latitude to plan and carry out the mission itself, within the parameters and guidelines provided by the high command. A second characteristic was that FES units continued to carry out reconnaissance up to the very moment of attack. Most missions were carefully and painstakingly planned at all levels.

Because of the painstaking attention to detail, from conceptualization to execution, a mission often took several months to prepare. This was possible largely because government forces left much of the military initiative up to the FMLN. So, rather than force the FMLN to react, the government reacted to FMLN operations. Hard evidence of this was that the FMLN hardly ever abandoned an objective, even when its plans had been compromised or detected. Compromise and detection only postponed the attack; they did not cancel it. The same principle applied in Colombia and elsewhere. In Colombia, plans were captured from the M-19 indicating that they planned to attack the Justice Palace in Bogota. Thinking that the plan was foiled, security increased for a time and then relaxed and returned to its prediscovery routine. In November 1985, the M-19 carried out one of its most spectacular and devastating attacks, taking the Justice Palace and causing an inferno that has gone down in Colombian annals as one of the greatest acts of infamy in the nation's history. A majority of the major installations attacked by the FMLN were known by the armed forces to be targets of guerrilla reconnaissance and operations planning.

A consequence of the lack of government initiative was that the FES were continually able to find and exploit government weaknesses despite the government's knowledge that it was being probed. Lack of initiative produced routine and sloppiness for which technology could not always compensate. FES units were designed to specifically take advantage of these weaknesses. Long periods of inaction will create a false sense of security and impunity, and long hours of boredom can cause sentries' senses to lose sharpness. Static defenses become penetrable if the obstacles impeding attack within that perimeter remain static. The FES were experts at discovering obstacles and developing methods to defeat them. FES operations were never carried out until the FES had conducted reconnaissance, found the weak points, and were sure they could rapidly penetrate their objective's defenses. There were only a few targets that the FES reconnoitered that they didn't eventually attack. Among these was the Artillery Brigade. The reason this unit survived unscathed was that it constantly detected and compromised FES planning around the installation. It constantly changed its security regime. By constantly being kept off balance, the guerrillas could never consolidate the information and plans to attack the base. By the end of the war, the base had not been attacked, although it had been the continual target of probes, reconnaissance, and planning.

The Attack

Once the planning stage was finished, the FES would attack. Surprise and speed were key principles used during the assault of the objective. The purpose of rapid, undetected penetration of objectives for the FES units was to gain the element of surprise. Surprise caught the enemy off balance and put him into a situation of severe initial disadvantage until he could recover. To capitalize on surprise and the moment of imbalance, the FES units made maximum use of explosives. The idea was to cause the maximum amount of damage to the enemy in the minimum time available before the enemy could bring his numerical and technological superiority to bear on the much smaller FES units. If they were completely successful, the enemy would not be allowed to recover from his surprise until it was too late, and he was destroyed.

An additional element of the attempt to produce imbalance was that FES units usually attempted to employ the principle of attacking from the inside out. Attacking from the inside enhanced surprise by attacking from the unexpected direction. It added to the surprise and confusion. The FES units capitalized on this by always conducting ruthless attacks with explosives on the dormitories of sleeping officers, soldiers, and vulnerable equipment first, and then eliminating the outer defenses: bunkers, trenches, and so on.

Most military installations are designed with layers of obstacles and fortified defensive positions on the outer perimeter. The more sensitive and vulnerable elements are located on the inside. The idea is to create a hard outer shell and put as much distance between the vulnerable elements and the hard outer shell, where the enemy is, as possible. The hard shell is manned by a minimum necessary defense element to keep the installation safe from outside direct attack, until the rest of the force can react. Defenses designed to defeat direct, large-scale attack are designed to defeat massed forces, the platoon, the company, the battalion, and so on. Because of this, there are often tiny gaps in the perimeter. Dead space, enough to allow a man to pass through, a hole in the wire, a gap in the minefield, a trench with a blind spot, and so on. FES tactics were intentionally designed to take advantage of these small holes to find a way to penetrate the defenses. Because these holes and gaps are small, no one believes that they will be used. Often they are not immediately detectable. As a consequence, they are not watched or covered. Infiltration techniques taught to special forces often emphasize finding routes into the enemy rear by finding gaps in the enemy lines. This same principle was applied by the FES, only the gaps they sought were measured in centimeters, not meters and kilometers. FES tactics were purposely designed to take advantage of just such small gaps and holes. By continually probing and testing, the FES soldiers would find the routes where they could crawl through the perimeter undetected. In the attack, the FES would use these routes through the gaps and holes to penetrate the defenses and eliminate the larger and more vulnerable internal elements first, thus defeating the purpose for the outer defenses. Since most of the outer defensive positions were intended to defend an attack from outside, subsequently eliminating the outer defensive positions from inside, once the inner elements had been eliminated, was a relatively simple task.

To further confuse and surprise government forces, the FMLN would coordinate other actions outside the base to confuse, delay, and protect the main attack. This was one of the outstanding characteristics of the FES, and the FMLN in general, this ability to coordinate numerous simultaneous operations. When the FMLN planned operations, it almost always planned a number of accompanying support operations. Its ability to keep track of its numerous scattered units and to coordinate these units for simultaneous action was an amazing feat of arms that many conventional armies are only now accomplishing with modern communications and satellite technology. Especially in the latter half of the war, the FMLN would mass scattered, platoon-size elements for a single successful attack, and then disperse the concentration before the armed forces could properly react. Simultaneously, numerous smaller actions would be carried out. This served a dual purpose. It made it very difficult for the armed forces to know what the real FMLN objective was, and therefore to know where to send the reaction force. Second, the numerous simultaneous attacks tied down and prevented potential reaction forces from reaching the real FMLN objective. In these types of operations, FES units often attacked the main objective, but they could also be assigned to one of the distraction attacks. These were the basic patterns of FES operations.

OTHER ROLES

Other major roles assigned to the FES included assignment as a coordinating and guiding force. Most notably, during the 1989 offensive, the FES brought large numbers of dispersed units together and then led them into their assigned positions. Secondary missions included shooting down aircraft, assassinations, kidnapping, robbing banks, and so on.

FIGHT MUCH WITH LITTLE

As was emphasized, FES troops were designed to eliminate the technological gap between the FMLN guerrillas and the Salvadoran armed forces through the mastery of soldier skills. Their typical mode of operation has been to seek out the enemy assets at their weakest point and eliminate them. The FMLN used the FES like many commanders of conventional armies would use artillery, airpower, and armor, to attack both tactical and strategic objectives. These included helicopters and planes, artillery pieces, bridges, and military bases. Instead of using technology, the FES accomplished their objectives through strict discipline, élan, and total mastery of basic guerrilla warfare skills. Their motto: "Fight Much with Little," aptly reflected their philosophy. The fact that they were able to carry out successful operations throughout the war speaks volumes for the validity of the basic FES concepts. Because of the success of the FES, it is likely that FES-type units will play a part in any future low-intensity guerrilla conflict, particularly in Latin America, but also in other parts of the world. Furthermore, the success of FES units should warn those likely to face units employing these techniques that despite technology, consistently effective countermeasures have only begun to be developed.

POSSIBLE COUNTERMEASURES

Disrupting Planning

Since FES units deny technological advantages by seeking the weaknesses in the system, it becomes obvious that the system weaknesses must be minimized. FES units have usually conducted their operations against fixed objectives. Fixed objectives are those that are permanent on the terrain and do not normally move or change over long periods of time. Countermeasures must begin with the simple and move to the complex. Since thorough planning was a hallmark of FES operations, an effective countermeasure would be to make this difficult or disrupt it. There are several counter-measures that, according to captured FES members, were effective against FES reconnaissance operations. The first was to surround the bases with a tall chain-link fence and top it with razor wire. This was less penetrable than rows of concertina wire. However, chain-link fences can still be crossed and still be seen through. Double rows of chain-link fence offer a little more protection. However, the easiest and most effective countermea-sure was the construction of a high, solid wall of brick, cinder block, ce-ment, and so on, with guard towers and bunkers around the outer edge of the perimeter. This was a difficult obstacle to cross undetected, and an effective barrier to observation from the outside. The second most effective measure was to equip the installation with bright lights. The lights were only effective if accompanied by guard towers and guard positions in areas that could visually cover the entire perimeter. In other words, a light with-out a person to check up on the lit area is not effective. Walls, fences, and lights were less effective if the FES could reach them undetected. The FES often operated on intelligence provided from infiltrators inside the bases who were part of the guerrilla intelligence units. The FES could blow down sections of the wall to create breaches, and could, with fire support from outside forces, use the violent in, violent out method of attack (see Chapter 2). If possible, the vegetation around the base should be cut down. How-ever, lack of vegetation did not always stop the FES. As mentioned above, they were experts at finding and exploiting gaps, such as folds in the terrain, drainage ditches, the shadows of large rocks, and so on. Because of this, in addition to cutting down the vegetation, the terrain around the perimeter should be made as flat and smooth as possible, if not by natural means, then by artificial means. This could mean pouring cement to fill in gaps, and so on. There are several examples in the text about how FES teams penetrated objectives by way of broken and vegetated terrain. In Colombia, the M-19 attacked the Cisneros engineers by crawling up to the fence through tall, uncut grass. In El Salvador, several penetrations were made by using streams and drainage ditches that ran underneath the perimeter wire. Unless the area was manned, booby traps and wire did not stop the FES from using these terrain features to their advantage.

Often, military bases in parts of the world where FES tactics are likely to be used are within cities and populated areas where it would be physi-cally or politically impossible to implement some of the above-suggested measures. A measure suggested by a captured FES guerrilla was that in these areas, a zone should be created around the base or installation through which civilians and pedestrians could not transit, or only transit after a thorough search and a proper ID check.

However, implementing the above measures did not always guarantee immunity from attack, as a number of bases that included these measures were hit by the FES. The 1986 attack on the 3rd Brigade base at San Miguel is a good example. Over time, FES reconnaissance elements can discover everything they need to know about fixed objectives. The FES objective was to attack when they were as close to 100 percent certain about the nature, strength, and disposition of the objective as possible. To defeat this certainty, another option is to become "mobile."

Internal Mobility

Internal base mobility would reduce FES-type units' ability to attain the desired amount of knowledge about the objective. Armed forces do need permanent bases. However, within those bases things could be made as mobile as possible. For example, different permanent units could constantly and randomly change positions within a given perimeter. The same could be done with CPs, key weaponry such as mortars, artillery, heavy machine guns, and so on. Multiple positions could be built for single units or weapons and then these positions randomly occupied over a period of time. The problem with all of the above-mentioned countermeasures is expense and inconvenience. Depending on the situation, however, preservation of forces from FES attack might override the added expense. Even if the measures mentioned above could not be taken due to multiple factors, certain vital elements (key support weapons) could randomly rotate their position.

Another measure could be to randomly expand and contract the perimeter. Minefields, searchlights, and wire entanglements could be continually shifted to prevent FES units from ever being able to plan a secure route through the obstacles. The obstacles themselves did not stop the FES, they just delayed them long enough to find a route around, over, under, or through. This was particularly true of minefields and wire. The FES had no trouble eventually finding their way through a fixed minefield. However, if that minefield had been constantly changing places and configurations, they would have found it very difficult to make it through. The case of El Roblar described in the text in Chapter 3 comes to mind. In urban perimeters where space is limited this could include setting up random roadblocks and fortified positions along the streets around the base. Another tactic could be, in conjunction with the shifting perimeter, to randomly place small ambush teams along suspected infiltration routes inside and outside the perimeter. FES teams rarely came face-to-face with an alert and waiting enemy. When they did, they were often caught in a position of disadvantage and killed.

Internal Defense

Because of the tendency to attack from the inside of an objective toward the outside, perimeter bunkers should be designed to provide all-around defense. Furthermore, similar bunkers should be built and manned by a reaction force in the center of the installations, near vital targets such as support weapons and command and control facilities. In fact, these vital targets should be placed in such bunkers and manned 24 hours a day. This would guarantee that no matter what, these vital elements would always be operational and available to supress attacks and call in reinforcements.

Compartmentalization

Another way to defeat or contain the inside-out method of attack would be to compartmentalize or disperse elements within a compound. In other words, set up the base so that the penetration and destruction of one portion of the base would not allow the collapse of the entire base. This could be done by having subcompounds within the main compound, complete with their own outer and inner barriers, command posts, defensive positions, and support weapons. If an FES unit penetrated one part of the compound, it could not run freely around the entire compound and wreak destruction on the entire base. Instead, it would have to cross a whole new set of internal barriers and obstacles. This would slow it down, bottle it up, and negate the opportunity to make maximum use of the element of surprise before the defending forces can react. Each subcompound should have its own heavy weapons that would be mutually supporting with other support weapons within the compound. Often, FES operations would target the support weapons first. Once these were destroyed, the defenders would be denied their most powerful assets to defeat guerrilla assaults on the base. By dispersing the support weapons to separate subcompounds, it would make the destruction of the heavy weapons by FES units more difficult. Setting them up to be mutually supporting would allow those heavy weapons not destroyed to bring down heavy and accurate fire on any position that FES sappers might take. Such measures would allow the defenders to bottle up and bring down heavy firepower onto a sapper force, thus negating the initial tactical advantage acquired by the attacking sappers in the first few moments of attack.

Barracks Construction

More expensive internal measures can also be taken. One objective of FES attacks is to eliminate unarmed soldiers first. As described in the manual, the FES attempt to do this by containing the soldiers in their barracks and eliminating them with explosives. To counter this, barracks could be constructed smaller, fortified, and designed to hold no more than a platoon. If this proved too expensive, a solution could be to partition existing barracks with blastproof walls. Windows and doors should be covered with screen mesh, and closed at night.

The FES would massacre soldiers in a barracks by containing them inside, covering all entrances/exits and hurling explosives and automatic fire through those openings. The comparison of shooting fish in a barrel comes to mind. This was not done merely out of malice, but as a survival tactic. The FES had to annihilate forces along their paths of exit to guarantee that nothing was left behind to shoot them in the back. If people are left in the FES team's rear that can still fight, the FES' job becomes much more difficult. To frustrate this, barracks or partitioned sections should have multiple entrances. Furthermore, alternative exits such as tunnels should be provided to allow the soldiers to escape without entering the FES line of fire. These tunnels could lead to fighting bunkers. Doors should be provided in the tunnels to allow soldiers to close them off if a bunker has been taken, or a barracks eliminated. FES tactics call for the destruction of a large force by a small force by gaining the element of surprise, attacking the enemy's weak point, and overwhelming the large force through the massive use of explosives. The ideas expressed above are designed to mitigate the effect of explosives, break up units so that only few can be destroyed by few, and eliminate or mitigate the element of surprise. While the ideas expressed above are not exhaustive, they are in keeping with frustrating the principles that made FES attacks so devastating.

Sentries

In terms of the troops, guards should not be on duty for long periods of time, especially at night. If guards are left alone for long periods of time at night, some usually will fall asleep. Furthermore, there should not be any permanent guard unit. Guard units should be rotated in and out of the field, and should not be on guard duty for more than a few days at a time. The idea is to never allow boredom and routine to settle in. The guard units should also be the ones to change the perimeter and carry out the anti-infiltration ambushes. This gives guard duty more variety.

The Military Initiative

One of the problems in El Salvador was that the military initiative was often left in the hands of the guerrillas, for no good reason. This allowed the guerrillas to take all the time they needed to thoroughly plan their operations. Continual operations needed to be conducted in the field to force the guerrillas off balance, so they would lose the initiative and have to react to government initiatives. This could have been done, if the armed forces had developed a similar capability to the FMLN.

Small, dispersed units could be permanently based in the field. Instead of staying in bases, they could develop mobile camps. Army offensives in El Salvador were never continuous. Units went out into the field and spent an average of only 15 to 20 days. During those 15 to 20 days they inflicted damage on the guerrillas, but afterward, the guerrillas were free to come back and rebuild. In other words, operations went in predictable cycles that allowed the guerrillas to make adjustments and carry on with their routine.

Units need to be able to permanently live in the field, and remain there several months at a time. If a unit is relieved, it needs to be replaced by another unit, so that presence is never broken. Furthermore, these units should be fairly small; platoon- and company-size elements would be preferred. However, in El Salvador, the guerrillas' ability to deploy battalion-size elements indicates that in each situation, circumstances dictate the size of unit that should be deployed. These units need to be able to rapidly and independently mobilize to attack or defend, just like the FMLN guerrillas were able to deploy, concentrating and dispersing as needed. The major difference would be that the armed forces units, unlike the guerrillas, could call up air, artillery, and armored units to support them. Using greater technology, the armed forces units should be able to concentrate and disperse faster, and with more efficiency than their guerrilla opponents. The units should, therefore, never be too far apart, within less than a couple of hours' march. Furthermore, like the guerrillas, these units need to be able to conduct, coordinate, and control multiple simultaneous attacks or patrols.

Last, but not least, good intelligence and counterintelligence effort needs to be carried out. The intelligence units need to be closely in touch with the operational units so that information can be acted on before it becomes historical. The Salvadoran military gathered a large amount of useful intelligence. However, it seems that too much of the information was not acted on because of lack of communication between gathering entities and operational units. It is unfair to suggest that this was always the case. The Salvadoran armed forces conducted some spectacularly successful operations through the proper use of intelligence. Unfortunately, much of their success remains classified. However, as mentioned earlier, much of the decline of FES capabilities later in the war can be attributed to attrition. A good portion of this attrition was the result of combat operations which were specifically directed at eliminating FES combatants, and not just a result of normal operational casualties, sickness, and so on. Good intelligence/counterintelligence is vital and can, if acted on effectively, make up for the lack of other countermeasures until these can be instituted.

Essentially, the ideas expressed above are aimed at permanently shifting the initiative away from the guerrillas. If the guerrillas are forced to react to government initiatives, then they will not be able to use their FES units to conduct effective special operations. The worst they will be able to do is conduct local, tactical operations that will have only minor tactical consequences, but not the major tactical results of knocking out a major base or runway.

THE LESSONS OF EL SALVADOR

The military community has been too eager to bury El Salvador. There was no clear victory, and the war was messy. Human rights violations and scandal (both real and imaginary) clouded the real lessons, at least from a military point of view. The guerrilla effort in El Salvador was the largest, the best funded, equipped, best internationally supported guerrilla effort in the Americas during the entire Cold War. The combatants on both sides were highly trained and capable of conducting well-planned, sophisticated military operations. Single engagements often involved thousands of men on both sides. The point here is that this was no phoney war. In a country of five million inhabitants, over 70,000 people, or 1.4 percent of the population died! Contrary to popular myth, most of these died in combat. The military admits it lost around 30,000, while the guerrillas admit to about half that number. The real figures are probably significantly higher. A high number of civilians were also killed, especially in the early part of the war.

Although small in absolute terms, El Salvador was probably the United States' single largest military effort made to date in Latin America, with perhaps the exception of Panama. The U.S. advisory group was heavily involved in training, planning, and operations from 1981 onward. A significant amount of experience was gained in this endeavor.

The troubling aspect of the lessons and experience gained in El Salvador is that it seems that because of the political problems of the experience, when the war came to an end there was a stampede to bury the files and acquire institutional amnesia. This seems to indicate that rather than learning from El Salvador, the same lessons will have to be learned all over again the next time a similar situation is faced. Often these lessons are heartbreaking; a case in point, the Vietnamese sapper techniques.

The Vietnamese tactics embodied in the FES were used to deliver devastating and demoralizing blows against the armed forces of El Salvador. It was not until late in the war that the FES' effectiveness diminished, or at least their capability to attack major installations. This loss of effectiveness was probably due to attrition as much as countermeasures taken. In other words, it is not clear that the FES were ever clearly understood, and effective countermeasures ever taken.

This could mean that despite two wars, these tactics have never been adequately studied or countered. The United States faced this threat in Vietnam. Sapper attacks were common, and Vietnam anecdotes are full of stories about the devastation caused by the sapper troops. Incredibly, when the sappers first appeared in El Salvador, the United States seems to have failed to pass on information gathered on Vietnamese sapper techniques to the Salvadorans. Institutional memory was short in this regard, and the Salvadorans had to learn through hard experience. However, it is not clear that the lessons were ever adequately learned by either the Salvadoran or U.S. military institutions in this conflict either. As a consequence, it is likely that U.S. forces or allies will run into FES tactics again. Logically, tactics that are considered effective are always passed on. Because of this, FES tactics are likely to appear again and again until they are adequately understood and countered. This book does not pretend to be the final word on this subject; rather, it is an attempt to describe a hitherto ignored aspect of guerrilla warfare and stimulate further study and understanding of the topic so that young men won't have to unecessarily be returned to their homes in body bags.

Bibliography

BOOKS

Behar, Olga. *Noches de Humo*. Bogota: Editorial Planeta, 1988.

Carrera, Alvaro. *Nicaragua: Frente Sur*. Caracas: Fondo Editorial Carlos Aponte, 1987.

Fernandez Salvatteci, Jose Antonio. *El Soldado y El Guerrillero* (Lima). N.d.

Guevara, Che. *Reminiscences of the Cuban Revolutionary War*. New York: MR Press, 1968.

Henriquez Consalvi, Carlos (Santiago). *La Terquedad del Izote*. Mexico City: Editorial Diana, 1992.

Lopez Vigil, Jose Ignacio. *Las Mil y Una Historias de Radio Venceremos*. San Salvador: UCA Editores, 1992.

Manwaring, Max G., and Court Prisk. *El Salvador at War: An Oral History*. Washington, DC: National Defense University Press, 1988.

Mattini, Luis. *Hombres y Mujeres del PRT-ERP: La Pasion Militante*. Buenos Aires: Editorial Contrapunto, 1990.

Mena Sandoval, Francisco Emilio, Captain. *Del Ejercito Nacional al Ejercito Guerrillero*. San Salvador: Ediciones Arcoiris, 1992.

Mendez, Eugenio. *Confesiones de un Montonero*. Buenos Aires: Editorial Sudamericana Planeta, 1985.

Miranda, Roger, and William Ratliff. *The Civil War in Nicaragua: Inside the Sandinistas*. New Brunswick, NJ: Transaction Publishers, 1993.

Prisk, Courtney E., ed. *The Comandante Speaks: Memoirs of an El Salvadoran Guerrilla Leader*. Boulder, CO: Westview Press, 1991.

Taibo II, Paco Ignacio. *La Batalla del Che*. Mexico City: Editorial Planeta, 1989.

Vick, Alan. *Snakes in the Eagle's Nest: A History of Ground Attacks on Air Bases*. Santa Monica, CA: Rand Corporation, 1995.

ARTICLES

Brown, Lawrence. "Special Operations in the Falklands." *Special Forces* (August 1988), pp. 40–43, 59–62.

Claver Tellez, Pedro. "Que Paso Realmente en el Batallon Cisneros de Armenia?" *Cromos* (October 1985), pp. 26–28.

Dye, Dale. "Showdown at Cerron Grande: Blooding the Airborne Battalion." *Soldier of Fortune* (November 1984), pp. 51–59.

FPL. *Revista Farabundo Marti: El Pueblo Salvadoreño en su Lucha.* No. 8. Managua, Nicaragua, 1981, pp. 4–5.

Grande, Marco Antonio. "La Estrategia Del FMLN Parte II: La Guerra Militar." *Analisis* (October 1989), pp. 294–317.

"Reportaje de las Americas." *Granma* (April 1987), p. 8.

Rosello, Victor J., Major. "Vietnam's Support to El Salvador's FMLN: Successful Tactics in Central America." *Military Review* (January 1990), pp. 71–78.

Scroft, Gene. "War Zone Bocay." *Soldier of Fortune* (September 1987), pp. 60–67, 99–101.

Semprun, Alfredo, and Mauricio Hernandez. "Sandinismo: La otra cara de ETA." *Blanco y Negro* (January 5, 1992), p. 16.

Walker, Greg. "Blue Badges of Honor." *Soldier of Fortune* (February 1992), p. 36.

———."Greg Fronius, Forgotten Warrior." *Behind the Lines* (March/April 1994), pp. 43–47.

———."Sapper Attack!" *Behind the Lines* (July/August 1993), pp. 9–11.

DOCUMENTS

Alejandro. *Report on the Status of the Final Offensive from Alejandro to Jovel.* January 14, 1981. Typed manuscript captured by Salvadoran army at an unknown date.

Armed Forces of El Salvador. *Activities in Which the Terrorist Guerrillas Have Participated.* March 1990.

———. *Report on the Events at Cerron Grande Dam.* July 1984.

ERP. *Combat Order #5.* Typed manuscript document on white letter paper, captured by the armed forces in Morazan on May 13, 1986.

ERP. *Informe a Alcatraz.* 1981.

ERP. *Mission for Team 2 of Platoon 2.* Handwritten order on lined notebook paper, captured by the armed forces in Morazan on March 31, 1986.

ERP. *Training of Special Forces.* Captured in Morazan in 1988.

FMLN. *Instruction Manual for Urban Commandos #3.* El Salvador: Publicaciones FMLN, 1987.

FMLN. *Manual de Instruccion Para los Comandos Urbanos: El Explosivo Como Arma Popular.* El Salvador: Publicaciones FMLN, 1987.

FMLN. *Military Line of the FMLN: High Command Meeting, May-June, Morazan 1985.* Sistema Venceremos, Morazan, 1986.

FMLN. *Sniper Shooting.* Printed document captured at an unknown date by the Salvadoran army.

FPL. *Centeno Clandestine Archive.* Captured from the FMLN in 1982.

FPL. *J-28 Commando Course.*

FPL. *Notes from the Meeting with David on the Special Select Forces.* April 15, 1981.

FPL. *Principales Experiencias Operativas de la D.A. #2 del Año 1985.* San Vicente, El Salvador: Ediciones Chinchontepec Heroico, 1986.

FPL. *Project of the Special Operation Detachment.* August 1980.

FPL. *Spiral notebook.* Handwritten document containing a variety of subjects, captured by the armed forces in 1983.

FPL. Untitled document listing diving equipment in the guerrillas' inventory. August 1980.

FPL. *Work Carried out on "Chocoyo."* Dated October 16, 1986, captured by the armed forces at an unknown date.

FPL-FMLN. *Experiences of the Conduct of Anti-Aircraft Defense.*

Guardia Nacional. *Investigation Report of the Circumstances Surrounding the Downing of the Bridge.* October 1981.

Servicio de Inteligencia del Estado (Argentine Intelligence). File entitled *JCR.* Given to the author by a former SIE operative in 1991.

Special Operations Group. *Know the Enemy.* Armed Forces of El Salvador, 1986.

Spencer, David. *FMLN FES: Fight Much with Little.* Provo, Utah, 1990. Unpublished manuscript.

Unknown FPL FES student. *Commando Course of July 7, 1989.* Notebook captured in 1989 in Cinquera.

PRISONER INTERROGATION TRANSCRIPTS

Interrogation Transcript of AIA, June 5, 1985.

Interrogation Transcript of Alejandro Montenegro, 1983.

Interrogation Transcript of JAFA, April 19, 1990.

Interrogation Transcript of JFFC, January 24, 1990.

Interrogation Transcript of JFR, August 24, 1986.

Interrogation Transcript of RAA, May 11, 1987.

Interrogation Transcript of RAC, May 12, 1987.

Interrogation Transcript of RAR, April 27, 1987.

Interrogation Transcript of SAJR, June 18, 1986.

Interrogation Transcript of SSG, April 5, 1982.

Interrogation Transcript of TA, September 17, 1987.

Index

About the Author

DAVID E. SPENCER has lived and travelled throughout Latin America, spending more than thirteen years in the region. From 1990 to 1992 he served as an independent political and public affairs adviser to the Salvadoran military. Currently he is a Ph.D. candidate at George Washington University in comparative politics. Among his earlier publications is *Strategy and Tactics of the Salvadoran FMLN Guerrillas* (Praeger, 1995).

ISBN 0-275-95514-1

HARDCOVER BAR CODE